THE STANZAIC ARCHITECTURE
OF EARLY GREEK ELEGY

The Stanzaic Architecture of Early Greek Elegy

CHRISTOPHER A. FARAONE

OXFORD
UNIVERSITY PRESS

OXFORD

UNIVERSITY PRESS

Great Clarendon Street, Oxford OX2 6DP

Oxford University Press is a department of the University of Oxford.
It furthers the University's objective of excellence in research, scholarship,
and education by publishing worldwide in

Oxford New York

Auckland Cape Town Dar es Salaam Hong Kong Karachi
Kuala Lumpur Madrid Melbourne Mexico City Nairobi
New Delhi Shanghai Taipei Toronto

With offices in

Argentina Austria Brazil Chile Czech Republic France Greece
Guatemala Hungary Italy Japan Poland Portugal Singapore
South Korea Switzerland Thailand Turkey Ukraine Vietnam

Oxford is a registered trade mark of Oxford University Press
in the UK and in certain other countries

Published in the United States
by Oxford University Press Inc., New York

© Christopher A. Faraone 2008

The moral rights of the author have been asserted
Database right Oxford University Press (maker)

First published 2008

British Library Cataloguing in Publication Data

Data available

Library of Congress Cataloging in Publication Data

Faraone, Christopher A.
The stanzaic architecture of early Greek elegy/Christopher A. Faraone.
p. cm.
ISBN 978–0–19–923698–5
1. Elegiac poetry, Greek—History and criticism. 2. Greek language—Metrics
and rhythmics I. Title.
PA3113.F37 2008
884'.0109—dc22   2007049194

Typeset by SPI Publisher Services, Pondicherry, India
Printed in Great Britain
on acid-free paper by
Biddles Ltd., King's Lynn, Norfolk

ISBN 978–0–19–923698–5

1 3 5 7 9 10 8 6 4 2

In memory of
Arthur W. H. Adkins and John J. Winkler

Preface and Acknowledgements

This book grows out of my classroom experience teaching a course on ancient Greek elegy to upper-level undergraduates and graduate students, and it is designed in part to answer some of the initially 'naïve' but ultimately fundamental questions they put to me about the poetic form of early Greek elegiac poetry: What is the typical length of an elegiac poem in the archaic period? Are any of the surviving fragments complete poems? Or if not complete, are they the beginnings and ends of lost poems? How can we tell? What formal devices did elegiac poets use to give a recognizable architecture to the shorter poems they sang around the symposium or to the much longer poems they composed on historical or political topics? And finally, how did archaic elegy change, as it was informally recited and reperformed in classical times at Athens and elsewhere?

It is fitting that I dedicate this book in part to the memory of Arthur Adkins, my congenial and thoughtful colleague. Long before my arrival at the University of Chicago he created and nurtured a popular reading course on archaic Greek elegy, which I inherited after he passed away. While preparing for and teaching this course in the autumn of 1998 and again in the winter of 2002, I first conceived and then tested the main arguments in this book. Prior to taking on this course, I was accustomed to teaching elegiac poems in a survey course devoted to 'Lyric Poetry', an odd setting generated by the persistent confusion over the melic status of elegiac poetry. (A confusion captured nicely in the repetition of the word 'lyric' in both the title and subtitle of perhaps the most popular text book for such courses in North America, Campbell's (1967) *Greek Lyric Poetry: A Selection of Early Greek Lyric, Elegiac and Iambic Poetry.*)

Arthur, however, insisted on devoting an entire course to reading all of the fragments of archaic elegy and in so doing created the perfect environment for formulating specific questions about the poetic form of elegy itself, rather than more global inquiries into the various features that elegy shares with the other early forms of monodic poetry, for example, its political content, sympotic setting or personal voice. My second and perhaps more obvious debt to Arthur is his book, *Poetic Craft in the Early Greek Elegists* (Chicago, 1985), which, like mine, grew out of his classroom experiences. In hindsight, it is quite clear to me that this book, with its emphasis on the craft of the elegiac poet and its close readings of individual fragments and their poetic structure, was a model for the style of analysis deployed here.

A great number of individuals helped in the creation of this book and it is a pleasure to recognize their contributions. First and foremost I am grateful to my students in those two memorable classes, especially to those who repeatedly pressed me to think harder about the poetic form of archaic elegiac poetry, and who assumed that the longer extant fragments, at least, could provide ample enough data to speculate about it. Secondly I wish to thank some of my friends and colleagues at the University of Chicago: Danielle Allen, James Redfield, Laura Slatkin, Peter White, and David Wray. They read the first and most tentative version of this study and offered penetrating but encouraging criticism. Elizabeth Adkins, Deborah Boedeker, Edward Courtney, Marta Cuypers, Mark Edwards, Susan H. Faraone, Scott Garner, Douglas Gerber, Kathryn Gutzwiller, Richard Hunter, Andre Lardinois, Jim Marks, Dirk Obbink, Allan Romano, David Sansone, David Sider, Susan Stephens, Greg Thalmann and Mark Usher all offered comments on subsequent drafts or individual chapters. The two anonymous readers for the press gave many helpful comments, and since they ultimately made themselves known to me, I can thank them by name as well: Ewen Bowie and Ian Rutherford. I am also grateful to Bob von Hallberg and David Wilson-Okamura for information and bibliography about the use of stanzas and rhyme in Italian and English poetry. The remaining faults are, of course, my own.

The bulk of this study was written during the summer and fall of 2002, while I was a fellow at the Franke Institute of Humanities at the University of Chicago. I am particularly grateful to Richard and Barbara Franke for their original and ongoing support of the Institute, and to its director, Jim Chandler, and his staff for creating such a wonderful and supportive environment for research and writing. I am especially grateful to Rana Al-Saadi, Dan Belnap, Neil Coffee, Martin Devecka, Elliott K. Goodman, Alex Lee and my daughter Amanda

M. Faraone for research and editorial help. Portions of this study appeared previously in *Classical Philology* (Faraone 2005*a*), the *Transactions of the American Philological Association* (Faraone 2005*b*) and *Mnemosyne* (Faraone 2006) and I am grateful to the editors of these journals for allowing me to republish much of that material here. The Greek text of selections of M.L. West (ed.), *Iambi et Elegi Graeci ante Alexandrum Cantati*, 2nd edn., Copyright Oxford University Press is printed with permission of the publishers. Likewise portions of the translations of D.E. Gerber are used here by permission of the publishers from *Greek Elegiac Poetry from the Seventh to the Fifth Centuries B.C.*, Loeb Classical Library, vol. 258, Cambridge, Mass.: Harvard University Press, Copyright 1999 by the President and Fellows of Harvard College. The Loeb Classical Library is a registered trademark of the President and Fellows of Harvard College.

C.A.F.

University of Chicago
April 2007

Contents

Note on Abbreviations and Transliterations

Wherever possible I have used the abbreviations for ancient authors, scholarly journals, collections of texts and the like as they appear in the second edition of the *Oxford Classical Dictionary*. In transliterating ancient Greek names it has seemed reasonable, if not entirely consistent, to use the familiar Latinized spelling for those names for which this has become normal English usage (e.g. 'Socrates' or 'Heracles'), and in other cases to use a direct transliteration of the Greek to avoid confusion, e.g. 'Dike' rather than 'Dice'.

1

Introduction

Recent scholarship on early Greek elegy suggests that there were two basic types: shorter poems sung at symposia on a variety of martial, political, and erotic themes and much longer historical narratives, such as Mimnermus' *Smyrneis* or Simonides' poem on the battle of Plataea.[1] There is less consensus on the existence of a third type, a formal elegiac lament sung in funerary contexts that was perhaps a specialty of the Doric world.[2] Our understanding of all forms of archaic elegy is, however, continually vexed by our inability to know what was the traditional length of a shorter elegiac poem and what—if any—was the size of a typical compositional unit in the more extended poems.[3] Such ignorance greatly limits our aesthetic appreciation, for example, of the poetry of Archilochus and Mimnermus, which survives antiquity only in small, isolated fragments quoted out of context by much later authors, who were generally more interested in mining these ancient poems for moral maxims than appreciating them as examples of archaic poetry.[4] This ignorance is equally debilitating when we turn our attention to the longer

---

[1] For recent overviews see e.g. Herington (1985) 31–39, Bowie (1986) and (2001), Pellizer (1990) 180, Bartól (1993) 51–57, Gerber (1997) 92–94, and Aloni (2001) 88–90. Slings (2000, 5–10) points out how much of this recent consensus is indebted to the important work of Reitzenstein (1893) 45–85.

[2] See Section 6.2 below.

[3] Bowie (1986) 13.

[4] Stobaeus—or the scribal tradition that transmits his *Florilegium*—seems to be particularly unreliable; see Campbell (1984) for his habit of stripping away personal information (and rewriting verses if necessary) in order to generalize a fragment, and Sider (2001*b*) 272–88 for evidence (in the recently discovered Simonides papyri) of other forms of Stobaean imprecision.

extant fragments, such as Tyrtaeus 12 or Solon 13, and try to discern any consistent signs of compositional design or architecture.

This problem of fragmentary and poorly preserved primary sources has in the past been exacerbated, because modern scholars—in some ways not unlike the ancient excerpters—traditionally used the fragments of archaic elegy more for evidence about the history of Greek ideas, warfare, society, or politics,[5] than for insight into their poetic form. Indeed, elegiac poetics, if it is commented upon at all, is usually assumed to be derivative of or dependent upon epic, on the grounds that the basic metrical unit of elegy (the couplet) and its Ionic dialect are closely related to the hexametrical verse and *Kunstsprache* of epic.[6] This tendency is especially exaggerated in the case of Tyrtaeus, because of his perceived proximity to epic: chronologically he is one of the earliest elegiac poets, and the military content of his poems allows for much easier comparisons, especially with a war-poem like the *Iliad*.[7]

In recent years, however, scholars have begun to re-examine the formal features of elegy and to underscore some of the ways it differs from epic. Dover, for example, has stressed some important linguistic variations in early elegiac poetry, which lacks many of the particles or paired particles that are characteristic of epic, and which seems to be unfamiliar with the digamma—an absence that is striking in the case of Tyrtaeus, who ignores it entirely even though his native Doric regularly acknowledges it.[8] More recently there have been some

---

[5] For the usefulness of the content of elegy in the study of early Greek ideas, see e.g. Adkins (1972) and Fränkel (1975); of military history, e.g. Snodgrass (1964) 181–82 and Adkins (1985) 77–78; of political and social history, e.g. Podlecki (1974) and Murray (1983) 124–36 and 159–80; and most recently even the history of organized crime: van Wees (1999).

[6] Adkins (1985, 21–23) summarizes this traditional approach, which seems to go back to Aristotle *Poetics* 1.

[7] Typical is Jaeger (1966) 107: 'The poems of Tyrtaeus in language, meter and mood are Homeric through and through.' See also Jacoby (1918) 19–31, Snell (1969), Adkins (1985) 87–92 or Gerber (1997) 106. Verrall (1896, 269) points out that this is a very old tradition, going back at least as far as Horace (*Ars Poetica* 410), who identifies Homer and Tyrtaeus collectively as those 'whose verses made the souls of men sharp in battle'.

[8] Dover (1967, 183–84 and 190–94) concludes that Tyrtaeus inherits elegy as an Ionic vernacular form, which draws to some degree on epic material and phraseology (p. 193). Barnes (1995, 148) shows, moreover, that—with regard to the frequency of clausular breaks within the hexameter—of all the extant elegists Tyrtaeus' verse is

suggestive shorter studies on the unique dynamics of elegiac metrics and formulas.[9] But the study of elegy has benefited perhaps most greatly from recent inquiries into the re-performance of archaic poetry in the classical period and the poetic traditions that evolve as a result. Herington, for example, has discussed the re-performance of Solon and Tyrtaeus in late-classical Athens, while Nagy has suggested that 'Theognis', like 'Homer' or the 'Anacreon' of the *Anacreonta*, represents a long poetic tradition or 'persona' in the guise of which the extant poems in the *Theognidea* were composed by a series of different Megarian symposiasts over a long period of time.[10]

In the present environment the time is right to revive a much older theory about the unique poetic form of early elegy. Henri Weil, around the time of the American Civil War, suggested that many of the early elegists organized their poems into 'strophes' that occasionally display a kind of responsion similar to that found in ancient Greek choral poetry.[11] Although his contemporaries rightly rejected the main argument of his study—that Solon 13 was primarily composed of four-couplet 'strophes'—they paid scant attention to some of his other, passing observations.[12] Weil's brief comments on Tyrtaeus 10–12 and Xenophanes 1 and 2 are, in fact, extremely insightful: he described

actually the *least* like Homeric verse, and dramatically so. More generally Bowie (1986, 14) notes: 'Elegy's metrical form relates to hexameter epic, but no evidence proves it a more recent genre. Not surprising for a dactylic metre, it shares much vocabulary with epic, but it is only a supposition that elegy is invariably the borrower and epic the lender.' Indeed, West (1995) argues that *Iliad* 22 may have been dependent on Tyrtaeus.

[9] See e.g. Greenberg (1985*a*) and van Raalte (1988) for meter, and for formulae Greenberg (1985*b*), who concludes (p. 260): 'elegy is not derived from the hexameter... It has its own rules.' Barnes (1995), focusing on patterns of enjambment, points out that the elegiac hexameter, because it functions as an integral part of the couplet, displays a number of important differences from the epic hexameter. An increase in necessary enjambment between hexameter and couplet, for example, leads to an increase in clause division at the bucolic diaeresis. There is also a general tendency to avoid an initial *hemiepes* at the start of the hexameter (and thus avoid couplets with one initial and two final *hemiepe*).

[10] Herington (1985) 48–50 and Nagy (1985). More recently Lardinois (2006) has asked similar questions about the poet named 'Solon'.

[11] Weil (1862).

[12] Weil's ideas about four-couplet Solonic 'strophes' were rejected by subsequent editors and pointedly refuted by Clemm (1883). Linforth (1919, 242–44) provides a concise overview of the controversy.

(without argument) two persistent features:[13] (i) the Tyrtaean fragments were composed in regular five-couplet 'strophes' and the Xeno-
phantic fragments in six-couplet ones; and (ii) verbal repetitions
highlight the 'strophic' architecture of these poems and create a formal
responsion, which, like metrical responsion in choral poetry, draws
attention to important thematic parallels and contrasts. As we shall
see, both of these observations can, in fact, be defended and augmen-
ted in ways that can tell us much about the unique poetic design of
early elegy.

Weil's thesis about 'strophes' and responsion was (as far as I can
tell) roundly ignored for nearly a century until Rossi in a lengthy and
detailed study confirmed that the first thirty lines of Tyrtaeus 10 were
indeed composed as three clearly marked five-couplet units. In
addition he noted that the first and last of these units were 'discur-
sive' in nature, while the middle one exhorted the audience to
action.[14] One goal of this study, then, is to combine Weil's initial
insight about the stanzaic divisions of the longer fragments of archaic
elegy, with Rossi's understanding of how the rhetorical structure of a
fragment fits comfortably within and is indeed creatively articulated
by these divisions.

Weil ventured no analysis of the extant elegiac fragments of Archilochus and Mimnermus, presumably because they are too short.
He completely ignored the *Theognidea* as well. Perhaps wisely so, for
this collection of nearly 700 elegiac couplets comes down to us in
manuscripts that bear little or no reliable indication of the beginnings or ends of separate poems.[15] This problem is, in fact, shared by
the entire corpus of archaic elegy. Indeed, aside from necessarily
subjective judgments about aesthetic or rhetorical unity and a few
scribal marks on papyri,[16] we have little external evidence at all for

[13] Weil (1862) devotes the first eight pages of his thirteen-page study to Solon 13, a
page and a half to Xenophanes 1 and 2 and four-and-a-half pages to Tyrtaeus 10–12.
[14] Rossi (1953/54) 414–15.
[15] The earliest and best manuscripts of the *Theognidea* do not distinguish individual poems, although some of the inferior manuscripts do; see West (1992) 173–74.
This suggests rightly to most scholars—see e.g. the recent comments of Friis-Johan-
sen (1991) 31—that these divisions are of doubtful authority.
[16] *POxy.* 854, uses a *paragraphos* and a *coronis* to mark the start of Archilochus 4, a
fragment that was at least four couplets long. Recently Obbink (2006) has shown that
this papyrus and a number of others all belong to the same 2nd-cent. CE book of

the length or boundaries of any archaic elegiac poem. To date scholars can generally agree on only one acceptable principle: that a vocative often indicates the beginning of a new poem. There is a fairly wide consensus, for example, that in the *Theognidea* the vocative forms of the name or patronymic of Cyrnus, the poet's primary addressee, regularly mark the start of a new poem, although disagreement remains about how often this is true.[17] Similarly, the use of the vocative ὦ νέοι at the beginning of line 15 of Tyrtaeus 10, was central to the long-standing, but now abandoned, thesis that lines 15–31 of the fragment comprised the start of a second poem unrelated to the first fourteen verses.[18]

As we shall see, Weil's notion of the 'strophic' design of elegy provides us with a more reliable method for discerning the beginnings and ends of individual poems or sections within them. I have, however, abandoned Weil's 'strophe', and borrow, instead, the term 'stanza' from the world of the Renaissance, where the idea of a poetic stanza seems to evolve from the lyrics of songs sung to musical accompaniment, an evolution very similar to that of archaic Greek elegy (see below).[19] According to the *Oxford English Dictionary*, English speakers in the sixteenth century borrowed the word 'stanza' directly from Italy, where the poetic connotation of the word apparently derived from the use of the Italian word *stanza* as 'a stopping

Archilochus' elegies that was 'an extensive edition, equipped with *coronides, paragraphoi*, accents, diareses, etc.' It included fragments of both short and long poems, including twenty-four continuous lines that seem to be a mythological exemplum about Telephus' rout of the Achaean army. The surviving text is, however, heavily damaged at the start and finish of most lines and too much has to be conjectured to know whether the poet has composed these lines in stanzas. The two papyrus fragments of the *Theognidea* (*POxy.* 2380 and *PBerlin* 21220) reveal that something like the extant corpus already existed in the Roman period; see Carriere (1962) and Kotansky (1993). The layout of the Oxyrhynchus papyrus suggests that some kind of symbol or short title marked line 255 as the beginning of a new poem, a point in the corpus where scholars have indeed always postulated the end of an earlier compilation. See Gronewald (1975) for full discussion. The Berlin papyrus, on the other hand, has some small bit of writing in between lines 930 and 931—another point where scholars have suggested a break between two different thematic sections.

[17] Hudson-Williams (1910, 2–4) provides a good summary. See also Section 4.2 below.

[18] See my discussion in Section 3.1.

[19] I am much indebted to Herrnstein-Smith (1968) 56–70 for much of this paragraph.

place' on a journey. The stanza, in short, originally designated not (as we usually understand it today) a repeated unit of verses, but rather the space or point of contact between them, where musicians and singers paused before repeating again the same melody with a new set of lyrics. In Renaissance England, however, a second, albeit incorrect, understanding of the term was intuited from an alternate meaning of the same Italian word as a 'room'.[20] These divergent derivations and definitions, in fact, provide different and productive ways of thinking about stanzas. The second, for example, imagines stanzas singly as a series of bounded 'rooms' into which poetic verses are distributed, like furniture or other household possessions, in a pleasing or logical pattern. Thus John Donne famously remarks in 'The Coronation': 'We'll build in sonnets pretty rooms.'

The stanza as a 'stopping place', however, turns our attention to the boundaries between successive units, where orally composing elegiac poets might pause briefly to collect their thoughts and then move on in a different direction, mood, or linguistic register, or where singers composing or improvising verses at a symposium might 'take up' a song as it moves from one performer to the next. For both ancient and Renaissance poets, moreover, stanzas provided extraordinary flexibility in terms of length and genre. Although the stanza may have evolved originally as a frame for short melodic songs, poets quickly recognized that repeated stanzas could be used to construct much larger and more complicated compositions. Indeed, there is theoretically no limit to the number of stanzas that a poet might use in an elegiac composition, some of which could apparently run as long as one or two thousand verses.[21] One thinks, of course, of the *terza rima* as a stanzaic vehicle for Dante's *Divine Comedy* or of the Spenserian stanza in *The Fairie Queen*.

My notion of the stanza emphasizes most of all the musicality of elegy, which in archaic times was most likely performed to the tune of the *aulos*, a kind of double oboe.[22] In the past scholars have assumed

---

[20] See e.g. Oliver (1994) 34. Rana Al-Saadi informs me that the Arabic word for stanza (*bêt*) is also the word for 'house'.

[21] Bowie (1986) 28–34 and Gerber (1997) 91–92.

[22] This has been a fraught question. In the 19th and early 20th cent. most scholars would have agreed that early elegy was sung to the *aulos*; see e.g. Page (1936) 211 ('beyond a reasonable doubt'). Campbell (1964) and Rosenmeyer (1969) mounted a

that the tune was short and simple, repeated over and over again with each couplet, an assumption that greatly limits the importance of the musical background and assigns to the elegiac performer, in comparison to the lyric one, an inferior status that blurs the lines between amateur and virtuoso.[23] I argue in this volume, however, that the stanza, and not the couplet, was probably the more important compositional unit of early Greek elegy, and that the aulete could in theory, at least, play a longer and presumably more complex melody that might span all five-couplets without repeating itself. Thus elegists probably had as great a challenge as lyric poets, at least until elegy loses its musical background in the classical period.

The musical accompaniment of early elegy has in the past created problems for the modern taxonomy of ancient Greek poetry, according to which there are two basic categories: (i) 'stichic' verse, in which a short metrical unit—for example, a single verse or couplet—is recited over and over again, usually without music, for example, the dactylic hexameters of epic or the iambic and trochaic 'speaking meters' of Greek drama; and (ii) 'melic' or 'melodic' verse sung to a stringed instrument or the *aulos*, in which longer sets of metrical units come to closure at regular intervals, for example, the stanzas of monodic poems, like those of Sappho or Alcman, or the strophic triads of choral poetry.[24]

strong challenge to this view, but gradually the *communis opinio* has swung back, see e.g. West (1974) 13–14, Henderson (1982) 24, Herington (1985) 31–36 and 192–93, and Bartól (1987). Rosenmeyer (1969) 217–18 depends heavily on Aristotle's understanding in *Poetics* 1 that elegiac poets, like epic ones, composed verse without music, but Aristotle is probably reflecting performance practices of the 4th cent. when elegy had already lost its musical background. For more recent views, see e.g. West (1974) 18–19, who classifies elegy as 'a variety of melic poetry'; and Bowie (1986) 13–21 (esp. p. 14, with his emphasis: 'archaic elegy was not spoken, but *sung*... and on almost all occasions it was accompanied by the *aulos*'). Gerber (1997, 96–98) provides a recent overview of the debate and concludes (p. 97): 'the sheer number of them [i.e. internal references to the *aulos*] strongly suggests that the instrument was a common accompaniment to elegy.'

[23] See e.g. Bowie (1986) 14: 'All an elegist must do is compose words within a regularly repeated metre and sing them to a tune that is presumably, like the couplet's metre, simple and repeated. ... This makes fewer demands than composing monody in metres of varying complexity for singing to the accompaniment of a stringed instrument played by the singer: the gap between the talented amateur and the virtuoso performer will be narrower.'

[24] See e.g. Dale (1965) 173. Nagy (1990*b*, 19–20) places elegiac couplets in the category of 'recitative' as opposed to 'melodic', while allowing that the former need

Scholars traditionally count elegiac poetry as stichic verse because it can be described metrically as the repetition of one elegiac couplet after another. But elegy's status as stichic verse conflicts with the consensus (see n. 22 above) that the Greeks in early times, at least, performed elegiac verses to the accompaniment of the *aulos*. Weil, on the other hand, presumably recognized the melic status of elegy (although he does not say so explicitly), when he pointed to the parallels between the 'strophes' he found in the elegiac fragments and those in choral poetry. I should stress, however, that this important musical feature of archaic elegy seems to have been abandoned by the time of Aristotle, who in the *Poetics* (1.1447^{a-b}) treats elegiac and epic poets together as examples of those, whose poetry features language and rhythm, but not music. Scholars suggest that archaic elegiac songs, indeed, gradually lose their specialized melodic accompaniment in the classical period, when they were re-performed in symposia by amateurs who spoke or chanted them as if they were non-melic poems,[25] an historical development that occurred in the Italian and English Renaissance as well, when the sonnet and various other kinds of stanzaic verse were gradually liberated from their musical settings. In Greece a similar trend helps explain why knowledge and appreciation of the stanza seem to weaken in the classical period and might, in fact, have been lost for good, had it not been for the scholarly revival of interest in the Hellenistic period.

Although the use of the term 'stanza' to describe repeated units of Greek elegiac poetry is potentially problematic, it has been used profitably in this way by modern scholars of Avestan and Propertian verse.[26] Use of the term does, nonetheless, threaten confusion with the other kinds of stanzas employed by archaic Greek poets. Thus, for

not mean 'monotone', because the Greek pitch accent provided some kind of 'patterning of pitch'.

[25] Herington (1985) 41–57 and Nagy (1990*b*) 23–27.

[26] One of the earliest forms of Indo-European poetry, the Gâthâs ('Divine Songs') of the Avesta, is stichic in form, having as its basic verse (called a *pada*) either a dimeter (8 syllables) or a trimeter (11 or 12 syllables). These 'Divine Songs' are composed in fixed units of metrically equal lines that are called 'stanzas'; see Malandra (2001) 320–21. Likewise Goold (1990, 19–20) uses 'stanza' as I do in this volume to refer to 'regular blocks of verses' within the corpus of Propertius, for example, 1.6 (six stanzas of three couplets), 1.10 (three stanzas of five couplets) and 1.14 (three stanzas of four couplets).

example, the traditional use of 'stanza' to describe the compositional unit of a Sapphic lyric poem is more apt because (as in the Italian or English case) metrical alteration of the final verse of each stanza makes it easier to isolate the stanzas as separate units. But after much consideration of Weil's 'strophe' (difficult because of its triadic associations) and such neologisms as 'monostrophs' or 'five-folders', I have opted to use the more familiar term 'stanza' throughout the volume, albeit in the more general meaning that has evolved in twentieth-century discourse on poetry, as a formal unit of verse, which is recurrently identical in length and metrical structure, and which often constitutes a division of a poem that corresponds to the paragraph in prose.[27] The analogy to the prose paragraph, in particular, captures one essential feature of the elegiac stanza that is not necessarily shared by the stanzas of the lyric genres of Greek poetry: the regular coincidence between the end of an elegiac stanza and the end of a sentence. The analogy offered above with the stanzas found in Renaissance poetry may also make sense of the relatively long length of the Greek elegiac stanza, which runs to ten or twelve verses, compared, for example, with the four-line Sapphic stanza. Indeed, like the fourteen-line Petrarchan stanza or the nine-line Spensarian, the relatively long length of the elegiac stanza provides more than adequate space for the full development of coherent arguments or ideas within the span of a single compositional unit, a feature that (as we shall see) lends itself especially well to the meditative or philosophical use of elegy.

This study has six central chapters. In Chapter 2, 'Internal Structure', I begin with a number of well-known elegiac fragments that ancient authors quote as complete five-couplet units or that modern editors and scholars almost universally identify on aesthetic or rhetorical grounds as free-standing poems. In my discussion, I begin by identifying a number of other salient features, such as ring-composition, internal rhymes, and word repetition, that can help us identify these fragments as unified and complete stanzas. In the second half of the chapter I discuss three kinds of elegiac 'set-pieces' that regularly appear in or among the fragments as discrete five-couplet units:

---

[27] See e.g. the discussions of Baum (1929) 53 or Wood (1940) 265. Oliver (1994, 54) identifies stanza as a 'sensible paragraph'.

prayers, catalogues, and priamels. In Chapter 3, 'Composition', the chapter most indebted to the work of Weil and Rossi, I examine a number of longer archaic fragments and suggest some additional criteria for identifying individual stanzas by the manner in which they are joined to and separated from those stanzas that precede and follow. I identify two general compositional patterns, the alternation between stanzas of exhortation and meditation, and the coordination of pairs of stanzas of the same linguistic type by often elaborate schemes of responsion.

In Chapter 4, 'Performance' and Chapter 5, 'Improvisation', I continue to examine the seams between five-couplet stanzas, this time looking for signs of a multiplicity of composers or performers. I begin with the sympotic practice of 'taking up the song' discussed by Reitzenstein and others, a type of elegiac performance during which one poet composes a five-couplet poem, to which another must respond with a second poem of equal length that commends, critiques, or challenges the first. My examples are drawn primarily from the *Theognidea*, but I suggest that some of the shorter fragments of Archilochus, Mimnermus, and Solon may have also been performed in a similar context. In Chapter 5, I turn to the case of re-performance, during which a performer of a later generation improvises a version of a traditional poem originally composed in elegiac stanzas. This creative re-performance of elegy is directly linked to its emergence as a popular spoken (i.e. no longer sung) form of entertainment in late-classical Athens and elsewhere. From this diachronic perspective, we see signs that the knowledge of or interest in the five-couplet stanza as a structural unit of elegy is fading.

In Chapter 6, 'Innovation and Archaism', I discuss two different cases of reaction to or reception of the archaic technique of stanzaic composition in the late archaic or classical period. The first involves the two long fragments of the iconoclastic philosopher-poet Xen-ophanes of Colophon, which (as Weil noted) are composed as pairs of six-couplet stanzas according to the same techniques discussed throughout the volume. I suggest, but cannot prove, that these six-couplet stanzas were an innovation of Xenophanes, who elsewhere challenges poetic tradition and authority. In the second half of this chapter I show that the elegiac lament sung by Andromache in her eponymous Euripidean play displays clear signs of stanzaic architecture. This fact, coupled with new epigraphical evidence for early elegiac epitaphs, suggests that unlike Xenophanes, Euripides is not innovating, but rather he is reflecting some real knowledge of traditional elegiac laments from an earlier time and from another part of Greece, the Doric-speaking world of the Peloponnese. Andromache's elegiac song, in short, is an exercise in archaism and perhaps exoticism, but not innovation. In Chapter 7, 'Revival', I conclude this study with a close reading of the famous 'Prologue' to Callimachus' *Aitia*, a programmatic manifesto where he lays out a defence of his own elegiac practices and castigates those of his rivals. I argue that the learned scholar-poet, who probably had at his fingertips the remains of most of archaic Greek poetry, consciously imitates the stanzaic compositions of his elegiac ancestors as a way of illustrating the poetic advice he gives in the 'Prologue'.

Finally, I append to this volume three short studies, which examine a number of individual poems that also illustrate my argument, but which, I felt, might ultimately detract from it, because of the lack of comparanda or the poor condition of an especially lacunose text. These appendices are offered, in short, as suggestions for further study. The first examines Mimnermus 12 as an example of a generic kind of elegiac digression that encompasses a single stanza. The second is devoted to Solon's famous Fragment 4 ('Eunomia'), which pulls together two earlier and tangential discussions (in Sections 3.2 and 4.2) of small portions of the same long fragment and offers a full reading of this striking, but woefully lacunose text as a single poem that was probably composed originally in at least five stanzas. The last appendix examines *Theognidea* 133–42, a somewhat clumsy composition that reveals how elegiac poets might use the stanza to collect a series of wisdom sayings into a fairly coherent stanza.

A few important caveats. In this study I offer only a handful of new insights into the literary interpretation of individual elegiac fragments. This is by design, since my primary goals are to describe and illustrate the salient features of the generic elegiac stanza and then to suggest how it lends structure to many of the longer fragments of early Greek elegy. In most cases the fairly stable body of scholarly interpretation of any individual fragment dovetails quite neatly with my added claim that it is composed in stanzas. In order to emphasize my agreements with this scholarly consensus and to highlight my rare disagreements with it, I have opted, with very few exceptions, to print the text of Martin West and the translation of Douglas Gerber[28] and to use similarly standard texts and translations of the elegiac compositions that do not appear there.

My second caveat concerns the unfolding of the argument. Of the six central chapters outlined above the first two are almost entirely descriptive and synchronic, and in them I offer a formal analysis of many extant fragments of early elegy. But if at the end of Chapter 3 my readers are not convinced that the stanza was an important compositional tool for the early elegiac poets, I advise them to stop reading, since the chapters that follow are designed to build on the basic arguments of the first three chapters and therefore assume some degree of acceptance of the ideas set forth in them. For the same reason it is inadvisable to dip into this study as a running commentary on individual poems and to skip, for example, directly to Chapter 4 to find out what I have to say about Tyrtaeus 12, since my arguments there are less likely to persuade someone who has not read the preceding two chapters.

A third disclaimer: there are a few occasions in this book where the stanzaic architecture of a longer poem leads me to suspect that a single end-stopped couplet has dropped out of the transmitted text of a particular fragment, usually in a repetitive list or description, such as the third stanza of Tyrtaeus 11, but especially in Solon 27 and Xenophanes 2, where the lacuna is confirmed by an obvious omission of a logical part of a series.[29] Scholars working on choral odes regularly use the same principle, of course, when they suspect lacunae in otherwise readily comprehensible texts, because of mismatches between the length or metre of responding strophes. Thus, for example, scholars agree that a whole verse has dropped out of a choral passage in Aeschylus' *Persians* that gives a repetitive list of the Persian war dead. They do so only because the metrical responsion between strophe and antistrophe demands a responding verse after line 995. In other words, without knowledge of the strophic

---

[28] West (1992) and Gerber (1999), who generally uses West's text, but in the rare cases that he does not, I discuss it in the notes.

[29] See Sections 3.2 and 6.1.

architecture of tragic choruses and the metrical responsion between strophes, this loss would never have been detected.[30] How is it then that modern scholars were so quick to discover the metrical responsion in passages of choral poetry and so slow to recognize the stanzaic structure of archaic elegy? The problem lies, I suspect, at the very origins of classical scholarship, for although the scholars at Alexandria in the Hellenistic and early Roman periods produced critical editions of and learned commentaries on Pindar, Bacchylides, and the tragedians and even discovered strophic responsion,[31] such critical editions and commentaries were either not produced or simply do not survive for the archaic elegiac poets,[32] except for the two polymetric masters Archilochus and Simonides, who were included in the canon of nine lyric poets.[33]

In fact the loss of single end-stopped elegiac couplets is common enough in the manuscript traditions of elegiac poems. We can see this process, for example, in the textual transmission of a five-couplet epigram of Leonidas of Tarentum: the last three couplets (all end-stopped) begin with the same verb in the same form and as a result the middle couplet has completely disappeared in the Palatine recension, a fact that would have been lost on us entirely were the full text not preserved in the alternate Planudean recension.[34] And in the case of the much larger collections of Latin elegy, scholars often are confronted with similar problems resulting from the excision or rearrangement of single end-stopped couplets, especially in sections where there is a series of similar end-stopped couplets in rigid

[30] Other Aeschylean examples include, e.g., the *Septem* (where we need a verse after 890 to correspond to 903), a lacuna in *Suppliants* 574–75, and missing lines after *Agamemnon* 1005 and 1522.

[31] Aristophanes of Byzantium apparently excised some extraneous words after line 27 of Pindar, *Olympian* 2, because they ruined the responsion. See Pfeiffer (1968) 187.

[32] See the comments of Gerber (1997, 103) on Tyrtaeus.

[33] Pfeiffer (1968, 205–06) discusses the canon of nine lyric poets, but nowhere does he mention Alexandrian or later editions of Callinus, Tyrtaeus, Mimnermus, Solon or Theognis. In fact, aside from a passing reference to Solon these poets do not appear at all in his study of the advent of classical scholarship. This is not to say that such editions did not exist. Indeed there are hints that some kind of edition, scholarly or not, was in circulation. In the case of Solon, for example, there are scattered hints that a formal corpus existed, which organized his poems by meter (see Ch. 5, n. 4).

[34] See the comments of Gow and Page (1965) on Leonidas no. 11 ad loc.

composition, as one finds, for example, in a catalogue.[35] This problem is, of course, greatly compounded in cases where the elegiac fragment in question survives in a single papyrus copy (for example, the 'Prologue' to Callimachus' *Aetia*) or is preserved solely by an often unreliable anthologist like Stobaeus (e.g. Mimnermus 2 or Solon 13).

Weil's thesis of the stanzaic composition of archaic elegy has some sobering, but not entirely unexpected, ramifications for our understanding of the survival and transmission of the earliest fragments of the elegiac poetry. The contrasts are remarkable. Whereas the longer fragments of Tyrtaeus and Xenophanes, for example, have survived antiquity with their stanzaic structures intact or at least still clearly visible, Solon 13 and the so-called 'Cyrnus Book' (*Theognidea* 19–254)—two other long fragments that are thought to preserve archaic elegiac compositions—reveal the unevenly corrosive effects of both oral re-performance and later scribal tampering. Stanzaic analysis reveals, for example, that although the midsection of Solon 13 (33–62) is composed fluently in three well-wrought five-couplet stanzas, the verses that precede and follow show few signs of stanzaic architecture at all, suggesting that if this fragment does indeed preserve the poetry of Solon, it does so in a corrupt form. We find a similar combination in the 'Cyrnus Book', where, for example, the first thirty verses and the last nine were apparently composed as stanzas, but much of the intervening material was not.

In neither case is this surprising, of course. Although the manuscripts of Stobaeus preserve Solon 13 as a single poem, scholars in the past have often complained about its loose syntactical organization and the 'stream of consciousness' displayed in its argument, and some argue that the last fourteen lines are probably two independent fragments unconnected with Solon.[36] And indeed, recent evidence regarding the new elegiac fragments of Simonides confirm long-standing fears that Stobaeus, his sources or the scribes that transmitted his work were capable of wrongly combining unrelated fragments.[37] Some modern scholars treat the *Theognidea* with the

---

[35] See e.g. the recent discussion of Butrica (1997) on the text of Propertius.

[36] For a good summary, see Gerber (1991) 176–79.

[37] Sider (2001*b*) 272–80.

same healthy skepticism, because it contains so many fragments that elsewhere are attributed to other poets.[38] This problem is, as we shall see, greatly exacerbated by the inconsistencies of transmission. It is easy to be critical of Stobaeus, but is also important to remember that he and his sources did manage to preserve in good condition two of the three longer Tyrtaean fragments that display stanzaic structure most vividly. Likewise in the 'Cyrnus Book' we find easily recognizable examples of single five-couplet stanzas side by side with an equal number of shorter and in some cases obviously truncated fragments that have presumably been excerpted from longer poems.

[38] Gerber (1991) 190–94.

2

Internal Structure

Of the two derivations of the word 'stanza' mentioned in the previous chapter, we shall explore first the idea of a stanza as a 'room', that is, a free-standing and internally coherent poetic unit. Many early archaic elegiac fragments do, in fact, seem to be composed in five-couplet stanzas, individually marked by thematic or rhetorical coherence but also by poetic devices common to other genres, for example, ring-composition and other forms of repetition that bring the stanza to satisfying closure. Single elegiac stanzas often take one of two recognizable forms with regard to content: (i) an A–B form, which begins with one theme or outlook, but then finishes—sometimes after a dramatic twist in the middle of the fifth line—with another, strongly contrary one; and (ii) an A–B–A form, which begins with one topic (A), shifts to a second (B), which challenges or illustrates the first, and then returns to the first (A) at the very end of the stanza. Elegiac poets also cast other kinds of rhetorical forms or generic set-pieces in the form of a single stanza. One persistent pattern consists of four couplets of meditation followed by a single one of exhortation. Set-pieces include the elegiac prayer, which often starts and ends with the name of the deity invoked, and the elegiac catalogue or priamel, which regularly begins with a general gnomic statement and then lists at least three illustrative examples of it.

2.1. STANZAS WITH AN INTERNAL TWIST

Later Greek authors quote a number of elegiac fragments that are five couplets in length, and modern editors tend to agree that most of these seem to be complete poems or, at least, rhetorically and logically complete sections of longer poems. One of the oldest is a well-known fragment of Archilochus that has a vocative in the very first line:[1]

> κήδεα μὲν στονόεντα, Περίκλεες, οὔτε τις ἀστῶν
> μεμφόμενος θαλίῃς τέρψεται οὐδὲ πόλις·
> τοίους γὰρ κατὰ κῦμα πολυφλοίσβοιο θαλάσσης
> ἔκλυσεν, οἰδαλέους δ᾽ ἀμφ᾽ ὀδύνῃς ἔχομεν
> πνεύμονας. ἀλλὰ θεοὶ γὰρ ἀνηκέστοισι κακοῖσιν,   5
> ὦ φίλ᾽, ἐπὶ κρατερὴν τλημοσύνην ἔθεσαν
> φάρμακον. ἄλλοτε ἄλλος ἔχει τόδε· νῦν μὲν ἐς ἡμέας
> ἐτράπεθ᾽, αἱματόεν δ᾽ ἕλκος ἀναστένομεν,
> ἐξαῦτις δ᾽ ἑτέρους ἐπαμείψεται. ἀλλὰ τάχιστα
> τλῆτε, γυναικεῖον πένθος ἀπωσάμενοι.   10

There will be no disapproval of our mourning and lamentation, Pericles, when any citizen or even state takes pleasure in festivities, since such fine men did the wave of the loud-roaring sea wash over, and our lungs are swollen from pain. But, my friend, for incurable woes the gods have set powerful endurance as an antidote. This woe comes to different people at different times. Now it has turned upon us and we bewail a bloody wound, but later it will pass to others. Come, endure with all haste, thrusting aside womanly mourning.

For a long time scholars were of the opinion that this is a fragment of a longer lament occasioned by a shipwreck that drowned the husband of Archilochus' sister,[2] but more recently some have cautiously suggested that the fragment is a complete poem.[3] This controversy need not detain us, however, for as we shall see time and again, either of these views could very well be true: Archilochus may have designed these verses as a complete and aesthetically pleasing compositional unit within a longer poem or he may have composed them as a single

[1] Archilochus 13, preserved by Stobaeus (4.56.3).

[2] See, e.g. Hudson-Williams (1926) 86, who like many earlier commentators is influenced by the mention in Plutarch (*Moralia* 33a–b) and Longinus (*On the Sublime* 10) of Archilochus' apparently famous poem about a shipwreck. West (1992) ad loc., bundles Fragments 9–13 in the traditional manner, but in his *apparatus criticus* to Fragment 13 comments: '*fort. carmen integrum.*' See Bossi (1990) 84–85 for a full review of recent opinions.

[3] See e.g. West (quoted in the preceding note), Campbell (1967) 145–46 ('[These lines] have the air of a complete poem: line 1 sounds like a beginning and 9–10 like an end, as well as echoing the central couplet'), Adkins (1985) 36, Bowie (1986) 22 n. 46 ('perhaps complete'), and idem (1997) 60: ('Stobaeus seems to have got hold of an elegy that might be complete') and Gerber (1997) 92 ('appearance of completeness').

poem. The question is moot for this study, which aims to show that
the elegiac stanza can serve either capacity.

Archilochus deploys a number of poetic devices in this fragment
that signal unity of design and closure. The final imperative τλῆτε,
for instance, clearly echoes an important word in the thematically
crucial central couplet (6: τλημοσύνην).[4] This fragment, moreover, is
knit together by the enjambment between couplets (at lines 5 and 7)
and within individual couplets,[5] and it is framed rhetorically by the
vocative in the first line and the imperative in the last.[6] Most commentators agree, moreover, that the fragment falls into two unequal
and somewhat contradictory parts: it begins by stating as a fact the
acceptability of mourning, but then ends by rejecting it entirely.
Archilochus dramatically emphasizes this change in outlook by
launching the second movement of the fragment in the second foot
of line 5 after the enjambed πνεύμονας—a turnabout that unsettles
the orderly rhythm of the poem, which begins with two rather
conservatively composed couplets, the first end-stopped. In the second half of the fragment, however, the poet follows up with the
strongly enjambed φάρμακον and other midline punctuation in
lines 7, 8, and 9.[7] The second half of this poem or stanza also
introduces the gods (θεοί) in an emphatic position between ἀλλὰ

---

[4] Campbell (1967) 145.

[5] Adkins (1985) 37. Note, too, that in the latter case, the verb is regularly placed at
the beginning of the pentameter: ἔκλυσεν (4), ἐτράπεθ᾽ (8), and τλῆτε (10).

[6] The shift in grammatical number is quite interesting, as Archilochus begins by
focusing on the personal loss of a single person, Pericles, the addressee of the poem,
but then he widens our sense of the magnitude of the devastation by revealing—
emphatically in the placement of words—the plurality of victims at the beginning of
the second couplet and by including himself in the first-person plural verb at the end
of line 4 and the pronoun at the end of line 7. Up to this point we might, nonetheless,
imagine a personal meditation of the Theognidean sort addressed to Cyrnus, but
then the poet ends with a plural vocative that implies a larger gathering of men, like
that usually imagined for the martial elegies of Callinus and Tyrtaeus.

[7] Adkins (1985) 39. Some scholars tend to attribute the energetic features in the
second half of the poem to Archilochean style generally. Thus, van Raalte (1988, 150)
cites Archilochus 13.3–8 as a good example of the 'maximum integration' produced
by the simultaneous enjambment of both hexameters and pentameters. Barnes (1995,
148) notes generally that Archilochus' surviving elegiac fragments display more
freedom and a 'more innovative and premeditated approach to composition, one
less dependent on traditional patterns.' I suggest here, and below, that these 'Archilochean' features may in fact be generic to elegiac stanzas of the A–B type, in which the
second half is more energetically and powerfully composed.

and γάρ, to counter the earlier emphasis on human perceptions and endeavors: the citizens (end of line 1), the city (end of line 2) and the collective victims of the shipwreck (beginning of line 3).⁸ Finally, this fragment contains within its brief compass the two most important parts of an early Greek elegiac poem: nearly nine lines of meditation on human nature, followed by a single command to act upon this meditation (τλημοσύνην ... τλῆτε).

We find a similarly coherent and dramatic internal structure in a well-known and widely admired five-couplet fragment of Mimnermus:⁹

> τίς δὲ βίος, τί δὲ τερπνὸν ἄτερ χρυσέης Ἀφροδίτης;
> τεθναίην, ὅτε μοι μηκέτι ταῦτα μέλοι,
> κρυπταδίη φιλότης καὶ μείλιχα δῶρα καὶ εὐνή,
> οἷ' ἥβης ἄνθεα γίνεται ἁρπαλέα
> ἀνδράσιν ἠδὲ γυναιξίν· ἐπεὶ δ' ὀδυνηρὸν ἐπέλθῃ   5
> γῆρας, ὅ τ' αἰσχρὸν ὁμῶς καὶ καλὸν ἄνδρα τιθεῖ,
> αἰεί μιν φρένας ἀμφὶ κακαὶ τείρουσι μέριμναι,
> οὐδ' αὐγὰς προσορέων τέρπεται ἠελίου,
> ἀλλ' ἐχθρὸς μὲν παισίν, ἀτίμαστος δὲ γυναιξίν·
> οὕτως ἀργαλέον γῆρας ἔθηκε θεός   10

What life is there, what pleasure without golden Aphrodite? May I die when I no longer care about secret intrigues, persuasive gifts, and the bed, those blossoms of youth that men and women find alluring. But when painful old age comes on, which makes even a handsome man ugly, grievous cares wear away his heart and he derives no joy from looking upon the sunlight; he is hateful to boys and women hold him in no honour. So harsh has the god made old age.

All recent commentators feel that this fragment is a complete poem.¹⁰ Even the particle δέ in the first line, once thought to be an impediment to such a claim, is now understood to belong to a group of typically adversative or continuative particles, including ἀλλά and γάρ, which often appear at the beginning of elegiac fragments and

---

⁸ Campbell (1967) ad loc. and Adkins (1985) 39.
⁹ Mimnermus 1, preserved by Stobaeus (4.20.16).
¹⁰ See e.g. Campbell (1967) ad loc., Gerber (1970) 106 ('air of completeness'), West (1974) 74–75, Adkins (1985) 96 ('[these lines] could be a satisfactory poem in themselves'), Bowie (1997) 60 ('complete') and again Gerber (1997) 93 ('appearance of completeness').

20 *Internal Structure*

seem to reflect the genre's close association with the symposium and the practice of 'taking up the song'.[11] The final line clearly brings closure: the asyndeton (here = γάρ) explains the cause for despair—the harshness of old age—while the adverb οὕτως sums up the negative descriptions that fill the second half of the fragment: 'For *so* harsh has the god made old age.'[12]

Like Archilochus, Mimnermus changes the mood of these verses dramatically in the middle of the fifth line from a fairly upbeat description of joyful youth to a gloomy assessment of the woes of old age, and he unsettles the balanced structure of the initial two couplets, each of which contains a complete thought.[13] He emphasizes, moreover, the bisection of the poem by deliberately mirroring the content and language of the two halves. The first line ends with the name of Aphrodite, who provides much of the joy of youth, while the last line closes with the anonymous and apparently hostile god who makes old age so harsh for mortals. And a string of neuter singular adjectives contrasts the joy of the opening line (1: τερπνὸν) with the lack of joy (8: οὐδ᾽... τέρπεται) and the pain and harshness of old age: ὀδυνηρὸν (5) and ἀργαλέον (10).[14] Similarly Mimnermus matches the men and women in line 5 (ἀνδράσιν ἠδὲ γυναιξίν), who are attracted by young men, with the boys and women in line 9 (παισίν... γυναιξίν), who reject the aging lover at the end of the poem.

Mimnermus uses many of these same techniques in another long fragment, which alludes to a famous Homeric simile:[15]

ἡμεῖς δ᾽, οἷά τε φύλλα φύει πολυάνθεμος ὥρη
ἔαρος, ὅτ᾽ αἶψ᾽ αὐγῆς αὔξεται ἠελίου,
τοῖς ἴκελοι πήχυιον ἐπὶ χρόνον ἄνθεσιν ἥβης
τερπόμεθα, πρὸς θεῶν εἰδότες οὔτε κακὸν

---

[11] See e.g. Verdenius (1974) 173–74, Allen (1993) 146–56, and Slings (2000), who all cite Reitzenstein (1893) 45–48. Allen (1993, 43) likewise connects it with the practices of sympotic singing. For further discussion see Section 4.1 below.

[12] Van Groningen (1958) 124.

[13] Adkins (1985, 97) notes that the second couplet is syntactically complete and the enjambment of ἀνδράσιν ἠδὲ γυναιξίν is unnecessary.

[14] I thank Peter White for this insight.

[15] Mimnermus 2, preserved by Stobaeus (4.34.12). As I will do throughout this study, I divide the Greek text and English translation of longer fragments into five-couplet units separated by a blank line in order to help clarify my argument by the visual layout. For discussion of the Homeric allusion, see Griffith (1976) and Allen (1993) ad loc.

οὔτ' ἀγαθόν· Κῆρες δὲ παρεστήκασι μέλαιναι,   5
ἡ μὲν ἔχουσα τέλος γήραος ἀργαλέου,
ἡ δ' ἑτέρη θανάτοιο· μίνυνθα δὲ γίνεται ἥβης
καρπός, ὅσον τ' ἐπὶ γῆν κίδναται ἠέλιος.
αὐτὰρ ἐπὴν δὴ τοῦτο τέλος παραμείψεται ὥρης,
αὐτίκα δὴ τεθνάναι βέλτιον ἢ βίοτος·   10
πολλὰ γὰρ ἐν θυμῷ κακὰ γίνεται· ἄλλοτε οἶκος
τρυχοῦται, πενίης δ' ἔργ' ὀδυνηρὰ πέλει·
ἄλλος δ' αὖ παίδων ἐπιδεύεται, ὧν τε μάλιστα
ἱμείρων κατὰ γῆς ἔρχεται εἰς Ἀίδην·
ἄλλος νοῦσον ἔχει θυμοφθόρον· οὐδέ τίς ἐστιν   15
ἀνθρώπων ᾧ Ζεὺς μὴ κακὰ πολλὰ διδοῖ.

We are like the leaves, which the flowery season of spring brings forth, when they quickly grow beneath the rays of the sun; like them we delight in the flowers of youth for an arm's length of time, knowing neither the bad nor the good that comes from the gods. But the dark spirits of doom stand beside us, one holding grievous old age as the outcome, the other death. Youth's fruit is short-lived, lasting as long as the sunlight spreads over the earth. And when the end of this season passes by, straightway death is better than life.

For many are the miseries that beset one's heart. Sometimes a man's estate wastes away and a painful life of poverty is his; another in turn lacks sons and longing for them most of all he goes beneath the earth to Hades; another has soul-destroying illness. There is no one to whom Zeus does not give a multitude of ills.

Most editors and commentators treat all sixteen lines as a coherent poem, but a few treat the first ten lines as well-balanced unit, as I have isolated it above.[16] In this first section of the poem, as in Mimnermus 1, the poet shifts dramatically in the midst of line 5 from a reflection on the springtime and sunny delights of youth to an abrupt warning that the dark demons of old age or death have taken a stand nearby. He brings these contrasting ideas and moods into sharp contrast by repeating and undercutting all three of the key images in the first half of the poem. The brief season of springtime, the light of the sun and the bloom of youth, he says, will all pass us by in good time. Poetic

---

[16] For the traditional assessment, see e.g. van Groningen (1958) 124, Schmiel (1974) or Griffith (1976). Barron and Easterling (1989, 94), on the other hand, discuss the first ten lines as if they were by themselves a coherent and pleasing unity and others (see next note) praise the ring-composition in them.

form, moreover, perfectly matches thematic content. In an amazing display of ring-composition Mimnermus sees to it that the key thematic words at the ends of lines 1–3 (ὥρη, ἠελίου, ἤβης) are systematically answered and thereby undone in reversed order by the same words, which appear in the second half of the poem at the ends of lines 7–9 (ἤβης, ἠέλιος, ὥρης).[17]

Mimnermus has, in short, put a good deal of thought and effort into composing the first ten lines of Fragment 2 as a discrete unit, whose internal structure is a marvel of precise word placement and balance. The final three couplets of the fragment quoted by Stobaeus (lines 11–16) do not, however, cohere well stylistically or rhetorically with the first five couplets: they are all end-stopped and their hexameters all have a strong penthemimeral caesura with a subsequent sense break at the bucolic diaresis, features that appear regularly (as we shall see) in elegiac catalogues.[18] Nor does this catalogue make complete sense rhetorically as the end of a poem begun at line 1, although it is perhaps a fitting start to another stanza designed to explain (γάρ) the first. But given the evidence mentioned earlier that Stobaeus or his copyists were capable of mistakenly combining two separate poems or excerpts into a single citation,[19] we need to be suspicious of the integrity of fragments like this one that survive only in his *Florilegium*. In any event, it is clear that Mimnermus or perhaps another poet constructs the last three couplets in a catalogue-style that differs greatly from the first ten lines, where he composes fluently with an elaborate triple ring of line-end repetitions and is in no way hemmed in by the stichic boundaries of the individual couplets.[20]

---

[17] See Gerber (1970) 108 and Donnet (1995) 265. Other scholars have commented on part of this pattern: Schmiel (1974, 248) notes the repetition of ἤβη and ὥρη, Griffith (1976, 78–79) of ὥρη, and Slings (2000, 18) remarks that the repetition of ἠέλιος in lines 2 and 8 is a form of ring-composition.

[18] Allen (1993) 144. The penthemimeral caesura creates an initial *hemiepes* in each couplet, which adds to the sense of regularity, since the pentameter is itself formed by two *hemiepe* in succession. As I discuss at the end of this chapter, lines 11–16 take the form of a truncated elegiac catalogue. They also begin with γάρ, suggesting that they may have been designed to explain or illustrate the contents of the preceding stanza (lines 1–10).

[19] Sider (2001*b*) 272–80.

[20] See Griffith (1976) 78–79, for the special artistry of the first ten lines.

2.2. RING-COMPOSITION AND PRAYERS

The early elegists, as we saw above in the case of Mimnermus and as we shall see throughout this volume, were enormously fond of ring-composition. We find a simple, but well crafted example in *Theognidea* 1341–50 (= Evenus 8c):[21]

> αἰαῖ, παιδὸς ἐρῶ ἀπαλόχροος, ὅς με φίλοισιν
> πᾶσι μάλ’ ἐκφαίνει κοὐκ ἐθέλοντος ἐμοῦ.
> τλήσομαι οὐ κρύψας ἀεκούσι⟨α⟩ πολλὰ βίαια·
> οὐ γὰρ ὑπ’ αἰκελίῳ παιδὶ δαμεὶς ἐφάνην.
> παιδοφιλεῖν δέ τι τερπνόν, ἐπεί ποτε καὶ Γανυμήδους   1345
> ἤρατο καὶ Κρονίδης ἀθανάτων βασιλεύς,
> ἁρπάξας δ’ ἐς Ὄλυμπον ἀνήγαγε καί μιν ἔθηκεν
> δαίμονα, παιδείης ἄνθος ἔχοντ’ ἐρατόν.
> οὕτω μὴ θαύμαζε, Σιμωνίδη, οὕνεκα κἀγὼ
> ἐξεφάνην καλοῦ παιδὸς ἔρωτι δαμείς.   1350

Alas, I am in love with a soft-skinned boy who shows me off to all my friends in spite of my unwillingness. I'll put up with the exposure—there are many things that one is forced to do against one's will—for it's by no unworthy boy that I was shown to be captivated. And there is some pleasure in loving a boy, since once in fact even the son of Cronus, king of the immortals, fell in love with Ganymede, seized him, carried him off to Olympus, and made him divine, keeping the lovely bloom of boyhood. So, don't be astonished, Simonides, that I too have been revealed as captivated by love for a handsome boy.

The poet argues that he is not ashamed to reveal his infatuation with a young boy (A), Zeus, after all, fell in love with Ganymede (B), therefore do not be amazed at the poet's infatuation (A). The mythological exemplum in the middle section is a rhetorical device typical of thematic ring-composition and it is effectively and humorously deployed here.[22] The poet enhances this thematic ring with a strong verbal one, when he repeats the same pair of aorist passive verb and

---

[21] This poem has also been assigned to Evenus because it is addressed to Simonides, a person who is addressed by Evenus in other poems. Harrison (1902), West (1992) and Gerber (1999) all treat it as a single poem, although some earlier editors treated 1345–50 as a separate poem; see West (1974) ad loc. for discussion.

[22] Fowler (1987) 74.

participle near the end of the first section A (1344: οὐ ... ὑπ' αἰκελίῳ
παιδὶ δαμεὶς ἐφάνην) and at the very end of the poem (1350: ἐξεφάνην
καλοῦ παιδὸς ἔρωτι δαμείς). The summary use of the adverb οὕτω at
the beginning of the last couplet, moreover, reminds us of the
emphatic placement of οὕτως at the beginning of the final pentameter of Mimnermus 1, and is a sure sign of closure in both stanzas.
The poet, however, overlays these complimentary patterns of thematic and verbal ring-composition with a rhetorical structure similar
to that used in Archilochus 13: four couplets of description followed
by one of advice.

A five-couplet stanza near the middle of the 'Cyrnus Book' (*Theognidea* 183–92) shows a similar degree of ring-composition:[23]

κριοὺς μὲν καὶ ὄνους διζήμεθα, Κύρνε, καὶ ἵππους
   εὐγενέας, καί τις βούλεται ἐξ ἀγαθῶν
185 βήσεσθαι· γῆμαι δὲ κακὴν κακοῦ οὐ μελεδαίνει
   ἐσθλὸς ἀνήρ, ἤν οἱ χρήματα πολλὰ διδῷ,
οὐδὲ γυνὴ κακοῦ ἀνδρὸς ἀναίνεται εἶναι ἄκοιτις
   πλουσίου, ἀλλ' ἀφνεὸν βούλεται ἀντ' ἀγαθοῦ.
χρήματα μὲν τιμῶσι· καὶ ἐκ κακοῦ ἐσθλὸς ἔγημε
190 καὶ κακὸς ἐξ ἀγαθοῦ· πλοῦτος ἔμειξε γένος.
οὕτω μὴ θαύμαζε γένος, Πολυπαΐδη, ἀστῶν
   μαυροῦσθαι· σὺν γὰρ μίσγεται ἐσθλὰ κακοῖς.

We seek out rams and asses and horses that are purebred, Cyrnus, and
everyone wishes that they mount (females) of good stock; but a noble
man does not mind marrying the base daughter of a base father if the latter
gives him a lot of money, and a woman does not refuse to be the wife of a
base man who is rich, but she wants a wealthy man instead of one who is
noble. It is money people honour; one who is noble marries the daughter of
one who is base and one who is base marries the daughter of one who is
noble. Wealth has mixed up blood. And so, Polypaïdes, do not be surprised
that the townsmen's stock is becoming enfeebled, since what is noble is
mixing with what is base.

Although, as in the preceding example, the manuscripts themselves
offer us no firm evidence about the beginning and end of this
fragment of the *Theognidea*, most scholars agree that the first line

[23] Stobaeus preserves some of these lines at 4.22.99, 4.29.53 (citing 'Xenophon' as
his source) and 4.30.11a.

of this fragment is the beginning of a poem, because the vocative
Κύρνε appears there and because the Athenian historian Xenophon
or another late-classical writer of the same name apparently knew of
a collection of Theognidean poems that began with line 183.[24]
Commentators, moreover, generally believe that line 192 is the end
of this fragment, because these five couplets are such a well-crafted
unity, both rhetorically and poetically.[25]

In part this impression arises from the complicated and somewhat
mind-numbing ring-composition that it displays. The statement in
the second couplet, for instance, γῆμαι δὲ κακὴν κακοῦ οὐ
μελεδαίνει | ἐσθλὸς ἀνήρ, ἤν οἱ χρήματα πολλὰ διδῷ, is reflected in
nearly reversed order in the fourth: χρήματα μὲν τιμῶσι· καὶ
ἐκ κακοῦ ἐσθλὸς ἔγημε.[26] As we shall see often in this study, verbal
echoes and parallel structures between the second and fourth couplets
of a stanza are common features of elegiac ring-composition. The
poet also emphasizes the internal structure and unity of the stanza by
creating a chiastic pattern in the progression of the main verbs—
βούλεται (184), οὐ μελεδαίνει, (185), οὐδὲ...ἀναίνεται, (187) and
βούλεται (188)—and by the reiteration of the word γένος near the
end of the poem (190 and 191), which recalls the adjective εὐγενέας
placed at the beginning of the first pentameter.[27] But, although this
poem contains an overabundance of verbal ring-composition, thematically it does not take the A–B–A form, like the Ganymede poem. Here
the three central couplets treat the same theme relentlessly and we see
how a Theognidean stanza can be used to collect and organize a series

[24] See e.g. Harrison (1902) 73–87, West (1974) 42 and 56–57, and Bowie (1997)
63. Gerber (1999, 175 n. 2) more cautiously suggests that the crucial word ἀρχή in
Xenophon's introduction means 'primary element' rather than 'beginning'.
[25] Garyza (1958, 166–67), van Groningen (1966, 72–75), Campbell (1967, 358),
Gerber (1970, 284–85), and Fowler (1987, 74) all treat these verses as a single poem.
Campbell (1983, 111) calls it a 'well constructed poem'. West (1992, ad loc.) agrees,
but suggests a lacuna after line 188, because he finds the μὲν at the beginning of the
fourth couplet inexplicable unless we posit a lacuna. Adkins (1985, 140) suggests,
however, that the γάρ in the version of 'Xenophon' quoted by Stobaeus removes the
problem entirely and should be adopted. He adds: 'Not only does Stobaeus' text make
sense, but it is difficult to imagine what could have appeared in the intervening lines
that would not weaken the tirade.'
[26] Nagy (1985, 55) and Kurke (1989, 543–44) both note the repetition of χρήματα
and other words for wealth in this poem.
[27] Adkins (1985) 140 and Nagy (1985) 55.

of wisdom-sayings and round them off into a fairly polished stanza. These verses do, however, have the same formal structure as the Ganymede poem: four couplets of meditation followed by a final couplet that begins with the same kind summary injunction (192: οὕτω μὴ θαύμαζε) followed by a vocative.[28]

I have up to this point identified two different ways of organizing content or theme within the five-couplet stanza. In the first (the A–B form), poets dramatically in the midst of the fifth line divide the stanza into two slightly unequal portions, in order to interrupt and then correct a meditation, with the result that the poet radically changes his mind or mood at the end: in this way Archilochus reverses the thought that it is permissible to mourn and Mimnermus revises his initially idyllic descriptions of youth and love, by suddenly imagining the onset of old age. The second type of internal stanzaic architecture (the A–B–A form) is a more continuous meditation or argument, in which the B section illustrates the assertions of A by providing examples, before the poet returns to and reiterates his initial thought (A). Such different thematic forms can, however, share other poetic and rhetorical structures. Archilochus 13 and *Theognidea* 183–92, for example, differ in their thematic organization, but they share the same rhetorical form: four couplets of meditation that begin with a vocative ('O Pericles!' or 'O Kyrnus!) and close with an exhortation in the final pentameter ('Be brave!' or 'Don't be amazed!'). Likewise Mimnermus 1 and *Theognidea* 1341–50, although they, too, have different kinds of thematic organization (the first A–B, the second A–B–A), both indicate closure by the summary use of the adverb οὕτως ('in this way') and by deploying verbal ring-composition.

The early elegists are also fond of using verbal ring-composition to frame five-couplet prayers to the gods. A well-known prayer to Zeus at *Theognidea* 341–50 is a good starting point, since it also displays

[28] *Theognidea* 429–38 are also treated by editors as an individual poem, because they contain a rhetorically complete argument; see ad loc., the comments of Harrison (1902), Garyza (1958), van Groningen (1966), and Gerber (1999). As in the Ganymede poem, they also display a clear and (in this case) even more overwrought ring-composition, which Fowler (1987, 74) summarizes as follows: 429–31 (theme: 'it easier to beget a man than educate him'), 432–34 (exemplum) and 435–38 (theme again).

the same internal twist that we observed earlier in the fragments of Mimnermus and Archilochus:

> ἀλλά, Ζεῦ, τέλεσόν μοι, Ὀλύμπιε, καίριον εὐχήν·
> δὸς δέ μοι ἀντὶ κακῶν καί τι παθεῖν ἀγαθόν.
> τεθναίην δ', εἰ μή τι κακῶν ἄμπαυμα μεριμνέων
> εὑροίμην. δοίην δ' ἀντ' ἀνιῶν ἀνίας:
> αἶσα γὰρ οὕτως ἐστί. τίσις δ' οὐ φαίνεται ἡμῖν   345
> ἀνδρῶν, οἳ τἀμὰ χρήματ' ἔχουσι βίῃ
> συλήσαντες· ἐγὼ δὲ κύων ἐπέρησα χαράδρην
> χειμάρρῳ ποταμῷ πάντ' ἀποσεισάμενος·
> τῶν εἴη μέλαν αἷμα πιεῖν· ἐπί τ' ἐσθλὸς ὄροιτο
> δαίμων, ὃς κατ' ἐμὸν νοῦν τελέσειε τάδε.   350

Come, Olympian Zeus, fulfill my timely prayer; grant that I experience something good to be set against my ills, or may I die if I do not find some relief from the anxieties that plague me. May I give pain in return for pain; for that is my due. But there is no retribution in sight for me against the men who have my possessions, which they robbed from me by force. I am like the dog that crossed the mountain stream in winter's flood and shook everything off. May I drink their dark blood! And may an avenging[29] spirit rise up so as to bring this to pass in accordance with my intent.

This is a complete prayer and all editors agree that it must end at line 350, in part because the very next line in the manuscripts (351) addresses Penia ('Poverty') and thus seem to introduce a new poem.[30] The ἀλλά at the beginning of the first couplet, moreover, is a common enough way to begin a prayer.[31] The two halves of this fragment are knit together by the same kind of verbal ring-composition we have seen before: the wish κατ' ἐμὸν νοῦν τελέσειε in the last line clearly recalls the imperative τέλεσόν μοι in the first, and the invocation of Olympian Zeus at the beginning of the first line is countered by the anonymous δαίμων at the start of the last, very much as Aphrodite, mentioned prominently at the end of the first

---

[29] Gerber (1999, 225 n. 2) is rightly uncomfortable with this odd translation of the adjective ἐσθλὸς, and he offers an alternative translation: 'may my guardian spirit watch over me.'

[30] See ad loc., the texts and comments of Garyza (1958), van Groningen (1966), Campbell (1967), West (1992) and Gerber (1999). Fränkel (1975, 416) and Campbell (1983, 109) discuss these lines as a single unit.

[31] See Hudson-Williams (1910) ad loc. for discussion and parallels.

line of Mimnermus 1, is recalled by the nameless θεός who replaces her at the end of the last (10).

The similarities do not, however, stop there. This poem contains a conditional wish to die near the start of the fragment (343; cf. Mimnermus 1.2) and also changes its tone dramatically in the middle of the fifth line (345): the poet starts with a deferential request to Zeus to stop his suffering and to punish his enemies, but then he interrupts himself and complains bitterly that in fact no revenge (τίσις) is forthcoming and he wishes that a 'noble spirit' (ἐσθλὸς δαίμων) might arise and fulfil his wish to drink the blood of his enemies. As in the other stanzas with a sharp internal twist, form follows content: the Theognidean poet begins with two rather orderly, end-stopped couplets, but then, after his emotional complaint in the middle of the fifth line, he produces two powerfully erratic verses, first by overrunning the couplet into the beginning of line 347 (συλήσαντες) and then by dividing the final hexameter with a strong pause after the first syllable of the fourth foot (349) in order to highlight the ghastly reference to the drinking of blood (αἷμα πιεῖν).

There is another well-known five-couplet prayer in the Theognidean corpus, which seems to have been composed during the Persian Wars (773–88):

> Φοῖβε ἄναξ, αὐτὸς μὲν ἐπύργωσας πόλιν ἄκρην,
> Ἀλκαθόῳ Πέλοπος παιδὶ χαριζόμενος·
> 775 αὐτὸς δὲ στρατὸν ὑβριστὴν Μήδων ἀπέρυκε
> τῆσδε πόλευς, ἵνα σοι λαοὶ ἐν εὐφροσύνῃ
> ἦρος ἐπερχομένου κλειτὰς πέμπωσ' ἑκατόμβας
> τερπόμενοι κιθάρῃ καὶ ἐρατῇ θαλίῃ
> παιάνων τε χοροῖς ἰαχῇσί τε σὸν περὶ βωμόν·
> 780 ἦ γὰρ ἔγωγε δέδοικ' ἀφραδίην ἐσορῶν
> καὶ στάσιν Ἑλλήνων λαοφθόρον. ἀλλὰ σύ, Φοῖβε,
> ἵλαος ἡμετέρην τήνδε φύλασσε πόλιν.
>
> ἦλθον μὲν γὰρ ἔγωγε καὶ εἰς Σικελήν ποτε γαῖαν,
> ἦλθον δ' Εὐβοίης ἀμπελόεν πεδίον
> 785 Σπάρτην δ' Εὐρώτα δονακοτρόφου ἀγλαὸν ἄστυ·
> καί μ' ἐφίλευν προφρόνως πάντες ἐπερχόμενον·
> ἀλλ' οὔτις μοι τέρψις ἐπὶ φρένας ἦλθεν ἐκείνων.
> οὕτως οὐδὲν ἄρ' ἦν φίλτερον ἄλλο πάτρης.

Lord Phoebus, since it was you who built the towering citadel, as a favour to
Pelops' son Alcathous, so now keep the Median army's aggression away from
this city, so that at the coming of spring the people may send you glorious
hecatombs amid festivity, delighting in the lyre and in lovely feasting and in
the dances of paeans and in cries round your altar. For indeed I am afraid
when I look upon the mindless, people-destroying strife of the Greeks.
Come, Phoebus, graciously protect this city of ours.

For I went once to the land of Sicily and I went to the vine-rich plain of
Euboea and to Sparta, the splendid city of the reed-nourishing Eurotas, and
they all treated me with kindly friendship on my arrival. But no delight came
to my heart from them, so true it is after all that nothing else is dearer than
one's homeland.

Although West and Gerber hesitantly treat all eight couplets as a
single continuous poem, most commentators and editors treat the
first five couplets of this fragment as a separate and complete poem
or compositional unit.[32] Indeed, at line 783 the poet switches somewhat abruptly from a formal prayer to an autobiographical narrative
of his travels to other parts of the ancient world.[33] But as in the case
of the last three couplets of Mimnermus 2, we need not deny that
these lines could have been designed to follow this five couplet
prayer—indeed one could argue that the poet is explaining (783:
γάρ) why he is praying so fervently to Apollo to protect his home
town.[34]

The stanzaic boundaries of the initial prayer are heavily marked by
the same vocative at the beginning of the first hexameter (773: Φοῖβε)
and at the very end of the last one (781: ἀλλὰ σύ, Φοῖβε), and by the
echo of the two similar requests: στρατὸν ... ἀπέρυκε | τῆσδε πόλεως
(775–6) and τήνδε φύλασσε πόλιν (782).[35] The verses are framed even
further by the concern for the god's friendly disposition towards the
Megarians (774: χαριζόμενος and 782: ἵλαος), and by the similarly
formulated descriptions of the external and internal threats facing

[32] See Carrière (1948) 193–94 for a summary of the majority opinion.
[33] The last three couplets also differ stylistically from those that precede; Carrière
(1948, 270–71) notes that in all of the pentameters of the prayer to Apollo, the initial
hemiepe are dactylic, whereas there is only one in the final three pentameters.
[34] In fact, the pattern here—a stanza of exhortation followed by verses of meditation introduced by γάρ—is common in early elegy (see Section 3.1 below).
[35] The final exhortation begins with ἀλλά at the bucolic caesura of the fifth
couplet—just as it does in Archilochus 13.

the city: στρατὸν ὑβριστὴν Μήδων (775) and στάσιν Ἑλλήνων
λαοφθόρον (781).[36] The middle portion, on the other hand, describes
the potential gifts that await the god if he responds positively: four
lines ending with significant nouns that alternate between images of
festivity and sacrifice: εὐφροσύνῃ (776); ἑκατόμβας (777); θαλίῃ (778);
and βωμόν (779). This prayer provides, in short, a good example of
how verbal ring-composition can enhance the A–B–A structure of a
stanza, for we have a request (A), the justification for it (B) and then
the renewed request (A).

Sometimes elegists place divine names at the beginning and the
end of five-couplet units that are not prayers, but the effect is similar.
Tyrtaeus 4, for example, recounts how a Spartan delegation famously
brought back from Delphi oracular instructions regarding the future
form of their government:[37]

> Φοίβου ἀκούσαντες Πυθωνόθεν οἴκαδ' ἔνεικαν
> μαντείας τε θεοῦ καὶ τελέεντ' ἔπεα·
> ἄρχειν μὲν βουλῆς θεοτιμήτους βασιλῆας,
> οἷσι μέλει Σπάρτης ἱμερόεσσα πόλις,
> 5   πρεσβυγενέας τε γέροντας· ἔπειτα δὲ δημότας ἄνδρας
> εὐθείαις ῥήτραις ἀνταπαμειβομένους
> μυθεῖσθαί τε τὰ καλὰ καὶ ἔρδειν πάντα δίκαια,
> μηδέ τι βουλεύειν τῇδε πόλει ⟨σκολιόν⟩·
> δήμου τε πλήθει νίκην καὶ κάρτος ἕπεσθαι.
> 10 Φοῖβος γὰρ περὶ τῶν ὧδ' ἀνέφηνε πόλει.

After listening to Phoebus they brought home from Pytho the god's oracles
and sure predictions. The divinely honoured kings, in whose care is Sparta's
lovely city, and the aged elders are to initiate counsel; and then the men of
the people, responding with straight utterances, are to speak fair words, act
justly in everything, and not give the city <crooked> counsel. Victory and
power are to accompany the mass of the people. For so was Phoebus'
revelation about this to the city.

As in the two prayers discussed above, Tyrtaeus marks this five-couplet
fragment as a unified and complete unit by beginning and ending
it with the divine name as the source of the oracular command

---

[36] I owe these last two examples to Mark Usher.

[37] This text combines overlapping verses quoted by Plutarch (*Lycurgus* 6) and
Diodorus Siculus (7.12.5–6). For a thorough discussion of the historical background,
see Andrewes (1938).

(1: *Φοίβου* and 10: *Φοῖβος*).[38] The last line, moreover, rhetorically brings the piece to closure by combining γάρ and the adverb ὧδ(ε): '*For* Phoebus *thus* revealed . . .' Because we can syntactically make sense of the four final hexameters (lines 3, 5, 7, and 9, which purport to be the text of Apollo's command) without the three pentameters that separate them, scholars have suggested plausibly that Tyrtaeus constructs these elegiac verses around an original four-line hexametrical response of the oracle.[39] If this is true, then it is significant that in the process of transforming oracular hexameters into elegiac couplets, the poet has framed them within a single elegiac stanza.

2.3. CATALOGUES AND PRIAMELS[40]

Scholars often note the important role that catalogues and priamels play in the longer fragments of early Greek elegy. Indeed, compositions like Solon's poem on the 'Ages of Man' (Fragment 27), the priamel at the beginning of Tyrtaeus 12, or the long catalogue in the midsection of Solon 13 are often singled out as exemplary of the type.[41] No one to my knowledge has noticed, however, that early elegiac poets tend to fashion such catalogues as single stanzas of five couplets or as coordinated groups of stanzas. To establish the basic form of the elegiac catalogue, I begin with a rather simple and poetically uninspiring example found on a Megarian inscription of late-Roman date, which preserves a poem that was apparently composed around the time of the Persian Wars:[42]

---

[38] Jaeger (1966, 126), Adkins (1985, 69), and Fowler (1987, 81) rightly cite this repetition as a classic example of ring-composition. Diodorus Siculus 7.12.6 preserves an entirely different version of the first couplet, which nonetheless preserves the bracketing feature of the repeated divine name: ⟨ὧ⟩δε γὰρ ἀργυρότοξος ἄναξ ἑκάεργος Ἀπόλλων | χρυσοκόμης ἔχρη πίονος ἐξ ἀδύτου·

[39] See e.g. West (1974) 184–85, Campbell (1983) 88, and Adkins (1985) 74.

[40] Most of this section appeared earlier as Faraone (2005a).

[41] See e.g. Race (1982) 57–62 and 64–71, who discusses Tyrtaeus 12.1–10, Xenophanes 2, Solon 13.43–64 and *Theognidea* 699–718.

[42] Page (1981) 213–15 Simonides no. 16 and Campbell (1991) Simonides no. xvi. I give the text and translation of the latter. The poem is preserved on an inscription of late-antique date that purports to be a new copy of an epigram of Simonides, the original of which had become 'destroyed with time'. Page states ad loc. that, although

32   *Internal Structure*

Ἑλλάδι καὶ Μεγαρεῦσιν ἐλεύθερον ἆμαρ ἀέξειν
ἱέμενοι θανάτου μοῖραν ἐδεξάμεθα,
τοὶ μὲν ὑπ' Εὐβοίαι καί Παλίωι, ἔνθα καλεῖται
ἁγνᾶς Ἀρτέμιδος τοξοφόρου τέμενος,
5   τοὶ δ' ἐν ὄρει Μυκάλας, τοὶ δ' ἔμπροσθεν Σαλαμῖνος
⟨   ⟩
τοὶ δὲ καὶ ἐν πεδίωι Βοιωτίωι, οἵτινες ἔτλαν
χεῖρας ἐπ' ἀνθρώπους ἱππομάχους ἰέναι.
ἀστοὶ δ' ἄμμι τόδε ⟨ξυνὸν⟩ γέρας ὀμφαλῶι ἀμφίς
10   Νισαίων ἔπορον λαοδόκωι 'ν ἀγορᾶι.

While striving to foster the day of freedom for Greece and the Megarians, we received the portion of death, some under Euboea and Pelion, where stands the sanctuary of the holy archer Artemis, others at the mountains of Mycale, others before Salamis… others again in the Boeotian plain, those who had courage to lay hands on the cavalry warriors. The citizens granted us this privilege in common about the navel of the Nisaeans in their agora where the people throng.

This epitaph purports to be the words of the dead men who are honoured by the inscription. They frame their boast by references to themselves as a collective—note the inclusive first-person plural verb 'we received' (ἐδεξάμεθα) in the initial couplet and the dative pronoun 'to us' (ἄμμι) in the last. In the body of the poem, however, the poet divides this large mass of troops into at least four discrete units of soldiers, who died fighting the Persians in different battles. The three central couplets each begin with a repeated pronoun (τοὶ μέν … τοὶ δ'… τοὶ δέ), have a strong break at the end of the couplet, and consistently display a penthemimeral caesura—all hallmarks, as we shall see, of elegiac catalogues. This kind of caesura, in particular, creates a regular rhythm in the couplet, which begins with a single *hemiepes* and ends with two.[43] The poet brings additional closure to the poem by referring to the Megarian people in the first

Simonidean authorship is most probably fictitious, 'there is nothing in the vocabulary, phrasing or metre incompatible with the early fifth-century'.

[43] Barnes (1995, 150) notes, in fact, that archaic elegists tend to avoid this caesura at a rate three times more than hexameter poets, because they wish to avoid having the regular and presumably monotonous pace of three *hemiepe* in the same couplet. I suggest that in the construction of elegiac catalogues poets use this caesura precisely to give an added sense of order to them.

and last lines (Μεγαρεῦσιν and Νισαίων), as if to reiterate the political unity of these warriors who died in different places and presumably at different times.

The first five couplets of Tyrtaeus 12 are likewise designed as a complete elegiac catalogue:[44]

οὔτ᾽ ἂν μνησαίμην οὔτ᾽ ἐν λόγῳ ἄνδρα τιθείμην
οὔτε ποδῶν ἀρετῆς οὔτε παλαιμοσύνης,
οὐδ᾽ εἰ Κυκλώπων μὲν ἔχοι μέγεθός τε βίην τε,
νικῴη δὲ θέων Θρηΐκιον Βορέην,
οὐδ᾽ εἰ Τιθωνοῖο φυὴν χαριέστερος εἴη,   5
πλουτοίη δὲ Μίδεω καὶ Κινύρεω μάλιον,
οὐδ᾽ εἰ Τανταλίδεω Πέλοπος βασιλεύτερος εἴη,
γλῶσσαν δ᾽ Ἀδρήστου μειλιχόγηρυν ἔχοι,
οὐδ᾽ εἰ πᾶσαν ἔχοι δόξαν πλὴν θούριδος ἀλκῆς·
οὐ γὰρ ἀνὴρ ἀγαθὸς γίνεται ἐν πολέμῳ...   10

I would not mention or take account of a man for his prowess in running or in wrestling, not even if he had the size and strength of the Cyclopes and outstripped Thracian Boreas in the race, nor if he were more handsome than Tithonus in form and richer than Midas and Cinyras, nor if he were more kingly then Pelops, son of Tantalus, and had a tongue that spoke as winningly as Adrastus, nor if he had a reputation for everything save furious valour. For no man is good in war...[45]

As in the Megarian inscription, the poet stresses the regular order and uniformity of the catalogue by placing strong pauses at the end of each couplet, by breaking all but one of the hexameters at the penthemimeral caesura, and by beginning each of the three middle couplets with the same repeating phrase 'not even if' (οὐδ᾽ εἰ). These middle couplets all have the same thematic structure as well, with each hexameter and pentameter providing at least one point of comparison (for example,

[44] Weil (1862, 9–10) was the first to note that lines 1–10 form a single unit, although other scholars have intuited it after him. Jaeger (1966, 119), for example, observes that lines 1–10 are 'a series of anaphoras whose irresistible crescendo does not come until line 10'—he is followed here by Tarditi (1982, 62)—and Fowler (1987, 82) refers to 'the strict symmetry of the first ten lines.' Adkins (1985, 74) refers to these lines as a complete priamel.

[45] The syntax of the final line extends into the beginning of the following stanza. See Faraone (2006) 36–38 and below at the end of Ch. 5 for detailed discussion of how this overrun of the stanzaic boundary is an artefact of a later re-performance of the fragment.

speed, beauty, or wealth) and at least one mythological exemplum of it (for example, Boreas, Tithonos, or Midas).

Although the final couplet begins with the same phrase ('not even if'), it breaks the pattern, because it introduces a summary statement that returns us to the generic man mentioned at the start of the stanza (1: ἄνδρα and 10: ἀνήρ), whose possible talents or skills are hypothetically described in the intervening verses. The three central couplets, moreover, each provide specific examples of these skills, much the same way that the three middle couplets of the Megarian epigram, break down the collective 'we' in the first verse into smaller discrete groups of warriors, who are identified more precisely by the site of their heroic deaths. In both cases, I should add, more than three examples are actually described within the three central couplets, but the repeating phrase or pronoun at the start of each couplet provides a regular rhythm or pattern to the series.

The final couplet of Tyrtaeus' catalogue differs from the Megarian epigram in one important way: it sums up the list in order to reject every item on it, by saying 'not even if he had a reputation for *everything* except furious valor'.[46] This popular variation of the catalogue is called a priamel, a poetic device consisting of a series of three or more paratactic statements of similar form, which serve to emphasize the last, usually by denigrating the rest.[47] The final line of this catalogue from Tyrtaeus 12 does not, however, provide the closure and rhetorical punch that one might expect from a priamel, because it is not a complete poem in and of itself, but rather a rhetorical device that Tyrtaeus uses to launch himself into a description in the next stanza of the noble warrior who is, in fact, excellent in the art of war. The priamel is, however, so artfully constructed, that were it stripped of its final couplet, we would not know that it was part of a martial elegy. Indeed, another poet in a different context might just as easily have ended it with a reference to love-making or wine-drinking as the prized activity, instead of warfare. We shall see,

[46] Race (1982, 57–59) gives an excellent discussion of lines 1–9, which he calls 'one of the best known priamels.'

[47] Race (1982) 9.

in fact, that the stanzaic priamel was a popular set-piece in elegiac composition.[48]

Solon seems to have been especially adept at expanding and manipulating the basic elegiac catalogue. In the second half of his Fragment 13, the famous 'Hymn to the Muses', for example, he uses the traditional frame of a five-couplet catalogue to compose a continuous thirty-line sequence (13: 33–62), which easily divides up into three separate stanzas.[49] The first stanza gives examples of faulty human self-perceptions and the false expectations that attend them (13.33–42):[50]

θνητοὶ δ᾽ ὧδε νοέομεν ὁμῶς ἀγαθός τε κακός τε,
†ἐν δηνην† αὐτὸς δόξαν ἕκαστος ἔχει,
πρίν τι παθεῖν· τότε δ᾽ αὖτις ὀδύρεται· ἄχρι δὲ τούτου   35
χάσκοντες κούφαις ἐλπίσι τερπόμεθα.
χὤστις μὲν νούσοισιν ὑπ᾽ ἀργαλέησι πιεσθῇ,
ὡς ὑγιὴς ἔσται, τοῦτο κατεφράσατο·
ἄλλος δειλὸς ἐὼν ἀγαθὸς δοκεῖ ἔμμεναι ἀνήρ,
καὶ καλὸς μορφὴν οὐ χαρίεσσαν ἔχων·   40
εἰ δέ τις ἀχρήμων, πενίης δέ μιν ἔργα βιᾶται,
κτήσεσθαι πάντως χρήματα πολλὰ δοκεῖ.

And thus we mortals, whatever our estate, think that the expectation which each one has is progressing well(?), until he suffers some mishap, and then afterwards he wails. But until then we take eager delight in empty hopes. Whoever is oppressed by grievous sickness thinks that he will be healthy; another man of low estate considers that it's high and that he's handsome though his form is without beauty. If someone is lacking means and is constrained by the effects of poverty, he thinks that he will assuredly acquire much money.

Here, as in the Megarian epigram, Solon uses inclusive first-person verbs in the first two couplets to describe the larger group of humanity ('we mortals think...' and 'we take eager delight...'), followed by

---

[48] See my discussions of the adapted priamel at Solon 13.43–52 (next in this section), at *Theognidea* 699–718 (Ch. 5) and Xenophanes 2.1–12 (Section 6.1)

[49] Scholars have long debated whether Fragment 13 is a single and unified poem and (if it is) how we are to identify its rhetorical or logical units. They generally see line 33 as the beginning of a new section that introduces the second half of the poem; see Gerber (1970, 124) and Anhalt (1993, 33–34) for a summary of earlier discussions.

[50] The verbal range and play of the Greek word δόξα is difficult to capture in translation. Campbell (1967, 234) concisely summarizes this double meaning as follows: 'Mortals, both good and evil, are (unlike Zeus, whose view is comprehensive) deluded by false beliefs and false hopes.'

three examples, each of which takes up a full couplet beginning with a pronoun that is linked syntactically as part of a regular series: χὦστις μέν (37), ἄλλος (39) and εἰ δέ τις (41).[51] The poet, moreover, enhances the unity of this section of the poem by replicating a key term and idea: he places the word δόξα in the first couplet to signal the beginning of this catalogue of (mis)perceptions, an idea that he reiterates in the last two couplets by using the cognate verb δοκεῖ to illustrate two specific cases, first in line 39 and then again in line 42, where it stands as the very last word of this five-couplet stanza.

If these five couplets had survived by themselves as a fragment of Solon's poetry, we would hardly think that they, like the Megarian epigram, constitute a complete catalogue, because we do not find here any sense of closure: the introductory couplet has been doubled in size and the summary statement is entirely missing. But like the Tyrtaean priamel, whose rhetorical ending was blunted to help ease the transition to the next stanza of the poem, the lack of closure here is quite purposeful, because this initial catalogue is followed, somewhat abruptly, by another, in which Solon shifts his attention away from the expectations of mortal men to their various vocations. This section of the fragment is ten couplets in length and can be separated on thematic and rhetorical grounds into two five-couplet stanzas (13.43–62):[52]

σπεύδει δ' ἄλλοθεν ἄλλος· ὁ μὲν κατὰ πόντον ἀλᾶται
ἐν νηυσὶν χρῄζων οἴκαδε κέρδος ἄγειν
45   ἰχθυόεντ' ἀνέμοισι φορεόμενος ἀργαλέοισιν,
φειδωλὴν ψυχῆς οὐδεμίαν θέμενος·
ἄλλος γῆν τέμνων πολυδένδρεον εἰς ἐνιαυτὸν

---

[51] Gerber (1999, ad loc.) and other editors suggest that lines 39–40 refer to *two* different cases (hence the comma at the end of 39): the low-born man, who thinks he is noble, and the ugly one, who believes he is handsome. If this is so, it violates the one-person-per-couplet rule that we see in most of the other elegiac catalogues. But Mülke (2002, 292) is surely right to think that Solon has the stock Greek phrase καλὸς κ' ἀγαθός in mind here and has produced, albeit in a chiastic manner, its poetic opposite: 'And another man of low estate thinks himself noble and handsome, though he has a displeasing shape.'

[52] Snell (1965, 89–90) seems to be the first to call these verses a 'catalogue of vocations' (*Berufekatalog*). Lattimore (1947, 166–67), Allen (1949, 55–56), Campbell (1967, 233–34), West (1974, 181), and Mülke (2002, 295–98) all recognize lines 43–62 as a ten-couplet unit. Buchner (1939, 170–90), and Maddalena (1943, 1–2) likewise think that 33–62 are a single unit, but offer no subdivision of the thirty lines. Race (1982, 65–67) treats lines 43–64 as a complete eleven-couplet priamel.

λατρεύει, τοῖσιν καμπύλ’ ἄροτρα μέλει·
ἄλλος Ἀθηναίης τε καὶ Ἡφαίστου πολυτέχνεω
ἔργα δαεὶς χειροῖν ξυλλέγεται βίοτον,   50
ἄλλος Ὀλυμπιάδων Μουσέων πάρα δῶρα διδαχθείς,
ἱμερτῆς σοφίης μέτρον ἐπιστάμενος·

ἄλλον μάντιν ἔθηκεν ἄναξ ἑκάεργος Ἀπόλλων,
ἔγνω δ’ ἀνδρὶ κακὸν τηλόθεν ἐρχόμενον,
ᾧ συνομαρτήσωσι θεοί· τὰ δὲ μόρσιμα πάντως   55
οὔτε τις οἰωνὸς ῥύσεται οὔθ’ ἱερά·
ἄλλοι Παιῶνος πολυφαρμάκου ἔργον ἔχοντες
ἰητροί· καὶ τοῖς οὐδὲν ἔπεστι τέλος·
πολλάκι δ’ ἐξ ὀλίγης ὀδύνης μέγα γίγνεται ἄλγος,
κοὐκ ἄν τις λύσαιτ’ ἤπια φάρμακα δούς·   60
τὸν δὲ κακαῖς νούσοισι κυκώμενον ἀργαλέαις τε
ἁψάμενος χειροῖν αἶψα τίθησ’ ὑγιῆ.

Everyone has a different pursuit. One roams over the fish-filled sea in ships, longing to bring home profit; tossed by cruel winds, he has no regard for life. Another, whose concern is the curved plough, cleaves the thickly wooded land and slaves away for a year. Another who has learned the works of Athena and Hephaestus, the god of many crafts, gathers in his livelihood with his hands; another, taught the gifts that come from the Olympian Muses and knowing the rules of the lovely art of poetry, makes his living.

Another has been made a seer by lord Apollo who works from afar and, if the gods are with him, he sees a distant calamity coming upon a man; but assuredly neither augury nor sacrifice will ward off what is destined. Others, engaged in the work of Paeon, rich in drugs, are physicians; for them too there is no guarantee. Often agony results from a slight pain and no one can provide relief by giving soothing drugs, whereas another, in the throes of a terrible and grievous disease, he quickly restores to health with the touch of his hands.

Here, as in the elegiac catalogues discussed earlier, we find a general statement ('Everyone has a different pursuit') followed by a list of examples. The first section describes four different vocations: the merchant (ὁ μέν), the ploughman (ἄλλος), the craftsman (ἄλλος), and the poet (ἄλλος). And as in the previous stanza, Solon casts each of the last three descriptions as a complete couplet beginning with the same pronoun and displaying the penthemimeral caesura in their hexameters.[53]

---

[53] In two of the three, moreover, the caesura falls after the same naturally long syllable: ἄλλος γῆν τέμνων (47) and ἄλλος Ὀλυμπιάδων (49). We find the same pattern in the preceding stanza: ἄλλος δειλὸς ἐὼν (39) and εἰ δέ τις ἀχρήμων (41).

The language of this first section, however, and the order of the human pursuits seem to reflect, albeit weakly, the form of the five-couplet priamel discussed earlier: Solon catalogues three kinds of work (merchant, ploughman and craftsman), and then ends with poetry, which is, of course, his own vocation. Although Solon does not emphatically single out poetry as any better than the rest, he nonetheless isolates and elevates it subtly, by treating the first vocation as dangerous (note the 'cruel winds' that beset the merchant) and the second two as contemptibly banausic: the ploughman 'slaves away' at his job while the craftsman gathers his livelihood 'with his hands,' thanks to the 'works' (50: ἔργα) he has learned from the gods. Only the final vocation, that of the poet, is the result of 'gifts' (51: the δῶρα of the Muses) and 'lovely skill' (52: ἱμερτῆς σοφίης), the latter a designation that recalls programmatic statements in Xenophanes and the *Theognidea* about the special craft of elegiac poetry.[54] Both the sequence, then, and the difference in tone between the first three vocations and the last poetic one suggest that this five-couplet stanza may have originally been composed as a priamel that boasted the virtues of elegiac poetry over all other pursuits.[55] Solon, however, seems to have taken this traditional elegiac priamel and adapted it as the first section of a longer catalogue of vocations that prizes but does not openly vaunt the work of the poet.

The second half of this catalogue superficially continues the structural design of the first—the pronouns ἄλλον and ἄλλοι each introduce a new vocation at the start of a couplet—but its form, content

---

[54] For σοφίη as the special skill of the elegiac poet, see e.g. Nagy (1985) 23–36 and Ford (1985) 82–83 and 89–93, on the *Theognidea* and my comments below in Section 6.1 on Xenophanes 2.12–14. See also Pigre's elegiac adaptation of the first line of the *Iliad*, which describes the Muse as she 'who holds the limit of all poetic skill (σοφίη)', where the word appears at the end of the pentameter and in an internal rhyme, i.e. two of the many features that distinguish elegy from epic. See Collins (2004) 136, for text and discussion.

[55] Two Latin examples of a five-couplet elegiac *recusatio* (a form of priamel), Propertius 3.9.35–44 and Petronius *Satyricon* 137.9.1–10, suggest that three foils may have been a typical number for a five-couplet elegiac priamel. Propertius, for example, lays out three themes that he refuses to treat. Each is treated to a full couplet or two that ends with a full stop, and each begins with a repeated first-person verbs: *non ego... findo... non flebo* (the Seven against Thebes)... *nec referam* (the Trojan War). The final couplet states his preference: he will sing like Callimachus. See Race (1982) 136–37 and 148.

and rhetorical purpose are different. In the preceding stanza each worker was the subject of his own sentence, which (with the exception of the first vocation) runs the length of a single couplet. In the second stanza, however, we find only two vocations and they differ from the first four in grammatical case or number: the seer appears in the accusative singular (ἄλλον) and takes up two couplets of description, and the healers appear in the nominative plural (ἄλλοι) and take up three. More important, however, is the change in focus and purpose. This stanza underscores the limits to or ambiguity of human efforts to protect or cure other mortals: the seer can predict the future, but is unable to ward off fate, while the healers have helpful drugs, but these cannot guarantee the life of a patient. Despite such variations, however, these two stanzas were clearly composed as a coordinated pair, with the second picking up from the first the notion that some groups—craftsmen and poets in the first stanza, and seers and healers in the second—receive their talents directly from their patron deities.

Solon, therefore, pieces together three somewhat different stanzas—each five couplets in length—into a fairly logical sequence:[56]

1. a catalogue of faulty human (self-)perceptions or expectations (δόξαι);
2. a priamel-like inventory of vocations that ends with a subtly favorable description of the poet;
3. an extension of (2) that turns into a meditation on the limitations of two additional god-given vocations.

None of these thematically coherent stanzas can, of course, stand as independent poems. Indeed, Solon cleverly deploys them as interlocked units, through which the listener moves quite effortlessly, thanks to their shared linguistic structure, especially the repetition of the pronoun ἄλλος at the start of the couplet and the consistent use of the penthemimeral caesura. But at the same time he manages to

---

[56] Lattimore (1947, 165–68) gives a similar analysis, but without noting the stanzaic structure. He acknowledges, for example, the new start made with lines 33–36 and describes 37–42 as an extension of 33–36. He then goes on to treat 43–62 as a single continuous unit.

vary each stanza by changing the focus, the number of individuals or
vocations described and the type or case of the initial pronoun at the
beginning of each descriptive couplet.[57]

Solon, Tyrtaeus, and the author of the Megarian epitaph all use the
five-couplet stanza to lend a regular structure to catalogues, and they
do so in a manner that nearly approaches generic composition: a
couplet-by-couplet series of *exempla*, each beginning their hexameters with the same or very similar pronouns and dividing them at
the penthemimeral caesura, all devices that are designed to enhance
the regular cadence of the catalogue. The final couplet is usually
reserved for a summation that sometimes uses the first-person plural
to include the poet ('we mortals') or the dramatic speaker (e.g. the
Megarian dead) within the group. Dryden and Pope composed
similar catalogues in heroic couplets, beginning with a general statement, followed by the individual items on the list, for which they
usually devote a single end-stopped and metrically similar couplet.[58]
There are also traces of more specialized forms. Tyrtaeus composes a
priamel at the start of Tyrtaeus 12, in which he contrasts a single
human possession ('furious valour') with a list of other prized, but
ultimately inferior, attributes of famous mythological heroes. I have
suggested, moreover, that the five-couplet priamel may have served
as a kind of elegiac 'set-piece', which is easily adaptable (by changing
the final line) to a wide variety of contexts. Indeed, we detected an
underlying priamel-structure in the first half of Solon's catalogue of
vocations, where he describes three preliminary examples in somewhat negative terms and then ends with the fourth and final example
of the poet, who is subtly praised above the others.

As we shall see in much greater detail below in Sections 3.2 and
6.1, knowledge of the regular architecture of elegiac catalogues—
especially the use of end-stopped couplets that begin with reiterated
pronouns—can help us to intuit places where truncated catalogues
may have lost entire couplets. Thus we saw at the start of this chapter

---

[57] Solon unifies this three-stanza sequence (33–62) by mentioning at the very end
the restoration of health (62: τίθησ' ὑγιῆ) to a man oppressed by terrible diseases (61:
νούσοισι ... ἀργαλέαις), words which recall the deluded man described in the first
stanza, who although oppressed 'by terrible diseases' (37: νούσοισιν ὑπ' ἀργαλέῃσι)
thinks that he will be healthy (38: ὡς ὑγιὴς ἔσται).

[58] Piper (1969) 19–23.

that Mimnermus 2 begins with a particularly well-crafted stanza framed by a complicated triple ring of chiastic repetitions to the spring season, the sun and youth. It ends somewhat disappointingly with three couplets composed in a more staid and repetitive style (lines 11–16):

> πολλὰ γὰρ ἐν θυμῷ κακὰ γίνεται· ἄλλοτε οἶκος
> τρυχοῦται, πενίης δ᾽ ἔργ᾽ ὀδυνηρὰ πέλει·
> ἄλλος δ᾽ αὖ παίδων ἐπιδεύεται, ὧν τε μάλιστα
> ἱμείρων κατὰ γῆς ἔρχεται εἰς Ἀΐδην·
> ἄλλος νοῦσον ἔχει θυμοφθόρον· οὐδέ τίς ἐστιν   15
> ἀνθρώπων ᾧ Ζεὺς μὴ κακὰ πολλὰ διδοῖ.

For many are the miseries that beset one's heart. Sometimes a man's estate wastes away and a painful life of poverty is his; another in turn lacks sons and longing for them most of all he goes beneath the earth to Hades; another has soul-destroying illness. There is no one to whom Zeus does not give a multitude of ills.

We can now appreciate the fact that these lines comprise an abbreviated elegiac catalogue that begins with a general statement (10: πολλὰ γὰρ ἐν θυμῷ κακὰ γίνεται), proceeds with three examples each introduced (as in Solon 13) with similar sounding words— ἄλλοτε (11); ἄλλος (13); and ἄλλος (15)—and then concludes by reiterating the theme of 'many miseries' (16: κακὰ πολλά). Since this catalogue displays most of the features of the elegiac catalogues discussed above (for example, ring-composition, as well as end-stopped couplets with penthemimeral caesurae and reiterated initial pronouns), since in the manuscripts of Stobaeus it follows a perfectly rendered elegiac stanza (Mimnermus 2.1–10), and since we have seen that Mimnermus is adept at composing such stanzas (see also Appendix I), we should leave open the possibility that two full end-stopped stanzas each beginning with ἄλλος might have dropped out of the manuscript before or after the middle couplet or may have even have been ignored by the excerpter himself. We shall see in the next chapter, moreover, that the particle γάρ, which appears at the start of this putative second stanza (line 1), is used repeatedly by early elegiac poets to introduce a new stanza of meditation, one which explains ideas or commands expressed in the stanza that preceded it.

The five-couplet stanza, then, serves as a useful frame for sharply defined compositional units, but with the exception of the Megarian epitaph, carved all by itself on a block of stone, we have little direct evidence that any of the elegiac stanzas discussed in this chapter was actually designed as an independent poem. It is true, for example, that Archilochus 13 and Mimnermus 1 seem to express full thoughts in carefully balanced verses, but are they complete compositions? It is, sadly, impossible to know this for certain on available information, although the shift or turnabout in the fifth line of each of these stanzas provides an added argument for completeness. Indeed, this shift recalls the traditional 'turn' in the ninth line of both the Petrarchan and the Shakespearian sonnet, which often questions or stops a thematic development, unsettles the regular movement of the poem, and thereby signals that the end of the poem (the final sestet) is near.[59] If this analogy is apt, then, we might speculate that five-couplet fragments with an internal twist may have a greater claim to being independent poems. The question is, in fact, even more complicated, because there lies a third possibility (which I take up in Chapter 4): the idea of Reitzenstein and others that some of the extant fragments of early elegy were performed by a series of symposiasts, each taking up the song from the previous singer, but adding his own coherent and complete addition, which from the perspective of the individual performer is a single composition, but from the perspective of the group represents a discrete part of the larger communal composition.

But for now it suffices to conclude that the early elegiac poet could deploy a single elegiac stanza in a variety of ways (e.g. in prayers or catalogues) and that the five-folder itself could take on a variety of forms. Indeed, among the scant surviving fragments I have identified at least four different internal structures. The first, the A–B form, has a dramatic shift in the middle that moves the audience suddenly from one mood or idea to a very different one. The second form, A–B–A, displays the classic device of thematic ring-composition. The four-plus-one form begins with four couplets of description or meditation and then ends with a fifth of advice. The basic shape of an elegiac catalogue and priamel, however, seems stiffer in format, since

59 Fussell (1965) 119–28 and Herrnstein-Smith (1968) 52–53.

it is usually built up on a series of single, end-stopped couplets, which each begin with the same or similar pronouns and have a regular cadence. I suggested in the previous chapter that the five-couplet stanza provided the unit for the melody performed by the *aulos*. The existence of these four types of internal stanzaic structure leads me to suggest further that the aulete may have played different, but somewhat standardized melodic patterns for each, in order to emphasize, for instance, the turnabout in the middle of the fifth stanza of the A–B type or the summary flourish of the final line of advice in the four-plus-one format. There are undoubtedly other, basic forms of the five-folder lurking in the extant corpus of Greek elegy, but those discussed here suffice to show that the five-couplet stanza provided a traditional, yet flexible frame that could be altered internally for different situations, moods or needs.

3

Composition

In the previous chapter, we examined the inner structure of individual stanzas, turning our attention only in the last instance, the catalogues of Solon 13, to how these stanzas might be arranged with others in a longer sequence. In what follows I shift entirely to this second, more complex order of analysis and once again I find it helpful to invoke the two different derivations of the term 'stanza'. Italian musicians and poets originally imagined stanzas as regular 'stopping points' on a journey, at which the poet could pause and then change the content, tone, or mode of his discourse, a model that is most apt for the first section of this chapter, where I discuss how elegiac poets regularly use the boundaries between stanzas as points of transition between advice and meditation, the two basic linguistic actions of the elegiac genre.[1] The second definition of stanza as a 'room', which proved useful in the previous chapter, will be invoked again in the second half of this chapter. Here, however, I draw upon a wider architectural metaphor and imagine the structure of a longer poem as a building of sorts assembled from a series of 'rooms', that are joined together in complimentary and coordinated ways. This use of individual stanzas as building blocks allows the poet to present and explore more complex ideas in an extended and orderly fashion, such as we find, for example, in Tyrtaeus' lengthy discussion of excellence ($ἀρετή$) in his Fragment 12 or Solon's 'Ages of Man' elegy (Fragment 24). In both sections, however, my goal is the same: to lay out a second set of criteria, in addition to the internal ones discussed in the

---

[1] See e.g. Jaeger (1966) 113–14, who describes the 'imperative' and 'indicative' components of elegy, or Gerber (1970) 91, who labels the two foci of elegy as 'hortatory' and 'philosophical.'

previous chapter, for isolating individual elegiac stanzas and describing how they work in a series within longer elegiac compositions.

3.1. ALTERNATION[2]

In the longer fragments of martial elegy we find a common pattern: the regular alternation between stanzas of meditation and exhortation. This pattern is most obvious in the extant fragments of Tyrtaeus, who makes regular use of the elegiac stanza in his fragment 10, the first thirty lines of which divide up quite easily into three alternating stanzas.[3] The first provides a meditation on the choice between bravery and cowardice (10.1–10):

> τεθνάμεναι γὰρ καλὸν ἐνὶ προμάχοισι πεσόντα
> ἄνδρ᾽ ἀγαθὸν περὶ ᾗ πατρίδι μαρνάμενον,
> τὴν δ᾽ αὐτοῦ προλιπόντα πόλιν καὶ πίονας ἀγροὺς
> πτωχεύειν πάντων ἔστ᾽ ἀνιηρότατον,
> πλαζόμενον σὺν μητρὶ φίλῃ καὶ πατρὶ γέροντι   5
> παισί τε σὺν μικροῖς κουριδίῃ τ᾽ ἀλόχῳ.
> ἐχθρὸς μὲν γὰρ τοῖσι μετέσσεται οὕς κεν ἵκηται,
> χρησμοσύνῃ τ᾽ εἴκων καὶ στυγερῇ πενίῃ,
> αἰσχύνει τε γένος, κατὰ δ᾽ ἀγλαὸν εἶδος ἐλέγχει,
> πᾶσα δ᾽ ἀτιμίη καὶ κακότης ἕπεται.   10

It is a fine thing for a brave man to die when he has fallen among the front ranks while fighting for his homeland, and it is the most painful thing of all to leave one's city and rich fields for a beggar's life, wandering about with his dear mother and aged father, with small children and wedded wife. For giving way to need and hateful poverty, he will be treated with hostility by

---

[2] Much of this section appeared previously as Faraone (2005b) 317–30.

[3] Noted by Weil (1862, 11) and first explained by Rossi (1953/54, 414–15): 'i primi 30 versi si lasciano disporre in tre gruppi di 10 versi ciascuno; il gruppo centrale contiene una serie di esortazioni all'azione, i due laterali ciascuno una tesi e un'antitesi di carattere discorsivo.' Until fairly recently editors separated Tyrtaeus 10 after line 14 into two poems of roughly equal length, taking as their primary clue the vocative ὦ νέοι in line 15 and the switch from first-person plural hortative subjunctives to second-person plural imperatives, an approach succinctly defended by Fränkel (1975, 154). West (1992), however, prints them as a single fragment and most recent commentators agree, e.g. Verdenius (1969, 347) and Gerber (1970, 72–73).

whomever he meets, he brings disgrace on his line, belies his splendid form, and every indignity and evil attend him.

Tyrtaeus presents us here with an extended gnomic reflection introduced by γάρ,[4] in which he describes first the brave warrior who dies defending his homeland and then the craven or defeated one, who flees and takes his family into exile. Although no obvious signs of ring-composition or repetition mark these five couplets internally as a complete unit, we are made aware of their autonomy when after a pause the poet continues on in a very different manner (10.11–20):[5]

> εἰ δ' οὕτως ἀνδρός τοι ἀλωμένου οὐδεμί' ὥρη
> γίνεται οὔτ' αἰδώς, οὐδ' ὀπίσω γένεος,
> θυμῷ γῆς πέρι τῆσδε μαχώμεθα καὶ περὶ παίδων
> θνήσκωμεν ψυχέων μηκέτι φειδόμενοι.
> 15   ὦ νέοι, ἀλλὰ μάχεσθε παρ' ἀλλήλοισι μένοντες,
> μηδὲ φυγῆς αἰσχρῆς ἄρχετε μηδὲ φόβου,
> ἀλλὰ μέγαν ποιεῖσθε καὶ ἄλκιμον ἐν φρεσὶ θυμόν,
> μηδὲ φιλοψυχεῖ τ' ἀνδράσι μαρνάμενοι·
> τοὺς δὲ παλαιοτέρους, ὧν οὐκέτι γούνατ' ἐλαφρά,
> 20   μὴ καταλείποντες φεύγετε, τοὺς γεραιούς.

But if there is no regard or respect for a man who wanders thus, nor yet for his family after him, let us fight with spirit for this land and let us die for our children, no longer sparing our lives. Come, you young men, stand fast at one another's side and fight, and do not start shameful flight or panic, but make the spirit in your heart strong and valiant, and do not be in love of life when you are fighting men. Do not abandon and run away from elders, whose knees are no longer nimble, men revered.

This second group of five couplets is distinguished from the first by linguistic mode and rhetorical purpose. Just as he marked the initial verse of the previous meditative stanza with γάρ, Tyrtaeus uses the

---

[4] There is some disagreement whether the first line of the Tyrtaeus 10 is the beginning of a poem. Traditionally it was thought that the γάρ explained some previous expression or thought, but Verdenius (1969, 337–38) and Adkins (1977, 75–89) suggest that γάρ, δέ and other so-called continuative particles are sometimes placed at the beginning of elegiac poems.

[5] At the beginning of line 11 West (1992, ad loc.) prints εἶθ' οὕτως with a dagger, but I follow Verdenius (1969, 347), Gerber (1999, ad loc.), Adkins (1977, 78–79) and others, who print Francke's simple emendation.

particle τοι (line 11) at the start of this stanza to signal the switch from generic speculation to the direct exhortation of the audience at hand.[6]

Indeed, whereas the first stanza is entirely descriptive or evaluative and focuses exclusively on the situations of two hypothetical soldiers, the second from beginning to end exhorts the audience of young men to fight bravely: Tyrtaeus distributes seven exhortations evenly over the ten lines: two first-person plural hortative subjunctives (13 and 14) followed by five second-person plural imperatives (15, 16, 17, 18, and 20).[7] And although he uses participles densely in both stanzas, he distinguishes them in number and grammatical case. He deploys singular and mainly accusative participles in the first stanza to describe how the generically good soldier falls bravely in battle (πεσόντα) while fighting (μαρνάμενον), but the cowardly one abandons (προλιπόντα) his city, wandering (πλαζόμενον) and eventually giving way (εἴκων) to poverty. In the second stanza, on the other hand, the participles are all plural and nominative, alternating between active and middle forms: μηκέτι φειδόμενοι (14); μένοντες (15); μαρνάμενοι (18); and μὴ καταλείποντες at the beginning of the final verse (20). The last two participles in the second stanza (18: μαρνάμενοι and 20: μὴ καταλείποντες), moreover, plainly recall and in some sense respond positively to the pair of participles placed near the beginning of the first stanza (2: μαρνάμενον and 3: προλιπόντα), the first of which describes the brave warrior fighting in the thick of battle and the second the craven one in the act of abandoning his city in disgrace. The advice supplied in the second stanza is, in short, based solidly on the 'theory' outlined in the first.

It seems, then, that the poet designed the first twenty lines of Tyrtaeus 10 as a pair of stanzas, the first of which—by means of generic description, comparison and evaluation—ruminates on the choices set before a soldier in time of war, while the second exhorts the audience to follow one of these paths and avoid the other. In addition to the subtle ring-composition created by the repeated

---

[6] See Denniston (1954) 537–38, and Verdenius (1969) on the force of τοι here.

[7] Rossi (1953/54) 415. Marta Cuypers points out to me how each of the last three pentameters begins with μή and has the same rhythmical structure—note especially the parallel placement of the two imperatives: ἄρχετε (16) and φεύγετε (20).

participles at the beginning of the first stanza and the end of the
second, Tyrtaeus links these two stanzas together in a more linear
fashion by the protasis at the start of the second ('But if there is no
regard or respect for a man who wanders thus, nor yet for his family
after him...'), which recalls the pathetic scene described in the first:
'wandering about with his dear mother and aged father, with small
children and wedded wife'.

Tyrtaeus continues on in the same manner in the third stanza of
this fragment, which, like the first, offers a meditation introduced by
γάρ (10.21–30):[8]

αἰσχρὸν γὰρ δὴ τοῦτο, μετὰ προμάχοισι πεσόντα
κεῖσθαι πρόσθε νέων ἄνδρα παλαιότερον,
ἤδη λευκὸν ἔχοντα κάρη πολιόν τε γένειον,
θυμὸν ἀποπνείοντ᾽ ἄλκιμον ἐν κονίῃ,
25   αἱματόεντ᾽ αἰδοῖα φίλαις ἐν χερσὶν ἔχοντα—
αἰσχρὰ τά γ᾽ ὀφθαλμοῖς καὶ νεμεσητὸν ἰδεῖν—
καὶ χρόα γυμνωθέντα· νέοισι δὲ πάντ᾽ ἐπέοικεν,
ὄφρ᾽ ἐρατῆς ἥβης ἀγλαὸν ἄνθος ἔχῃ,
ἀνδράσι μὲν θηητὸς ἰδεῖν, ἐρατὸς δὲ γυναιξὶ
30   ζωὸς ἐών, καλὸς δ᾽ ἐν προμάχοισι πεσών.

For this brings shame, when an older man lies fallen among the front ranks
with the young behind him, his head already white and his beard grey,
breathing out his valiant spirit in the dust, clutching in his hands his
bloodied genitals—this is a shameful sight and brings indignation to be-
hold—his body naked. But for the young everything is seemly, as long as he
has the splendid prime of lovely youth; while alive, men marvel at the sight
of him and women feel desire, and when he has fallen among the front ranks,
he is fair.

Here, as in the first stanza of the fragment, Tyrtaeus explores and
compares the appropriateness of men falling in battle, a theme that
he once again examines in two hypothetical and diametrically opposed cases, which are neatly bracketed and contrasted by the repetition—in nearly identical phrases—at the end of the first and last
lines: it is shameful for the old men to fall in the front ranks while
the young hang back (21: αἰσχρὸν γὰρ... μετά προμάχοισι πεσόντα

---

[8] Barron and Easterling (1989, 92) discuss these verses as if they were a discrete
and coherent unit.

κεῖσθαι πρόσθε νέων) whereas the young man is virtuous, brave and beautiful, whenever he falls among the fore-fighters (30: καλὸς δ᾽ ἐν προμάχοισι πεσών).⁹

And Tyrtaeus, just as he does at the start of the second stanza, picks up a theme that appears in the command at the end of the previous stanza ('Do not abandon older warriors in the fray'), when he begins this new stanza by giving the rationale that lies behind the exhortation (21–27 midline: 'For it is shameful…'). He then ends with the alternate case: a young man is desirable and beautiful both alive and dead—in the latter case if he falls in the first ranks of the warriors. The poet heightens the contrast first by repeating the adjectives αἰσχρὸν and αἰσχρὰ at the beginning of lines 21 and 26, and then by focusing our attention almost voyeuristically on the sight of the two different bodies, in each case filling up an entire verse and using a similar construction: αἰσχρὰ τά γ᾽ ὀφθαλμοῖς καὶ νεμεσητὸν ἰδεῖν (26); and ἀνδράσι μὲν θηητὸς ἰδεῖν, ἐρατὸς δὲ γυναιξὶ (29).¹⁰ Tyrtaeus further unifies this stanza by its linguistic consistency. He deploys five singular accusative participles to describe the shamefully abandoned older man (21: πεσόντα; 23: ἔχοντα; 24: ἀποπνείοντ᾽; 25: ἔχοντα; and 27: γυμνωθέντα) and two in the nominative case to describe the young man who dies nobly (both in 30: ἐών and πεσών). The shift, moreover, from the accusative case in construction with an infinitive (21–2: αἰσχρὸν γὰρ … κεῖσθαι πρόσθε νέων) to the nominative (30: ζωὸς ἐών … πεσών) follows the pattern established in the first stanza (1–2: τεθνάμεναι γὰρ καλὸν and 8: χρησμοσύνῃ τ᾽ εἴκων καὶ στυγερῇ πενίῃ).

There emerges, then, a significant pattern of alternating stanzas in the first thirty lines of Tyrtaeus 10:¹¹

[10 lines] Meditation introduced by γάρ
(indicative verbs and singular participles, primarily in the accusative, but then ending in the nominative)

⁹ Weil (1862) 12–13.
¹⁰ Adkins (1977, 95) stresses the special use here and elsewhere in Tyrtaeus 10 of the visual or aesthetic range of Greek moral vocabulary (i.e. καλός = 'beautiful') to urge young men to fight. Stehle (1997, 120–21) rightly notes that the young male bodies are eroticized as well.
¹¹ Rossi (1953/54) 414–15.

50   *Composition*

[10 lines] Exhortation introduced by τοι
(plural hortative subjunctives and imperatives with plural nominative participles)

[10 lines] Meditation introduced by γάρ
(indicative verbs and singular participles, primarily in the accusative, but then ending in the nominative)

Weil also noted how the last line of the third stanza in addition to
recalling the first line of its own stanza also echoes the very first line
of the fragment:[12]

τεθνάμεναι γὰρ καλὸν ἐνὶ προμάχοισι πεσόντα (1 = 1st of 1st stanza)
αἰσχρὸν γὰρ δὴ τοῦτο, μετὰ προμάχοισι πεσόντα (21 = 1st of 3rd stanza)
ζωὸς ἐών, καλὸς δ᾽ ἐν προμάχοισι πεσών. (30 = last of 3rd stanza)

This triple responsion of nearly identical verse-ending phrases at the
beginnings of both meditative stanzas and the end of the last one
emphasizes important differences in their moral evaluation: it is a
fine thing, Tyrtaeus asserts, when brave men fall fighting in the front
ranks, but a shameful thing when elderly warriors fall in the same
position, while the young hang back. This combination, therefore, of
ring-composition within stanzas and responsion between them
serves two important functions: similar line-endings articulate the
architecture of the fragment by calling attention to the beginnings
and endings of individual units, while at the same time diametrically
opposed moral terms at or near the start of these same lines
(καλόν... αἰσχρόν... καλός) highlight the great moral differences
between these choices.

Is it the case, then, that the first thirty lines consist of a complete
three-stanza elegiac poem? Perhaps, but there remains one difficulty.
According to our primary source for this fragment—the manuscripts
of the fourth-century Athenian orator Lycurgus (*Against Leocrates*
107)—Tyrtaeus 10 continues on with a single couplet:

ἀλλά τις εὖ διαβὰς μενέτω ποσὶν ἀμφοτέροισι
στηριχθεὶς ἐπὶ γῆς, χεῖλος ὀδοῦσι δακών.

---

[12] Weil (1862) 11 and Rossi (1953/54) 415. The result, as Adkins (1977, 96) puts it,
is that line 30 'constitutes the conclusion of, if not quite an argument, the movement
of Tyrtaeus' thought.'

Come, let everyone stand fast, with legs set well apart and both feet fixed
firmly on the ground, biting his lip with his teeth.

These words would seem to introduce yet another round of exhortation, but some editors, beginning with Brunck, have traditionally
dismissed them as a scribal intrusion or mistake of some sort, since
an identical couplet also appears in Tyrtaeus 11.21–22, where it does,
in fact, introduce a stanza of exhortation (see below in Section 3.2).
Others have suggested, however, that this final couplet provides a
fitting peroration for an elegiac poem of this sort, which ideally
should end with a final call to battle.[13]

The stanzaic structures outlined above clearly isolate the last
couplet in an awkward manner, and at first glance they might
encourage us to follow Brunck's lead and excise lines 31–32. This
couplet is not, however, so easily dismissed since it has not one, but
two perfectly good fourth-century Athenian witnesses: in addition to
Lycurgus, Plato seems to have known a version of this fragment that
included these final two verses.[14] If, then, we accept the fact that in
the fourth century both Lycurgus and Plato knew a version of the
poem that contained verses 31–32, and the fact that the preceding
lines were artfully composed as three stanzas that alternate between
meditation and exhortation, I suggest that we can add a third
hypothesis to the two debated by scholars: the 32-line fragment
quoted in the manuscripts of Lycurgus is incomplete and Tyrtaeus
10 was, in fact, originally composed as a series of at least four five-
couplet stanzas, articulated by the regular alternation between
stanzas of meditation introduced by γάρ and those of exhortation
introduced by τοι or ἀλλά.[15]

In the first twenty lines of Tyrtaeus 11, the poet once again uses the
boundary between five-couplet stanzas to shift from one linguistic

[13] Prato (1968, 100–1) provides a detailed survey of both sides of the argument.

[14] Verdenius (1969, 348) points out that Plato paraphrases Fragment 10—albeit in
condensed fashion—at *Laws* 630b: διαβάντες δ' εὖ καὶ μαχόμενοι ἐθέλοντες
ἀποθνήσκειν (cf. Tyrtaeus 10.31: εὖ διαβὰς; and 10.13–14: μαχώμεθα καὶ...|
θνήσκωμεν ψυχέων μηκέτι φειδόμενοι).

[15] In Faraone (2005*b*) I also suggest that the piling up of vivid participles in
the final couplet (31–32)—'with legs set well apart' (εὖ διαβὰς), 'firmly fixed'
(στηριχθείς) and 'biting' (δακών)—continues Tyrtaeus' practice throughout this
fragment of deploying densely and prominently placed participles, here (as in the
second stanza) closely linked with an imperative verb.

mode to another. He begins by directly addressing an audience of Spartan soldiers (1–10):[16]

> ἀλλ', Ἡρακλῆος γὰρ ἀνικήτου γένος ἐστέ,
> θαρσεῖτ'—οὔπω Ζεὺς αὐχένα λοξὸν ἔχει—
> μηδ' ἀνδρῶν πληθὺν δειμαίνετε, μηδὲ φοβεῖσθε,
> ἰθὺς δ' ἐς προμάχους ἀσπίδ' ἀνὴρ ἐχέτω,
> 5   ἐχθρὴν μὲν ψυχὴν θέμενος, θανάτου δὲ μελαίνας
> κῆρας ⟨ὁμῶς⟩ αὐγαῖς ἠελίοιο φίλας.
> ἴστε γὰρ ὡς Ἄρεος πολυδακρύου ἔργ' ἀΐδηλα,
> εὖ δ' ὀργὴν ἐδάητ' ἀργαλέου πολέμου,
> καὶ μετὰ φευγόντων τε διωκόντων τ' ἐγένεσθε
> 10   ὦ νέοι, ἀμφοτέρων δ' ἐς κόρον ἠλάσατε.

Come, take courage, for your stock is from unconquered Heracles—not yet does Zeus hold his neck aslant—and do not fear throngs of men or run in flight, but let a man hold his shield straight toward the front ranks, despising life and loving the black death-spirits no less than the rays of the sun. You know how destructive the deeds of woeful Ares are, you have learned well the nature of grim war, you have been with the pursuers and the pursued, you young men, and you have had more than your fill of both.

This initial stanza of exhortation falls into two parts. The first three couplets contain a stream of imperatives, nearly all of which encourage the appropriate martial spirit or mental attitude of the young men, rather than reiterate (as we saw in Tyrtaeus 10) the details of hoplite warfare: 'be brave', the poet implores them, 'hate life', 'love death', and so on. The reasons for this more abstract approach are, however, given in the final two couplets, where the poet continues to use second-person plural verbs to acknowledge that the men in the audience already know all about the grim realities of war and are, in fact, experienced in both victory and defeat.

Although only half of these first ten verses actually exhort—lines 1 and 7–10 use the indicative throughout—this stanza nonetheless pays consistent attention to the performative context of the poem: it contains eight second-person plural verbs which address or describe the audience of young Spartan men.[17] The stanza is, moreover,

---

[16] Weil (1862) 11–12.

[17] Of the eight imperatives, two appear at the start of the line (lines 2 and 6), four at the end (1, 3, 9, and 10), one after the midline break (3) and one before it (8). The third-person imperative at the end of line 4 (ἐχέτω) should also be added to this list,

framed with presumably specific references to their particular circumstances (paraphrase): 'Since (γὰρ) you are of Heracles' race (1)...since
(γὰρ) you know (i.e. personally) the horrors of military rout from both
perspectives (8–10).' The ring-composition is especially effective here:
the paired names and epithets of 'unconquered Heracles' and 'woeful
Ares' appear in similar sounding phrases ('because you are the race...'
and 'because you know the works...') and straddle the mid-line caesura
of the verse (1: Ἡρακλῆος γὰρ ἀνικήτου γένος ἐστέ and 7: ἴστε γὰρ ὡς
Ἄρεος πολυδακρύου ἔργ᾽ ἀΐδηλα). There is, then, no generic advice here
about what a typical soldier usually does in war: Tyrtaeus exhorts a group
of Spartan men to fight by reminding them of their own special heritage
and their own previous experience on the battlefield.

But as in Tyrtaeus 10, the boundaries of this individual stanza are
best illuminated by the stark contrast with the stanza that follows,
where Tyrtaeus changes gears entirely and—in a meditation once
again introduced by γὰρ—examines the moral choice between alter-
natives (11:11–20):[18]

> οἳ μὲν γὰρ τολμῶσι παρ᾽ ἀλλήλοισι μένοντες
> ἔς τ᾽ αὐτοσχεδίην καὶ προμάχους ἰέναι,
> παυρότεροι θνήσκουσι, σαοῦσι δὲ λαὸν ὀπίσσω·
> τρεσσάντων δ᾽ ἀνδρῶν πᾶσ᾽ ἀπόλωλ᾽ ἀρετή.
> οὐδεὶς ἄν ποτε ταῦτα λέγων ἀνύσειεν ἕκαστα,   15
> ὅσσ᾽, ἢν αἰσχρὰ πάθῃ, γίνεται ἀνδρὶ κακά·
> ἀργαλέον γὰρ ὄπισθε μετάφρενόν ἐστι δαΐζειν
> ἀνδρὸς φεύγοντος δηΐῳ ἐν πολέμῳ·
> αἰσχρὸς δ᾽ ἐστὶ νέκυς κατακείμενος ἐν κονίῃσι
> νῶτον ὄπισθ᾽ αἰχμῇ δουρὸς ἐληλάμενος.   20

Those who dare to stand fast at one another's side and to advance towards
the front ranks in hand-to-hand conflict, they die in fewer numbers and they
keep safe the troops behind them; but when men run away, all esteem is lost.
No one could sum up in words each and every evil that befalls a man, if he
suffers disgrace. For to pierce a man behind the shoulder blades as he flees in
deadly combat is gruesome, and a corpse lying in the dust, with the point of
a spear driven through his back from behind, is a shameful sight.

since in martial elegy and elsewhere it is the functional equivalent of the second-
person plural imperative.

[18] Aside from Bowra (1969, 56–57) and Fowler (1987, 81), few scholars have
discussed these lines as a discrete unit.

In this second stanza Tyrtaeus sets up a formal contrast in the first three couplets between those (11: οἳ μὲν) who stand fast in the battle line, and others (14: τρεσσάντων δ' ἀνδρῶν) who break the hoplite line and flee.[19] The same comparison is then expressed differently in the final two couplets, which seem to reiterate again the contrast—described at the end of the previous section (lines 9–10)—between fleeing and pursuing a rout. This stanza also provides a good example of ring-composition between the second and fourth couplets: the spondaic genitive phrase that takes up the first half of the fourth pentameter (18: ἀνδρὸς φεύγοντος) echoes darkly the sense, words, and prosody of the first half of the second pentameter (14: τρεσσάντων δ' ἀνδρῶν). And as he does in Fragment 10, here the poet contrasts an exhortative stanza, that begins with ἀλλά and focuses directly and continually on the audience in front of him, with a meditative stanza that begins with γάρ and describes the facts of war using generalizable third-person examples. This contrast is significant, because the poet could easily have used second-person plural verb forms in the second stanza, for example, in the first sentence: 'For if *you* dare to stand fast ... and advance ... *you* will die in fewer numbers.' That he does not do so here, or in his other two long fragments, suggests some kind of generic or rhetorical constraint.

This pattern of alternating stanzas in Tyrtaeus 10 and 11.1–20 is partially visible among the ruins of Callinus 1, which is perhaps the oldest extant example of martial elegy:

> μέχρις τέο κατάκεισθε; κότ' ἄλκιμον ἕξετε θυμόν,
> ὦ νέοι; οὐδ' αἰδεῖσθ' ἀμφιπερικτίονας
> ὧδε λίην μεθιέντες; ἐν εἰρήνῃ δὲ δοκεῖτε
> ἦσθαι, ἀτὰρ πόλεμος γαῖαν ἅπασαν ἔχει
>
> . . . .
>
> 5   καί τις ἀποθνῄσκων ὕστατ' ἀκοντισάτω.
> τιμῆέν τε γάρ ἐστι καὶ ἀγλαὸν ἀνδρὶ μάχεσθαι
> γῆς πέρι καὶ παίδων κουριδίης τ' ἀλόχου
> δυσμενέσιν· θάνατος δὲ τότ' ἔσσεται, ὁππότε κεν δὴ
> Μοῖραι ἐπικλώσωσ'. ἀλλά τις ἰθὺς ἴτω
> 10 ἔγχος ἀνασχόμενος καὶ ὑπ' ἀσπίδος ἄλκιμον ἦτορ
> ἔλσας, τὸ πρῶτον μειγνυμένου πολέμου.
>
> οὐ γάρ κως θάνατόν γε φυγεῖν εἱμαρμένον ἐστὶν
> ἄνδρ', οὐδ' εἰ προγόνων ᾖ γένος ἀθανάτων.

---

[19] Fowler (1987) 82.

πολλάκι δηϊοτῆτα φυγὼν καὶ δοῦπον ἀκόντων
ἔρχεται, ἐν δ᾽ οἴκῳ μοῖρα κίχεν θανάτου.   15
ἀλλ᾽ ὁ μὲν οὐκ ἔμπης δήμῳ φίλος οὐδὲ ποθεινός,
τὸν δ᾽ ὀλίγος στενάχει καὶ μέγας, ἤν τι πάθῃ·
λαῷ γὰρ σύμπαντι πόθος κρατερόφρονος ἀνδρὸς
θνήσκοντος, ζώων δ᾽ ἄξιος ἡμιθέων·
ὥσπερ γάρ μιν πύργον ἐν ὀφθαλμοῖσιν ὁρῶσιν·   20
ἔρδει γὰρ πολλῶν ἄξια μοῦνος ἐών.

How long are you going to lie idle? Young men, when will you have a courageous spirit? Don't those who live round about make you feel ashamed of being so utterly passive? You think that you are sitting in a state of peace, but all the land is in the grip of war... even as one is dying let him make a final cast of his javelin. For it is a splendid honour for a man to fight on behalf of his land, children, and wedded wife against the foe. Death will occur only when the Fates have spun it out. Come, let a man charge straight ahead, brandishing his spear and mustering a stout heart behind his shield, as soon as war is engaged.

For it is in no way fated that a man escape death, not even if he has immortal ancestors in his lineage. Often one who has escaped from the strife of battle and the thud of javelins and has returned home meets with his allotted death in his house. But he is not in any case loved or missed by the people, whereas the other, if he suffer some mishap, is mourned by the humble and the mighty. All the people miss a stout-hearted man when he dies and while he lives he is the equal of demigods. For in the eyes of the people he is like a tower, since single-handed he does the deeds of many.

The final ten lines of this fragment (12–21) form a rhetorically complete stanza that explains (γάρ) why a generic hoplite should fight hard. The infinitive construction at its start (οὐ γάρ ... φυγεῖν εἱμαρμένον ἐστὶν), moreover, recalls, at least superficially, the beginning of both meditative stanzas in Tyrtaeus 10 (1: τεθνάμεναι γὰρ καλὸν and 21–22: αἰσχρὸν γάρ ... κεῖσθαι), raising the possibility that the use of such constructions at the beginning of meditative stanzas may have been a generic feature of early elegy and not simply an idiosyncrasy of Tyrtaeus.

The final stanza of Callinus 1 has, moreover, a consistent and remarkable style. Unlike the lines that precede it, where only two of six couplets are end-stopped, each of these couplets forms a single sentence. Callinus increases this sense of order in the final stanza by inserting a series of identical internal rhymes in the first, fourth, and fifth pentameters (13: προγόνων ... ἀθανάτων; 19: ζώων ... ἡμιθέων; 21: πολλῶν ... ἐών)—a sonorous effect that is heightened by the use of five long syllables at the beginning of each of the last four lines,[20] and by the echoing repetition—in close proximity to some of the rhyming words—of the adjective ἄξιος after the mid-line caesura of lines 19 (ἄξιος ἡμιθέων) and 21 (ἄξια μοῦνος ἐών).[21] The clustering of all these poetic features in this stanza is all the more notable when we realize how greatly they contrast with the rest of the extant fragment, in which there are no other internal rhymes and no other verses with purely spondaic first halves. These last five couplets of Callinus 1, then, seem to have been composed both rhetorically and stylistically as a meditative stanza of the type favoured by Tyrtaeus, and they are so powerfully rendered that a number of scholars have suggested that they may have provided a stately conclusion to an entire poem.[22]

Does Callinus 1 show signs of any other five-couplet stanzas or the alternation between meditation and exhortation? This is impossible to say for certain since a lacuna of unknown length after line 4 hampers our appreciation of the overall structure of the remaining lines. The seven verses that sit between the missing hexameter (after line 4) and the complete elegiac stanza at the very end (12–21) begin and end with exhortations rendered in the third-person singular imperative ('Let each man ...') suggesting that the preceding verses were primarily exhortative, although, as we saw in Tyrtaeus 11, they need not be uniformly so.[23] The four opening lines of this fragment— those that lie before the lacuna—neither advise nor exhort the audience, but like the initial stanza of Tyrtaeus 11 they do focus attention tightly on the here-and-now of the performance, in this case abusing the young men in the audience for their sloth or indifference rather than praising them as Tyrtaeus does. It is possible, therefore, that

---

[20] These are usually called spondaic *hemiepe*. Van Raalte (1988, 148 n. 8) notes that this is a rare phenomenon that also occurs at the very end of Tyrtaeus 12, suggesting that it is a device used to slow the pace and bring a longer poem to closure.

[21] Giannoti (1978) 421.

[22] See e.g. Adkins (1985, 61) 'a powerful conclusion', or Gerber (1997) 100–1: 'the poem may well be complete. It has an effective opening and a satisfying ending.'

[23] These verses end with the word 'war' (11: πολέμου), which may have been a traditional boundary marker in martial elegy; see the end of Ch. 5 for my discussion of Tyrtaeus 12, where the same word appears at the very end of three of its four stanzas.

these four verses were also part of a stanza of exhortation, but given
the lacunose state of the text, the only assertion one can make with
confidence is that the last five couplets of Callinus 1 were designed as a
well-rounded meditative stanza that is differentiated both linguistic-
ally and rhythmically from the hortative verses that directly precede it.

All of these examples of alternating stanzas are culled from martial poems, and indeed this compositional form seems especially
suited to this early species of elegy. The same pattern does show up,
however, in at least one poem that has nothing to do with war: the
famous *sphragis* or 'Seal-Poem' that sits at the very beginning of
the 'Cyrnus Book', which scholars identify as the earliest stratum
of the *Theognidea* (19–38):[24]

> Κύρνε, σοφιζομένῳ μὲν ἐμοὶ σφρηγὶς ἐπικείσθω
>   τοῖσδ᾿ ἔπεσιν, λήσει δ᾿ οὔποτε κλεπτόμενα,   20
> οὐδέ τις ἀλλάξει κάκιον τοὐσθλοῦ παρεόντος,
>   ὧδε δὲ πᾶς τις ἐρεῖ· "Θεόγνιδός ἐστιν ἔπη
> τοῦ Μεγαρέως· πάντας δὲ κατ᾿ ἀνθρώπους ὀνομαστός·"
>   ἀστοῖσιν δ᾿ οὔπω πᾶσιν ἁδεῖν δύναμαι.
> οὐδὲν θαυμαστόν, Πολυπαΐδη· οὐδὲ γὰρ ὁ Ζεὺς   25
>   οὔθ᾿ ὕων πάντεσσ᾿ ἁνδάνει οὔτ᾿ ἀνέχων.
> σοὶ δ᾿ ἐγὼ εὖ φρονέων ὑποθήσομαι, οἷάπερ αὐτός,
>   Κύρν᾿, ἀπὸ τῶν ἀγαθῶν παῖς ἔτ᾿ ἐὼν ἔμαθον·
> πέπνυσο, μηδ᾿ αἰσχροῖσιν ἐπ᾿ ἔργμασι μηδ᾿ ἀδίκοισιν
>   τιμὰς μηδ᾿ ἀρετὰς ἕλκεο μηδ᾿ ἄφενος.   30
> ταῦτα μὲν οὕτως ἴσθι· κακοῖσι δὲ μὴ προσομίλει
>   ἀνδράσιν, ἀλλ᾿ αἰεὶ τῶν ἀγαθῶν ἔχεο·
> καὶ μετὰ τοῖσιν πῖνε καὶ ἔσθιε, καὶ μετὰ τοῖσιν
>   ἵζε, καὶ ἄνδανε τοῖς, ὧν μεγάλη δύναμις.
> ἐσθλῶν μὲν γὰρ ἄπ᾿ ἐσθλὰ μαθήσεαι· ἢν δὲ κακοῖσι   35
>   συμμίσγῃς, ἀπολεῖς καὶ τὸν ἐόντα νόον.
> ταῦτα μαθὼν ἀγαθοῖσιν ὁμίλει, καί ποτε φήσεις
>   εὖ συμβουλεύειν τοῖσι φίλοισιν ἐμέ.

---

[24] Van Groningen (1966, 25), Friis Johansen (1991) and Gerber (1997, 124) and
(1999, ad loc.) treat all twenty of these lines as a single poem (marked at the
beginning by Κύρνε), which is followed by another poem that begins (at line 39) in
the same way. Campbell (1967, ad loc.) and West (1992, ad loc.), on the other hand,
both mark the end of the poem at line 26, presumably because Cyrnus' name appears
in the next couplet (in the pentameter at line 28) and thus putatively signals the
beginning of a new poem. Xenophanes 1 provides another example of a non-martial
elegy with alternating stanzas; see Section 6.1 below.

For me, a skilled and wise poet, let a seal, Cyrnus, be placed on these verses. Their theft will never pass unnoticed, nor will anyone take something worse in exchange when that which is good is at hand, but everyone will say, 'They are the verses of Theognis of Megara, and he is famous among all men'; but I am not yet able to please all the townsmen. It's not surprising, Polypaides, since not even Zeus pleases everyone when he sends rain or holds it back. It is with kind thoughts for you that I shall give you advice such as I myself, Cyrnus, learned from noble men while still a child.

Be sensible and do not, at the cost of shameful or unjust acts, seize for yourself prestige, success or wealth. Know that this is so, and do not seek the company of base men, but always cling to the noble. Drink and dine with them, sit with them, and be pleasing to those whose power is great. For from the noble you will learn noble things, but if you mingle with the base, you will lose even the sense you have. Knowing this, associate with the noble, and one day you will say that I give good advice to my friends.

These verses appear to be composed as a linked pair of elegiac stanzas. The poet, for instance, uses ring-composition to signal the boundaries of the first stanza by placing σοὶ δ᾽ ἐγὼ at the beginning of the fifth hexameter (27), where it answers σοφιζομένῳ μὲν ἐμοὶ at the beginning of the first (19).[25] The repetition of the vocative Κύρνε at the beginning of the first hexameter and last pentameter—similar to the repetition of Apollo's name in Tyrtaeus 4—also helps to bracket these verses as a freestanding unit.

But here, too, the unity of this initial stanza cannot be fully appreciated until we see what comes next. Indeed, as was true for the fragments of the martial elegists, the second stanza (29–38) switches from the mainly descriptive language of the first stanza—it is a mix of prophecy and meditation—and devotes itself almost entirely to exhortation. The contrast remarkable: the second stanza bristles with ten imperatives directed at Cyrnus, whereas the first has none.[26] To the modern ear these commands may seem to be a rather disjointed collection, but this appears to be a peculiar feature of some Theognidean stanzas, namely to use ring-composition to collect and organize a series of different wisdom sayings into a single unit, as we saw earlier, for example, in *Theognidea* 183–92 (see Section 2.2) and as we can

---

[25] Friis Johansen (1991) 11–12.

[26] The imperative at the end of the first line (19: ἐπικείσθω) is vague and figurative—'let a seal be placed'—and we need not and should not assume that the poet is commanding Cyrnus to do so.

also see in *Theognidea* 133–42 (see Appendix III). Here, in fact, the second stanza displays a bit of thoughtful ring-composition: the summary command in the final hexameter, 'associate with the noble, once you have learned these things' (37: ταῦτα μαθὼν ἀγαθοῖσιν ὁμίλει) combines and reiterates in different form the dual commands near the beginning of the stanza, (31): ταῦτα μὲν οὕτως ἴσθι· κακοῖσι δὲ μὴ προσομίλει.[27]

The poet, then, plainly distinguishes these two stanzas from one another by content and linguistic form, and yet like some of the stanzas discussed above, he has designed them as a well-balanced and responding pair. The pedagogic advice in the final couplet of the second stanza (37: ταῦτα μαθὼν ἀγαθοῖσιν ὁμίλει), for instance, also echoes the final words of the first (28: ἀπὸ τῶν ἀγαθῶν ... ἔμαθον), and the last thought in the second stanza—'someday you will say that I gave good advice' (37–38: ποτε φήσεις | εὖ συμβουλεύειν... ἐμέ)—plainly recalls the prediction at the very end of the first (27): σοὶ δ' ἐγὼ εὖ φρονέων ὑποθήσομαι.[28] These are not, of course, examples of the stricter kind of nearly verbatim responsion that we have seen in Tyrtaeus 10 or 11, but they are extremely effective. The last-mentioned echo in line 37, for example, nicely underscores the prediction in the first stanza that the chain of oral tradition will remain unbroken: the advice that the poet received from an older generation of ἀγαθοί while he was still a youth (28: παῖς ἔτ' ἐών), is now passed along to another παῖς, Cyrnus, in the exhortations of the second stanza, which is a repository for this inherited wisdom. The boundary between these two stanzas is, moreover, marked strongly by a transition formula that identifies the introduction of embedded speech. The first stanza ends emphatically with the performative future[29]—'I shall (hereby) advise you, regarding the very sorts of things I myself once learned'—followed in the very next stanza by the content of those childhood lessons, which the poet recalls and recites for the benefit of Cyrnus.[30]

---

[27] Friis Johansen (1991) 28.   [28] Friis Johansen (1991) 29–30.

[29] For a discussion of the performative future, usually in combination (as here) with a variety of deictic pronouns or adverbs, see Faraone (1995).

[30] Van Groningen (1966, 22) and Friis Johansen (1991, 20) both note how the asyndeton at the beginning of the second stanza (line 29) introduces the advice immediately.

Scholars have long noted the existence of generic themes in early elegy, for example: the contrast between brave fighting and craven flight or between noble friends and base ones. We can see here, however, evidence of a generic structure as well: Tyrtaeus and the Theognidean poet—and probably Callinus as well—seem to compose their elegies in stanzas that alternate between vigorous exhortation and thoughtful meditation, the latter typically accomplished by generic description and moral evaluation. Alternating stanzas, moreover, give longer fragments a formal and logical structure, especially (as in the beginning of Tyrtaeus 11) when a meditative stanza refers to and provides a defence for a preceding stanza of exhortation, or (as we saw in the 'Seal Poem' from the *Theognidea*) when an exhortation is based upon the logic or claims of a preceding meditation. These meditations, moreover, often seem to take a generic form: they are regularly introduced by γάρ and use impersonal constructions with the infinitive to explore various human values or courses of action in abstract evaluative terms. The exhortations, on the other hand, are introduced by ἀλλά, τοι or asyndeton and usually call attention to the situation of performance before an audience, by using imperative, vocatives and various forms of deictic language.

3.2. COORDINATION

The poets of the archaic period use another important technique to organize their longer compositions: coordinated pairs of stanzas of similar linguistic mode and purpose, which are joined by a shared architecture and contrasted by close responsion. Here the idea of stanza as a room provides a best model for analysis, precisely because these pairs generally seem to work as building blocks in more complicated sequences of thought or argument. It is, I suggest, this kind of stanzaic construction that allows early elegists like Solon or Tyrtaeus to organize their longer ruminations into a logical sequence, for example, the discussion of the nature of ἀρετή in Tyrtaeus 12 or of the different life-stages of man in Solon 27. Here, too, the notion of a stanza as a 'verse paragraph' is especially helpful, since it seems to have been used as a tool, well in advance of the development of Greek prose, for organizing extended and more philosophical arguments.

The end of Tyrtaeus 11, however, serves as an initial counter-example to remind us that it was possible, although for some reason rare among the extant fragments of archaic elegy, to use the same techniques to coordinate a pair of purely exhortative stanzas (11.21–38):[31]

ἀλλά τις εὖ διαβὰς μενέτω ποσὶν ἀμφοτέροισι
στηριχθεὶς ἐπὶ γῆς, χεῖλος ὀδοῦσι δακών,
μηρούς τε κνήμας τε κάτω καὶ στέρνα καὶ ὤμους
ἀσπίδος εὐρείης γαστρὶ καλυψάμενος·
δεξιτερῇ δ' ἐν χειρὶ τινασσέτω ὄβριμον ἔγχος,   25
κινείτω δὲ λόφον δεινὸν ὑπὲρ κεφαλῆς·
ἔρδων δ' ὄβριμα ἔργα διδασκέσθω πολεμίζειν,
μηδ' ἐκτὸς βελέων ἑστάτω ἀσπίδ' ἔχων.

ἀλλά τις ἐγγὺς ἰὼν αὐτοσχεδὸν ἔγχεϊ μακρῷ
ἢ ξίφει οὐτάζων δήϊον ἄνδρ' ἑλέτω,   30
καὶ πόδα πὰρ ποδὶ θεὶς καὶ ἐπ' ἀσπίδος ἀσπίδ' ἐρείσας,
ἐν δὲ λόφον τε λόφῳ καὶ κυνέην κυνέῃ
καὶ στέρνον στέρνῳ πεπλημένος ἀνδρὶ μαχέσθω,
ἢ ξίφεος κώπην ἢ δόρυ μακρὸν ἑλών.
ὑμεῖς δ', ὦ γυμνῆτες, ὑπ' ἀσπίδος ἄλλοθεν ἄλλος   35
πτώσσοντες μεγάλοις βάλλετε χερμαδίοις
δούρασί τε ξεστοῖσιν ἀκοντίζοντες ἐς αὐτούς,
τοῖσι πανόπλοισιν πλησίον ἱστάμενοι.

Come, let everyone stand fast, with legs set well apart and both feet fixed firmly on the ground, biting his lip with his teeth, and covering thighs, shins below, chest, and shoulders with the belly of his broad shield; in his right hand let him brandish a mighty spear and let him shake the plumed crest above his head in a fearsome manner. By doing mighty deeds let him learn how to fight and let him not stand—he has a shield—outside the range of missiles,

but coming to close quarters let him strike the enemy, hitting him with long spear or sword; and also, with foot placed alongside foot and shield pressed against shield, let everyone draw near, crest to crest, helmet to helmet, and breast to breast, and fight against a man, seizing the hilt of his sword or his long spear. You light-armed men, as you crouch beneath a shield on either side, let fly with huge rocks and hurl your smooth javelins at them, standing close to those in full armour.

---

[31] Lines 1–20, a pair of alternating stanzas, were discussed earlier in Section 2.3. Fowler (1987, 81) suggests that the ἀλλά in line 21 starts a new section of the fragment. My discussion of these lines first appeared in Faraone (2006) 30–34.

Most editors do not recognize the break that I have marked in the
text after line 28, suggesting instead that the poem continues on with
a mere pause for a comma.[32] At the turn of the nineteenth century,
however, some scholars intuited textual problems here. Wilamowitz,
for example, believed that these two sections (21–28 and 29–38)
were doublets of one another, since both mention a complete set of
battle gear: shield, helmet, crest, and spear.[33] This is a potentially
attractive suggestion, as it might explain why the second half of the
fragment does not continue the pattern of alternation between exhortation and meditation that we saw in the first half (1–20).

If we set aside for the moment the problem that the first stanza
(lines 21–28) contains only four couplets, we can, I think, identify a
different kind of design in the final part of this poem by noting a
pattern of interaction between these two stanzas. I limit myself to two
observations, one about content and another about response.
Although Tyrtaeus exhorts young men to battle throughout lines
21–38, there is one important difference in the content of his advice.
In the first four couplets (21–28) he advises them how to withstand
an attack from the enemy, for example: by standing firm 'with legs set
well apart and both feet fixed firmly on the ground,' by covering
themselves with their shields and by shaking their spears and helmet-
crests vigorously. He emphasizes his concern for a strong defensive
posture, moreover, by exhorting them twice to use their shield (24
and 28) and by beginning and ending the section with pleas regard-
ing the static position of each soldier: 'let him wait' ($\mu\epsilon\nu\acute{\epsilon}\tau\omega$) and 'let
him not stand ($\mu\eta\delta$' $\acute{\epsilon}\sigma\tau\acute{a}\tau\omega$) beyond the range of missiles'. In the
second section of this exhortation (29–38), however, Tyrtaeus advises
the warriors to approach the enemy aggressively, to kill them by
stabbing with their spears or swords (29–30: $o\mathring{v}\tau\acute{a}\zeta\omega\nu\ldots\acute{\epsilon}\lambda\acute{\epsilon}\tau\omega$),
and to fight while thrusting their fully armed bodies against them
(31–33: $\acute{\epsilon}\rho\epsilon\acute{\iota}\sigma a s\ldots\mu a\chi\acute{\epsilon}\sigma\theta\omega$). Likewise he urges the light-armed
troops in the last two couplets to take the offensive and hurl their
stones and javelins (35–39: $\beta\acute{a}\lambda\lambda\epsilon\tau\epsilon\ldots\acute{a}\kappa o\nu\tau\acute{\iota}\zeta o\nu\tau\epsilon s$). Now there is
no waiting or covering up with the shield: the poet strenuously urges
all to move forward and attack.

---

[32] See e.g. Gerber (1970), Adkins (1972), and West (1992), all ad loc.
[33] Wilamowitz (1900) 114.

One might object, of course, that in the general mayhem of battle these differences between defensive and offensive warfare are too subtle, but Tyrtaeus has, in fact, prepared us for this distinction by an intricate series of responsions between the opening couplets of the last three stanzas of the fragment:

οἳ μὲν γὰρ τολμῶσι παρ᾽ ἀλλήλοισι μένοντες
  ἔς τ᾽ αὐτοσχεδίην καὶ προμάχους ἰέναι, (11–12)

ἀλλά τις εὖ διαβὰς μενέτω ποσὶν ἀμφοτέροισι
  στηριχθεὶς ἐπὶ γῆς, χεῖλος ὀδοῦσι δακών, (21–22)

ἀλλά τις ἐγγὺς ἰὼν αὐτοσχεδὸν ἔγχεϊ μακρῶι
  ἢ ξίφει οὐτάζων δήϊον ἄνδρ᾽ ἑλέτω, (29–30)

In the first couplet of the second stanza (the meditative one discussed earlier in Section 3.1), Tyrtaeus sums up the behaviour of the hypo-thetically best fighters as (11–12): 'those who dare to stand fast (μένοντες) at one another's side and to advance towards the front ranks in hand-to-hand conflict (ἔς τ᾽ αὐτοσχεδίην... ἰέναι).' This distinction between waiting and plunging into battle may puzzle the modern reader, but it summarizes neatly the difficult discipline of hoplite battle: the individual soldier must never break the line in which he is stationed, because the shield in his left hand protects not only his own body but also that of the soldier to his left. Tyrtaeus, therefore, in his compact description at the start of the second stanza (11.11–12) urges two different but equally important modes of fighting: at times the soldier must wait bravely in proper formation and withstand the assaults against the line, but at other times he must move forward and attack aggressively.

In the second half of Tyrtaeus 11, the poet recalls this dual strategy for hoplite fighting by devoting one stanza of the ensuing exhort-ation to defensive techniques and another to offensive ones. He underscores the logical organization of these last two stanzas, more-over, by beginning each with a responding hexameter: Here, as in other cases of Tyrtaean responsion, the verbal repetition at the beginning of one portion of the responding verse (21: ἀλλά τις εὖ and 29: ἀλλά τις ἐγ-) draws attention to the contrasting words that follow, which highlight defensive persistence (11.21: μενέτω) and aggressive attack (11.29: ἰὼν αὐτοσχεδόν) in the first lines of each, while echoing (as shown above) the vocabulary used at the start of the second stanza (11.11–12). This is yet another good example of how elegiac response performs two basic tasks: the repetition of words or phrases at the beginnings and ends of stanzas allows the poet to mark the boundaries of individual stanzas and to emphasize the parallels between them, while at the same time highlighting important differences by placing contrasting words in parallel positions in the responding verses.

I suggest that in the first half of Tyrtaeus 11 the poet uses the same architecture of alternating stanzas that he deploys in Tyrtaeus 10, but that when he swings into his third stanza (this one of exhortation), he decides, for the reasons discussed above, to double the length of it to reflect his dual perspectives on hoplite combat:

[10 lines] Exhortation to the right attitude introduced by ἀλλά
  (second-person plural verbs focused on immediate performance)

[10 lines] Meditation introduced by γάρ
  (third-person indicative verbs).

[8 lines] Exhortation to defence introduced by ἀλλά
  (τις + third-person singular imperative)

[10 lines] Exhortation to attack introduced by ἀλλά
  (τις + third-person singular imperative and then second-person plural imperative)

If I am correct in my analysis here, the third stanza (as transmitted in the manuscripts of Stobaeus) is missing a couplet, not an uncommon hazard for the survival of elegiac fragments that are often composed, like this one, in end-stopped couplets—especially in a section of the poem that provides a repetitive catalogue of wartime actions.[34] But the most powerful argument for assuming a lacuna here rests on the simple fact that (as we have seen) Tyrtaeus uses the five-couplet stanza throughout Fragments 10 and 11, and (as we shall see presently) in Fragment 12 as well. In the specific case of Tyrtaeus 11, moreover, where we can trace the wider architecture of the fragment with its triple responsion at the start of the final three stanzas, we are in an especially good position to observe where an individual couplet has indeed dropped out—just as we can identify a damaged passage of

---

[34] Adkins (1985, 78) notes that Tyrtaeus 11 has an exceedingly high percentage of end-stopped lines (twenty-seven out of thirty-eight).

choral lyric by noting where the metrical responsion between strophe and antistrophe breaks down in the transmitted text.

Solon also makes good use of coordinated pairs of stanzas. We have already seen one excellent example in his corpus, where he organizes a series of meditative stanzas into a larger edifice: the three contiguous stanzas of catalogues in the second half of Solon 13, the last two of which—the catalogue of vocations (13.43–62)—form a coordinated pair of stanzas that exhibit a seamless rhetorical and syntactic structure, while at the same time managing to distinguish themselves as discrete entities (see the end of Section 2.3). As it turns out, Solon shows a repeated interest in such coordinated pairs. When we recall, for example, that he composed an elegiac poem on the ten stages of a man's life, we might think that this would be the perfect subject for a pair of five-couplet stanzas. The surviving verses, however, disappoint us—at least initially (Solon 27):[35]

παῖς μὲν ἄνηβος ἐὼν ἔτι νήπιος ἕρκος ὀδόντων
   φύσας ἐκβάλλει πρῶτον ἐν ἔπτ' ἔτεσιν.
τοὺς δ' ἑτέρους ὅτε δὴ τελέσῃ θεὸς ἔπτ' ἐνιαυτούς,
   ἥβης ἐκφαίνει σήματα γεινομένης.
τῇ τριτάτῃ δὲ γένειον ἀεξομένων ἔτι γυίων   5
   λαχνοῦται, χροιῆς ἄνθος ἀμειβομένης.
τῇ δὲ τετάρτῃ πᾶς τις ἐν ἑβδομάδι μέγ' ἄριστος
   ἰσχύν, ᾗ τ' ἄνδρες σήματ' ἔχουσ' ἀρετῆς.
πέμπτῃ δ' ὥριον ἄνδρα γάμου μεμνημένον εἶναι
   καὶ παίδων ζητεῖν εἰσοπίσω γενεήν.   10
τῇ δ' ἕκτῃ περὶ πάντα καταρτύεται νόος ἀνδρός,
   οὐδ' ἔρδειν ἔθ' ὁμῶς ἔργ' ἀπάλαμνα θέλει.
ἑπτὰ δὲ νοῦν καὶ γλῶσσαν ἐν ἑβδομάσιν μέγ' ἄριστος
   ὀκτώ τ'· ἀμφοτέρων τέσσαρα καὶ δέκ' ἔτη.

---

[35] This fragment is quoted in its entirety by Philo of Alexandria (1st cent. CE) in his *Creation of the World* (104) and by Clement of Alexandria (2nd–3rd cents. CE) in his *Stromata* (6.144.3). The fragment has not found as much favour with modern readers. Campbell (1967, 246–47) is typical of the scholarly reaction ('rigid', 'monotonous', 'intractable material'). West (1992, ad loc.) does not think this fragment is a complete poem and Adkins (1972, 128) rightly notes that it seems to lack a proper introduction, although he does seem to feel that line 18 is an adequate ending. Weil (1862, 6–7) divides the poem into three three-couplet stanzas. The analysis that follows first appeared in Faraone (2005a) 260–64.

15   τῇ δ' ἐνάτῃ ἔτι μὲν δύναται, μαλακώτερα δ' αὐτοῦ
        πρὸς μεγάλην ἀρετὴν γλῶσσά τε καὶ σοφίη.
        τὴν δεκάτην δ' εἴ τις τελέσας κατὰ μέτρον ἵκοιτο,
        οὐκ ἂν ἄωρος ἐὼν μοῖραν ἔχοι θανάτου.

A boy while still an immature child, in seven years grows a fence of teeth and loses them for the first time. When the god completes another seven years, he shows the signs of coming puberty. In the third hebdomad his body is still growing, his chin becomes downy, and the skin changes its hue. In the fourth everyone is far the best in strength, whereby men show their signs of manliness. In the fifth it is time for a man to be mindful of marriage and to look for a line of sons to come after him.

In the sixth a man's mind is being trained for everything and he is no longer as willing to commit acts of foolishness. In the seventh and eighth, a total of fourteen years, he is far the best in thought and speech. In the ninth he still has ability, but his speech and wisdom give weaker proof of a high level of excellence. If one were to complete stage after stage and reach the tenth, he would not have death's allotment prematurely.

As we saw in the catalogues discussed in the previous chapter, Solon has given this fragment a persistent formal structure, by allotting one couplet to each of the ten seven-year periods (the so-called 'hebdomads'), by dividing five of the nine hexameters at the penthemimeral caesura, and by beginning each with the appropriate ordinal number—with one glaring exception: in lines 13–14 Solon interrupts the pattern with two cardinal numbers, crowds the seventh and eighth hebdomads into a single couplet, and leaves us with an oddly organized nine-couplet composition.[36]

There are, in fact, internal indications that this poem was originally designed as a pair of five-couplet stanzas and that the rather lame combination of the seventh and eighth hebdomads within a single couplet is the work of a scribe trying to repair the loss of the full couplet that once described the eighth stage of life. In the first place, although both sections of this poem share the same rigid format,

---

[36] Hudson-Williams (1926) 129: 'The ten-fold division [i.e. of human life] is very rare and the poet evidently found much difficulty working it out: cf. vv. 13–14, where he is unable to distinguish between the seventh and eighth hebdomads'; Campbell (1967) 247: 'the structure of the poem collapses when the seventh and eighth ages are combined.' Falkner (1995) 138: 'the results are…even ungrammatical, as in 13–14, where the literal values of the cardinals (ἑπτά and ὀκτώ) cannot be sustained.'

there are some subtle but important differences in content and emphasis, just as we saw in the twinned stanzas on human vocations in Solon 13. The first five couplets of Solon 27, for example, deal only with the physical growth of a baby to a young man, focusing on various parts of his body: the teeth, the physical signs of puberty, the chin, the skin color, the strength, and the outward signs of maturity and manliness.[37] There is no mention at all of his mental or rhetorical skills. There are also hints of formal unity within this first stanza: the second and fourth couplets close with similar *hemiepe*—σήματα γεινομένης (4) and σήματ᾽ ἔχουσ᾽ ἀρετῆς (8)[38]—and all three of the middle couplets end with the same sound (-ης). Solon also frames his descriptions of the first five hebdomads, by mentioning in the final couplet the need at this point in life to start having children (παίδων), a word that harks back to the very first word of the poem (παῖς) and reminds us of the generational reproduction of male bodies.

Just as in his catalogue of professions (13.43–62), where we saw signs that the first five-couplets probably once served as a freestanding priamel, here too Solon might have ended the catalogue after the fifth hebdomad if he so chose or if he needed it for another rhetorical purpose. But instead he goes on to describe the stages of the mature adult, focusing on a man's non-physical faculties: the training of the mind (νοῦς), the avoidance of foolishness, the skill in thought and speech (νοῦς and γλῶσσα), and in the ninth stage the waning of speech and wisdom (γλῶσσά τε καὶ σοφίη). And as in Solon's catalogue of vocations, verbal echoes between the two halves of the catalogue develop this second section as a suitable partner to the first. The phrase ἐν ἑβδομάδι μέγ᾽ ἄριστος, for instance, at the end of the penultimate hexameter of the first stanza (line 7) is echoed by the nearly identical phrase ἐν ἑβδομάσιν μέγ᾽ ἄριστος at the end of the second hexameter of the second section (line 13)—a repetition that

---

[37] Siegman (1970) points out the important differences in content between the first five couplets and those that follow.

[38] I follow Gerber and most modern editors, who print the manuscripts' σήματ᾽ here. West, on the other hand, prefers πεῖρατ᾽, a conjecture of Städtmüller. For the second and fourth couplets as a traditional site of stanzaic ring composition, see e.g. the second stanza of Tyrtaeus 11 (see Section 3.1) or *Theognidea* 183–92 (see Section 2.2).

in fact highlights (as elegiac responsion regularly does) the thematic differences between the two sections: 'the very best in physical strength' is contrasted against 'the very best in thought and word.'[39] He also brings up the idea of seasonality at the end of the second stanza (οὐκ ... ἄωρος ἐὼν) in a manner that echoes the closing line of the first (ὥριον ... εἶναι).[40]

In sum: the architecture of this fragment suggests that Solon composed it as a pair of elegiac stanzas, and that he organized them as a regularly paced and continuous list that divides up human life into an earlier period of thirty-five years, during which the development and reproduction of the physical body is of paramount importance, and a later period of equal length, focused on the evolution and eventual devolution of a man's mental and rhetorical skills. Since Solon in every case but the seventh and eighth grants each hebdomad a complete couplet that begins with ordinal number, and since he generally pursues this practice of equal representation in the individual couplets of the catalogues in Solon 13, it is natural to suspect that at some point in its transmission from antiquity an entire couplet dropped out of our text, a couplet that once described fully the features of the eighth hebdomad. And that at some later point in time a scribe, realizing that the eighth hebdomad was missing, rewrote lines 13–14 with their telltale cardinal numbers, and in so doing ejected yet another pentameter.[41] Was Solon 27, then,

---

[39] See Adkins (1985) 130 for the repetition and the contrast. I should point out that this is not a typical case of parallel responsion, since the repeated phrases occur in the fourth couplet of the first stanza and the second couplet of second stanza. This kind of responsion might better be labeled 'mirroring responsion'. It is rare, but shows up elsewhere, especially in Xenophanes 2, for which see Section 6.1. We saw in Section 2.1 a similar phenomenon (albeit within a single stanza) in the chiastically organized ring-composition in Mimnermus 2.1–10.

[40] Adkins (1985) 131. And in the final couplet the participle τελέσας (17) occupies the same *sedes* as τελέσῃ in the second couplet (3). The shift in subject, from the 'god' who successfully brings the young boy to the age of fourteen and the old man who successfully completes his life by himself, is especially poignant. Falkner (1995, 161) notes the repetition, but gives a different interpretation.

[41] This thoughtful solution was suggested to me independently by Mark Usher and Marta Cuypers and I thank them both for it. If we imagine, moreover, a lacuna of a full couplet before line 15, there emerges another good example of ring-composition between the second and fourth couplets of this second stanza, for the phrase νοῦν καὶ γλῶσσαν at the start of line 13 (in the second couplet of the reconstructed stanza) is echoed by γλῶσσά τε καί σοφίη at the end of line 16 (in the fourth).

a complete two-stanza poem? Probably not. His practice as illustrated in Solon 13 suggests that he, like Tyrtaeus, treated such
catalogues as useful set-pieces, that he could adapt and work into a
longer poem whenever an appropriate need arose.

Traces of stanzaic design in his Fragment 4 suggest that Solon
could employ these same techniques in even longer poems, where
unlike in his catalogues the individual stanzas are part of the narrative and argument itself. Fragment 4 is unfortunately quite lacunose
and the difficulties involved in analysing its structure force me to
discuss it separately and in greater detail in Appendix II. But suffice it
to say that amid the wreckage of this fine poem one can make out
two well-preserved stanzas at the start and finish (1–10 and 30–39)
and the ruins of a pair of coordinated stanzas in the middle, one
which describes the collapse of the city and civic life (12–20) and
another the destruction of individual homes and family life (21–30).
Solon emphasizes the differing sites of these disasters, moreover, by
placing a pair of closely responding hexameters in the fourth couplet
of each stanza, that compares and contrasts the destruction that
approaches the whole city and the individual homes alike: $τοῦτ'$
$ἤδη$ $πάσῃ$ $πόλει$ $ἔρχεται$ $ἕλκος$ $ἄφυκτον$ (17: 'Already this inescapable
wound approaches the whole city') and $οὕτω$ $δημόσιον$ $κακὸν$ $ἔρχεται$
$οἴκαδ'$ $ἑκάστῳ$ (26: 'In this way a public disaster comes homeward for
each individual'). In contrast, however, to the paired stanzas in Solon
13 and 27, these matching stanzas are not rhetorical set-pieces like
catalogues, but rather they are firmly embedded and indeed crucial
to the ongoing narrative about the demise of the poorly ruled city.

In contrast, then, to the rhetorically and poetically crafted single
stanzas of Archilochus and Mimnermus analyzed in the previous
chapter, the longer fragments of Tyrtaeus, Solon and the Theognidean poet reveal two additional sets of techniques that early elegiac
poets used to separate and organize individual stanzas in pairs or
even longer series. In the case of alternation, although the individual
stanzas often show few signs of ring-composition or the other forms
of internal structure documented in the previous chapter, their
rhetorical and linguistic unity is nonetheless easily apparent thanks
to the stark contrast with the stanzas that precede or follow. The
elegiac audience, in short, intuits the boundaries between stanzas less

by feeling closure at the end of the stanza, and more by experiencing the sudden change at the start of the next one. In addition to alternating stanzas, early elegists also composed pairs of coordinated stanzas (usually meditative ones) that are linked and contrasted by an elaborate set of responsions and structural parallels. Such paired stanzas are, of course, a perfect vehicle for the binary thinking popular among the ancient Greeks. They provide room, moreover for longer and therefore deeper meditations than are possible in single-stanza compositions or in longer poems structured by alternating stanzas, and thereby they offer an opportunity for breaking down more complex topics into two or more stanzas and examining each sub-topic in much greater detail.

4

Performance

Now that we have a good sense of how poets constructed individual elegiac stanzas and used them to organize longer compositions, a different question arises: can the stanzaic design of these fragments give us any insight into how this genre was performed? In recent years, for example, scholars have suggested that the extant elegiac fragments might be more polyphonic and complex than previously imagined. Reviving the work of Reitzenstein and others, some have returned to the idea that most if not all shorter elegiac compositions, like Greek drinking songs (*skolia*), were sung at symposia by a series of individuals, with each in turn 'taking up the song' and adding to or reacting against the verses of the previous singer.[1] Reitzenstein himself suggested in particular that contrary opinions in the transmitted text of the *Theognidea* might in fact preserve traces of such communal performances at the symposia of the archaic period.[2] In what follows, I suggest that the stanzaic structure of early elegy allows us, in fact, to postulate for the earlier periods, at least, a fixed five-couplet length for these individual contributions and to locate in the *Theognidea* examples of short elegiac songs—in one case a string of three together—that seem to react, extend and even correct the poem that came before.

---

[1] See. e.g. Vetta (1980) xxviii–xxxi and (1984), Herington (1985) 31–39, Bartól (1993) 51–57, Bowie (1997) and Aloni (2001) 88–90. Slings (2000, 5–10) points out how much of this recent work is deeply indebted to Reitzenstein (1893) 45–85.

[2] Reitzenstein (1893) 61–62; cf. West (1974) 17 and Vetta (1984). All of their examples, however, involve single couplets or pairs of them.

4.1. THE SYMPOTIC SETTING

Two relatively unknown elegiac stanzas from the classical period bear witness to this kind of communal performance in the round and were apparently designed to be sung at two different points in a sequence of such stanzas. The first is an elegiac poem inscribed, after three short *skolia*, on a papyrus from Elephantine that was apparently used as an *aide-mémoire* for a participant at a symposium (Adespota Elegiaca 27):[3]

χαίρετε, συμπόται ἄνδρες ὁμ[ήλικες · ἐ]ξ ἀγαθοῦ γὰρ
ἀρξάμενος τελέω τὸν λόγον [ἐ]ἰς ἀγα[θό]ν.
χρὴ δ᾽, ὅταν εἰς τοιοῦτο συνέλθωμεν φίλοι ἄνδρες
πρᾶγμα, γελᾶν παίζειν χρησαμένους ἀρετῇ,
5   ἥδεσθαί τε συνόντας, ἐς ἀλλήλους τε φ[λ]υαρεῖν
καὶ σκώπτειν τοιαῦθ᾽ οἷα γέλωτα φέρειν.
ἡ δὲ σπουδὴ ἐπέσθω, ἀκούωμέν [τε λ]εγόντων
ἐν μέρει· ἥδ᾽ ἀρετὴ συμποσίου πέλεται.
τοῦ δὲ ποταρχοῦντος πειθώμεθα· ταῦτα γάρ ἐστιν
10   ἔργ᾽ ἀνδρῶν ἀγαθῶν, εὐλογίαν τε φέρει.

Hail, fellow drinkers, [age-mates]. Fine was my beginning and fine will be the end of my discourse. Whenever we friends gather for such an activity, we ought to laugh and joke, behaving properly, take pleasure in being together, engage in foolish talk with one another, and utter jests such as to arouse laughter. But let seriousness follow and let us listen to the speakers in their turn: this is the best form of symposium. And let us obey the symposiarch: this is the conduct of good men and it wins praise.

This poem is five-couplets in length and, as befits its elegiac metre, it is almost entirely hortatory, consisting of a salutation, followed by a pair of quatrains that urge us first to play (3–6) and then to move on to a more serious form of discourse (7–10).[4] The similarities

[3] It is preserved, along with three *skolia*, on an early Hellenistic papyrus from Elephantine (*PBerol.* 13270). The scribe has isolated these verses as a separate elegiac poem or sympotic contribution by writing the verses out line by line, by indenting them and by placing a *paragraphos* before the first couplet. For discussion, see Ferrari (1988) and Collins (2004) 65–66. Gentili and Prato (1985, 139) date this poem to the 5th-cent. BCE.

[4] This fragment, especially in its use of the construction χρή plus the infinitive and its emphasis on moderate behaviour, is similar to Xenophanes 1, for which see below Section 6.1.

and differences between these two injunctions are marked at the end
of each section by the repetition of the verb φέρειν with highly
contrasted objects, 'laughs' and 'good discourse': οἷα γέλωτα φέρειν
(6) and εὐλογίαν τε φέρει (10).[5] The summary explanation in the
final couplet, moreover, employs the typical language of closure
(9: ταῦτα γὰρ...) as well as the phrase 'deeds of good men' (10:
ἔργ᾽ ἀνδρῶν ἀγαθῶν), which recalls the opening couplet (1–2):
χαίρετε ... ἄνδρες ... ἐξ ἀγαθοῦ... εἰς ἀγαθόν. These verses, then,
display many of the internal signs of a unified and self-sufficient
stanza that were discussed in Chapter 2. And in this case, as in the
case of the Megarian epitaph, we can be confident that we have a
complete poem.

A similar five-couplet fragment is attributed to the fifth-century
poet Ion of Chios:[6]

> χαιρέτω ἡμέτερος βασιλεὺς σωτήρ τε πατήρ τε·
> ἡμῖν δὲ κρητῆρ᾽ οἰνοχόοι θέραπες
> κιρνάντων προχύταισιν ἐν ἀργυρέοις· ὁ δὲ χρυσοῦν
> δῖνον ἔχων χειροῖν νιζέτω εἰς ἔδαφος.
> σπένδοντες δ᾽ ἁγνῶς Ἡρακλεῖ τ᾽ Ἀλκμήνῃ τε, 5
> Προκλεῖ Περσείδαις τ᾽ ἐκ Διὸς ἀρχόμενοι
> πίνωμεν, παίζωμεν· ἴτω διὰ νυκτὸς ἀοιδή,
> ὀρχείσθω τις· ἑκὼν δ᾽ ἄρχε φιλοφροσύνης.
> ὅντινα δ᾽ εὐειδὴς μίμνει θήλεα πάρευνος,
> κεῖνος τῶν ἄλλων κυδρότερον πίεται. 10

Greetings to our king, our saviour and father; and for us let the wine-pouring
attendants mix the bowl from silver pitchers; and let him who holds in his
hands the golden jug wash our hands on to the floor. Let us make holy
libation to Heracles and Alcmena, to Procles and Perseus' descendants,
beginning with Zeus, and let us drink and play; let the singing last all night,
let there be dancing; begin the jollity with a will; and if anyone has a shapely
woman waiting to share his bed, he will drink more confidently than the rest.

Like the stanza from Elephantine, this poem is primarily exhortative.
Even if we discount the opening greeting to the god Dionysus

---

[5] The papyrus has the infinitive φέρειν in the final line and this is what West (1992,
ad loc.) prints. Gerber (1999, ad loc.) follows Wilamowitz and corrects to φέρει.

[6] Ion 27, quoted by Athenaeus (463a). The translation is from Campbell (1991)
ad loc.

(χαιρέτω), there are no fewer than five imperatives and two hortative subjunctives aimed at encouraging both the servants and the guests to help stage a successful symposium. Barring any sure signs of ring-composition or verbal repetition it is difficult to know for certain if this is an entire poem, but it does give a complete, albeit abbreviated, description of the preliminary rites of a symposium.

It bears, moreover, obvious similarities to the poem from Elephant-ine, which is certainly complete. Both begin in like fashion (χαίρετε and χαιρέτω) and exhort the gathered company to various kinds of activities. But the implied timing of the performance of these two poems is different. Ion appears to have composed his stanza for the start of the symposium, because the first actions he recommends—the washing of hands and the triple libations—usually take place before the symposium begins. The poem from Elephantine, on the other hand, seems designed for some later point during the enter-tainment, because it refers in the first couplet to some poem that had been apparently been performed earlier: 'Fine was my beginning and fine will be the end of my discourse (λόγος).' The verses that follow also seem to suggest, albeit in very general terms, that it is time for the discourse to shift from playful banter to more serious topics.[7] But to precisely which genre of discourse does the Elephantine poem refer? We get one important clue at lines 7–8, where the poet says 'let us listen to the speakers in turn' (ἀκούωμέν [τε λ]εγόντων | ἐν μέρει). Most readers are likely to think of Plato's *Symposium*, perhaps, and the series of prose speeches recorded there, but if we are meant to think of oratory, why does the poet use the related noun λόγος (line 2) to refer to his own contribution, which is, in fact, a finely composed elegiac stanza?[8]

[7] This is, in fact, confirmed by the sequence of poems on the papyrus itself: the elegiac stanza comes after the three *skolia*, suggesting that it would have been per-formed after the *skolia*, perhaps at the start of a string of more serious elegiac compositions. The shift is not, however, marked by any clear deictic language in the poem itself, for example by placing a νῦν in line 7 ('now let seriousness follow'), but rather by the shift from a generalized desideratum (2–6: 'whenever we meet, we should laugh') to a direct command with a contrastive δέ: 'But let seriousness follow' (7).

[8] Bowie (1993, 359–60) rightly allows that the λόγοι here could be either spoken or sung and Bartól (1993, 46–47) notes a number of instances where Greek authors—albeit not the elegiac poets themselves—seem to use the verb λέγειν to refer to the content of elegiac verses and ἀείδειν to refer to their mode of presentation, similar to the difference in epic between ἐννέπειν and ἀείδειν.

It seems *a priori* more likely that, when he encourages the participants to take up a serious theme 'in turn' (ἐν μέρει), the poet from Elephantine is referring to the traditional sympotic form of elegiac performance and has composed this stanza to prompt the transition from some initially playful poems on love and drinking to more serious compositions, presumably on political or philosophical themes. In any event, it is easy to imagine that these two complete five-couplet stanzas were composed by or for a symposiarch as a vehicle for outlining or recalling the procedures of a symposium, and in the case of the Elephantine poem, to signal the appropriate tone and content of the songs sung there. The five-couplet length of both poems, moreover, suggests that the songs sung by the other symposiasts were of equivalent length. This is certainly the case with the drinking songs (*skolia*) that were likewise performed in the round, both the more famous ones in lyric metres (for which see notes 17–18 below) and those of probably Hellenistic date, which are preserved on a first-century CE papyrus and were apparently performed in stanzas of four 'mouse-tailed' hexameters.[9] In the case of the hexametrical *skolia* in particular it is clear from the arrangement of the stanzas on the papyrus—each poem is separated by spaces and set down in alphabetical order according to the first letter of the first line—that this document, like the one from Elephantine, was designed as a prompt for sympotic performance. And each four-line stanza is separated from the next by the command 'Pipe for me!' (αὔλει μοι), which suggests that the symposiasts marked the end of each individual contribution by a musical fanfare of some sort or perhaps by a repeated refrain.[10] Each stanza, finally, is devoted to a single theme and half of the surviving examples are heavily marked by ring-composition in the first and last lines, for example (11–14):[11]

---

[9] *POxy.* 1795. In a mouse-tailed hexameter the penultimate syllable is always short.

[10] Higham (1936) 314–15.

[11] Hopkinson (1988, 80–81 and 271–74) provides a convenient text and discussion. He notes (p. 271) that the content of these verses 'has less in common with other surviving scolia...than with certain poems in the Theognidean collection (esp. 1039–70b).'

Λύδιος αὐλὸς ἐμοὶ τὰ δὲ Λύδια παίγματα λύρας
κα[ὶ] Φρύ[γι]ος κάλαμος τὰ δὲ ταύρεα τύμπανα πονεῖ·
ταῦτα ζῶν ἆισαι τ᾽ ἔραμαι καὶ ὅταν ἀποθάνω
<u>αὐλὸν</u> ὑπὲρ κεφαλῆς <u>θέτε μοι</u> παρὰ ποσσὶ λύρα[ν.

The Lydian pipe labors for me and the Lydian ditties of the lyre
And the Phrygian reed and the bull-hide tambourines.
When I am alive I desire to sing these things, but whenever I die
Set the pipe above my head and the lyre at my feet.

These stanzas of mouse-tailed hexameters are shorter than the elegiac
ones discussed in this study, but they do give us good insight into
what a collection single elegiac contributions to a symposium might
look like, especially those, like Mimnermus 1 or the Theognidean
Ganymede poem, which offer a compact and rhetorically complete
meditation. In fact any single stanza that displays strong ring-
composition or the four-plus-one format would be a fit contribution
to a round of single-stanza songs at the symposium, as long as it
presented a complete idea and stayed within the thematic bounds laid
out by the symposiarch, whether these be broadly established—as in
the 'serious' themes decreed by the Elephantine poem—or dictated
informally by the sequence of contributions that have preceded it.

4.2. GENERIC 'CITY-POEMS' AS VEHICLES FOR POLITICAL DEBATE

We can see amidst the flotsam and jetsam of the *Theognidea* the
outlines of the kind of serious, communally performed poems that
the Elephantine poet seems to imagine. Near the start of the 'Cyrnus
Book' we find two five-couplet stanzas in close proximity (39–48 and
53–62) that record different opinions about the cause of an impending political disaster in the city. The first (39–48) appears in the
collection directly after the seal-poem discussed in the previous
chapter:

Κύρνε, κύει πόλις ἥδε, δέδοικα δὲ μὴ τέκῃ ἄνδρα
40   εὐθυντῆρα κακῆς ὕβριος ἡμετέρης.
ἀστοὶ μὲν γὰρ ἔθ᾽ οἵδε σαόφρονες, ἡγεμόνες δὲ

τετράφαται πολλὴν εἰς κακότητα πεσεῖν.
οὐδεμίαν πω, Κύρν’, ἀγαθοὶ πόλιν ὤλεσαν ἄνδρες,
ἀλλ’ ὅταν ὑβρίζειν τοῖσι κακοῖσιν ἄδῃ
δῆμόν τε φθείρωσι δίκας τ’ ἀδίκοισι διδῶσιν   45
οἰκείων κερδέων εἵνεκα καὶ κράτεος,
ἔλπεο μὴ δηρὸν κείνην πόλιν ἀτρεμίεσθαι,
μηδ’ εἰ νῦν κεῖται πολλῇ ἐν ἡσυχίῃ . . .[12]

Cyrnus, this city is pregnant and I am afraid she will give birth to a man who
will set right our wicked insolence. These townsmen are still of sound mind,
but their leaders have changed and fallen into the depths of depravity. Never
yet, Cyrnus, have noble men destroyed a city, but whenever the base take
delight in outrageous behaviour and ruin the people and give judgments in
favour of the unjust, for the sake of their own profit and power, do not
expect that city to remain quiet long, even if it is now utterly calm . . .

Editors and commentators have assumed, as I do, that the vocative
(Κύρνε) in the initial position of line 39 as well as the clear change in
subject (politics) and linguistic mode (meditation) marks the beginning of a new poem.[13] These five couplets, moreover, comprise a self-
contained and coherent stanza of the Theognidean type discussed in
Chapter 2: four couplets of meditation followed by a single one of
exhortation to a recommended mental state. Compare for example,
the prohibition at the start of the final couplet here (47 ἔλπεο μὴ . . .
πόλιν ἀτρεμίεσθαι) with the one that appears at the end of the poem
on dangers of aristocratic miscegenation discussed earlier in Section
2.2 (191–192: οὔτω μὴ θαύμαζε γένος . . . μαυροῦσθαι).

The poet also frames verses 39–48 with a sophisticated bit of ring-
composition. In the first couplet, 'this city' is likened to a pregnant

---

[12] Lines 39–48 are followed in the *Theognidea* by two additional couplets (49–52),
which in their present state cannot stand alone as an independent composition or the
beginning of another stanza. The first of the two is dependent syntactically on the
imperative in the final line of the stanza quoted here, and the mention of 'this city' in
the very last line (52) must refer to 'this city' in the first line (39). I believe (but
cannot prove) that these couplets are the ruins of a second stanza designed to follow
29–38, because they begin (εὖτ’ ἂν τοῖσι κακοῖσι φίλ’ ἀνδράσι ταῦτα γένηται) in a
manner similar in form to the protasis of a condition that Tyrtaeus often uses to
begin a new stanza, e.g.: (10.11–12) εἰ δ’ οὕτως ἀνδρός τοι ἀλωμένου οὐδεμί’ ὥρη |
γίνεται οὔτ’ αἰδώς . . . Note the parallels between ταῦτα and οὕτως, and generic use of
ἀνδράσι and ἀνδρός. At the end of the next chapter I argue that an earlier version of
the second stanza of Tyrtaeus 12 also began in similar fashion.

[13] Every edition I have consulted begins a new poem or section at line 39.

woman, who has not yet experienced her labour pains, and the poet expresses fear for her future. In the last couplet he repeats this same idea in the form of the prohibition discussed above:

> Κύρνε, κύει πόλις ἥδε, δέδοικα δὲ μὴ τέκῃ ἄνδρα (39)
>
> ἔλπεο μὴ δηρὸν κείνην πόλιν ἀτρεμίεσθαι (47)

But by a clever sleight of hand the poet has, in fact, tricked us: the framing verses of the stanza do not, in fact, refer to the same city. Although the poet repeats the word πόλις in the first, fifth, and final hexameters, he subtly but effectively contrasts 'this city' (39), which is presumably Megara or the city in which these verses are being sung, with a hypothetical city, introduced at the very middle of the stanza (43, also a hexameter) as a way to explain his apprehension (the asyndeton here having the force of γάρ): 'For never yet have good men destroyed a city [i.e. any city].' The poet then asserts (again in a negative expression) the conditions under which 'any city' might be destroyed, closing with the sad thought that if these conditions are fulfilled, there can be no hope or expectation that 'that city' (47) will survive. Syntactically he must be referring here to the hypothetical city raised at the center of the poem, because he uses the demonstrative pronoun κείνην ('that city' i.e. the doomed one imagined in the fifth line of the stanza), to distinguish it from πόλις ἥδε in the first line ('this city here'), and because at lines 43 and 47 he deploys the word πόλις (both times in the accusative case) in the same position in the hexameter.

There follows close by in the 'Cyrnus Book' another stanza concerned with the fate of the city, that pointedly disagrees with the one just examined (53–62):[14]

> Κύρνε, πόλις μὲν ἔθ' ἥδε πόλις, λαοὶ δὲ δὴ ἄλλοι
>
> οἳ πρόσθ' οὔτε δίκας ᾔδεσαν οὔτε νόμους,
>
> 55 ἀλλ' ἀμφὶ πλευραῖσι δορὰς αἰγῶν κατέτριβον,
>
> ἔξω δ' ὥστ' ἔλαφοι τῆσδ' ἐνέμοντο πόλεος.
>
> καὶ νῦν εἰσ' ἀγαθοί, Πολυπαΐδη· οἱ δὲ πρὶν ἐσθλοὶ
>
> νῦν δειλοί. τίς κεν ταῦτ' ἀνέχοιτ' ἐσορῶν;
>
> ἀλλήλους δ' ἀπατῶσιν ἐπ' ἀλλήλοισι γελῶντες,
>
> 60 οὔτε κακῶν γνώμας εἰδότες οὔτ' ἀγαθῶν.

---

[14] West (1992, ad loc.) and Gerber (1999, ad loc.) follow the *communis opinio* when they print these lines as the first part of an eight-couplet poem (53–68).

μηδένα τῶνδε φίλον ποιεῦ, Πολυπαΐδη, ἀστῶν
ἐκ θυμοῦ χρείης οὕνεκα μηδεμιῆς·

Cyrnus, this city is still a city, but the people are different, people who formerly knew neither justice nor laws, but wore tattered goatskins about their sides and lived outside this city like deer. And now they are noble, Polypaïdes, while those who were noble before are now base. Who can endure the sight of this? They deceive one another and mock one another, knowing neither the distinctive marks of the base nor those of the noble. Make none of these townsmen your sincere friend, Polypaïdes, because of any need.

This stanza is designed much like the first city-poem (39–48). In both the poet addresses Cyrnus at the start of the first line, provides four couplets of meditation on the political health of 'this city', and then closes with a single prohibition in the final couplet. This second city-poem (53–62) also shows signs of ring-composition. The reference to 'these citizens' at the end of the final hexameter (τῶνδε ... ἀστῶν), for example, refers back in summary fashion to the 'people' (λαοί) mentioned at the end of the first, as does the appearance of the vocative Πολυπαΐδη in the final hexameter, which recalls Κύρνε in the first. Indeed, the final hexameter, with its prohibition and vocative is yet another example of what seems to be a stock Theognidean marker of closure. Note too how the combination of Cyrnus' patronymic and the word ἀστῶν at line-end closely match the final hexameter of the Theognidean poem about miscegenation:

μηδένα τῶνδε φίλον ποιεῦ, Πολυπαΐδη, ἀστῶν (61)

οὕτω μὴ θαύμαζε γένος, Πολυπαΐδη, ἀστῶν (191)

This second city-poem, then, seems to have been composed as a typical Theognidean stanza.

How, then, might we explain the close resemblances between these two city poems? I suggest that the second city-poem (53–62) was composed in reaction to the first, in the kind of *catena simposiale* that scholars often imagine for elegiac performance at a symposium.[15] Indeed, it not only recalls the first city-poem, it also critiques it by identifying a different threat to the city. The first poem made it quite clear that 'these citizens (ἀστοί) are still of sound mind' and that the

---

[15] The term is borrowed from Vetta (1980) xxviii–xxxi.

leaders of the city are to blame for the current civic woes (41–42). In the mid-stanza description of the hypothetical city, too, the citizens are absolved from any blame, when the poet tells us that the κακοί ruin 'the people' (45: δῆμος). The sources of evil are, in short, neither 'the citizens' nor 'the people'. In the second city-poem, however, the poet says somewhat enigmatically that 'this city is still a city' but the people (53: λαοί) have changed, a group that is likewise equated at the end of the poem with the citizens (61: ἀστῶν). The singer's position has, in short, either changed radically or (more likely) the song has at this point been taken up by another performer: in the first poem the citizens are of sound mind and implicitly good, but the political leaders are bad, whereas in the second poem 'this city is still a city', i.e. it still has the same political institutions, but it is now endangered because the citizens themselves are of a different (and inferior) type.

The composer of the second city-poem artfully uses response to underscore this contrast in opinion, by imitating and conflating the form and wording of the opening verses of the first city-poem:

> Κύρνε, κύει πόλις ἥδε, δέδοικα δὲ μὴ τέκῃ ἄνδρα
> εὐθυντῆρα κακῆς ὕβριος ἡμετέρης.
> ἀστοὶ μὲν γὰρ ἔθ᾽ οἵδε σαόφρονες, ἡγεμόνες δὲ
> τετράφαται πολλὴν εἰς κακότητα πεσεῖν (39–42)

> Κύρνε, πόλις μὲν ἔθ᾽ ἥδε πόλις, λαοὶ δὲ δὴ ἄλλοι,
> οἳ πρόσθ᾽ οὔτε δίκας ᾔδεσαν οὔτε νόμους (53–54)

The responsion is more complicated than we have seen before, but it is carefully wrought. The poet begins the second city-poem with Κύρνε, πόλις μὲν ἔθ᾽ ἥδε πόλις (53), thus echoing the reference to 'this city' in the first hexameter of the first city-poem: Κύρνε, κύει πόλις ἥδε (39). But not exactly. By overrunning the midline caesura with the repetition of the word πόλις, the second poem calls attention to the close parallelism between the two stanzas, but also to the unsettling statement that follows: 'but the people are different'.[16] And here lies the cleverness of the repetition and its complexity:

---

[16] For consistency I give the translation of Gerber (1999) here, but the contrast between μέν and δέ strongly suggests that λαοί should be the predicate rather than the subject. Thus a better paraphrase (as I give below) would be 'This city is still a city, but different men (ἄλλοι) indeed are (i.e. now) its people.'

the first line of the second city-poem also imitates the second couplet of the first city-poem. Indeed, the expression πόλις μὲν ἔθ᾽ ἥδε (53), recalls ἀστοὶ μὲν γὰρ ἔθ᾽ οἵδε (41) as well as Κύρνε, κύει πόλις ἥδε (39). And here the responsion is even stronger thanks to the closer parallels in the overall syntax of the couplet: both couplets (41–42 and 53–54) are composed as marked comparisons (μὲν and δέ) in which the allegedly non-offensive parties (41: ἀστοὶ and 53: πόλις) are defined in a brief predicate sentence that is closely followed in the same hexameter by a more ominous description of the alleged trouble-makers (41: ἡγεμόνες and 53: λαοί) in a sentence that then concludes in the pentameter. To paraphrase: the first poet sings 'This city is pregnant for disaster, for although the citizens here are still good, their leaders are depraved' (41–42), to which the second responds 'This city is still the same city, but the citizens are now of a different sort' (53–54). In the second case, the charge is—as we later learn—that the influx of rough-and-tumble outsiders has changed the citizen body to such an extent that it threatens the traditional political system.

It is difficult, then, to avoid the conclusion that the beginning of this second city-poem was carefully designed to recall and then refute the assertions of the first. I suggest, moreover, that we can see in these two discordant city-poems the bare outlines of the kind of antagonistic symposiastic play that we also find in the collection of Athenian *skolia* preserved by Athenaeus (695a),[17] where in close proximity we find two short poems, which begin in identical fashion: 'In a myrtle branch I will carry my sword, as did Harmodius and Aristogeiton', but then end quite differently: (i) 'when they slew the tyrant and made Athens a city of equal rights (ἰσονόμους τ᾽ Ἀθήνας ἐποιησάτην)'; and (ii) 'when at the feast of Athena they slew the tyrant'. Here the difference in expression is subtle, but important: for a radical democrat, the first version, with its mention of *isonomia* is preferable, whereas a singer with oligarchic leanings might prefer to describe the event as a squabble at a festival between two aristocrats that brought no real political change to Athens.[18] I suggest, then, that

---

[17] Lambin (1979) and Collins (2004) 112–24.

[18] Another pair seem to contend playfully over the superiority of hetero- or homosexual attraction (695d): 'Would that I might become a lovely ivory lyre and that lovely lads might take me to join the chorus of Dionysus' and 'Would that

these two *skolia* stand in the same relationship to each other as the two Theognidean city-poems: they appear close to one another in the collection and take up the same subject, but nevertheless seem to express significantly different political views.

Were these two city-poems, in fact, composed at the same banquet with the second in immediate response to the first? It is difficult to say, since it is easy to imagine another scenario: the first city-poem became part of the traditional repertoire of Theognidean poetry, was re-performed regularly, and at some later point in time (perhaps a whole generation or even century later) another talented poet composed the second poem to refute or update the first, when political circumstances or opinions had changed. And then once both city-poems are in the repertoire, one can certainly imagine that they could be recited at the same event, especially if both of these contrary views still prevailed in the city. This is certainly what we must imagine for the repeated performances of the discordant Harmodius and Aristogeiton *skolia* in classical Athens. A practice of combining old and new poems in sympotic performances may help explain, in fact, a number of chronologically dubious anecdotes about famous poets disagreeing with one another in their songs. Diogenes Laertius (1.6) reports, for example, that when Mimnermus wrote (Mimnermus 6) 'Would that my fated death might come at sixty, unattended by sickness and grievous cares,' Solon rebuked him saying (Solon 20) 'But if even now you will listen to me, remove this [i.e. verse] ... and changing it, Ligyaistades, sing as follows: "May my fated death come at eighty".'[19] Diogenes living in the fully literate Roman world presumably imagines that Solon somehow disputed with Mimnermus from the printed page ('when Mimnermus wrote'), an unlikely

I might become some large new lovely golden jewel and that a lovely woman, whose heart is pure, might wear me.'

[19] Translation by Gerber (1999) ad loc. For a recent discussion see Tuomi (1986). Plutarch, *Comparison of Solon and Publicola* 1.5 records another disagreement that Solon had with him about the 'duration of life' and cites Solon 21, which many scholars assume to be from the same poem as Solon 20. West (1974, 181–82) suggests that in Solon 20 the poet quoted Mimnermus' verses in his own poem before refuting him, offering as a parallel the manner in which Simonides 8.1–2 quotes Homer's simile about the leaves. The Homeric verses, however, by Simonides' time, if not before, had the status of an aphorism and Simonides does not challenge the truth of it, the way Solon challenges Mimnermus.

scenario in the sixth-century. The format of taking-up-the-song, however, suggests another possibility for this interchange, namely that famous songs like Mimnermus' were repeated at symposia and that, when Solon made his famous rebuke, he was in fact responding on the spot to a version of the Mimnerman poem that had just been performed by a person at his side. Thus when he says in his elegiac rejoinder 'changing it, Ligyaistades, sing as follows' he presumably directed his words to a fellow symposiast, who had just performed Mimnermus' poem. Such dramatic re-performance of the archaic repertoire is, indeed, one of the basic premises of the *Theognidea*, namely, that the original poet is present in the voice of those who take up his persona and repeat his verses.

It seems, in fact, that Solon himself composed a poem that shares some of the language and concerns of the two Theognidean city-poems. Solon 4, the so-called 'Eunomia' fragment, begins with a five-couplet section that frets in similar ways about the future of 'our city' (1: ἡμετέρη δὲ πόλις) and expresses fears that both the citizens (6: ἀστοὶ) and the leaders (7: ἡγεμόνες) are acting in a manner that will doom the city:[20]

> ἡμετέρη δὲ πόλις κατὰ μὲν Διὸς οὔποτ᾽ ὀλεῖται
> αἶσαν καὶ μακάρων θεῶν φρένας ἀθανάτων·
> τοίη γὰρ μεγάθυμος ἐπίσκοπος ὀβριμοπάτρη
> Παλλὰς Ἀθηναίη χεῖρας ὕπερθεν ἔχει·
> αὐτοὶ δὲ φθείρειν μεγάλην πόλιν ἀφραδίῃσιν   5
> ἀστοὶ βούλονται χρήμασι πειθόμενοι,
> δήμου θ᾽ ἡγεμόνων ἄδικος νόος, οἷσιν ἑτοῖμον
> ὕβριος ἐκ μεγάλης ἄλγεα πολλὰ παθεῖν·
> οὐ γὰρ ἐπίστανται κατέχειν κόρον οὐδὲ παρούσας
> εὐφροσύνας κοσμεῖν δαιτὸς ἐν ἡσυχίῃ   10

Our state will never perish through the dispensation of Zeus or the intentions of the blessed immortal gods; for such a stout-hearted guardian, Pallas Athena, born of a mighty father, holds her hands over it. But it is the citizens

---

[20] Quoted by Demosthenes 19.254–56. Since this poem was inserted at a later date into the MSS of Demosthenes, it is not clear that the orator wanted all thirty-nine lines of the transmitted text to be read, since this would detract valuable time from his speech. MacDowell (2000, 312) suggests in passing that these first ten lines could have illustrated all the points that the orator wanted to make. Fränkel (1975, 220) quotes and discusses lines 1–10 as if they were a discrete unit.

themselves who by their acts of foolishness and subservience to money are willing to destroy a great city, and the mind of the people's leaders is unjust; they are certain to suffer much pain as a result of their great arrogance. For they do not know how to restrain excess or to conduct in an orderly and peaceful manner the festivities of the banquet that are at hand.

The rhetorical unity of this stanza is manifest: it is one long sentence divided into two sections, each of which contains a prediction followed by an explanation. The first (1–4: μὲν followed by γὰρ) predicts the benevolent intentions of Zeus and the other gods toward Athens, whereas the second and longer section (5–10: δὲ followed by γὰρ) depicts the malevolence and bad behavior of its citizens and their leaders and predicts much suffering for the city.[21] The poet, moreover, highlights these parallel movements by repeating key ideas and words in the first part of each section: the destruction of the city (1: ἡμετέρη ... πόλις ... οὔποτ᾽ ὀλεῖται and 5: φθείρειν μεγάλην πόλιν ... βούλονται) and the varying mental states or inclinations of the divine and then human participants (2: φρένας, 3: μεγάθυμος, 5: ἀφραδίῃσιν, 6: βούλονται, 7: ἄδικος νόος and 9: οὐκ ... ἐπίστανται).[22]

There are signs, moreover, that this stanza was composed on the same generic model as the two Theognidean city-poems. The similarities in content are obvious enough:[23] the survival of the city in which the poet is performing ('this city' or 'our city') hangs in the balance of civil discord between different political groups. But there are some important formal parallels as well, although Solon's treatment is more expansive at the start. In the first Theognidean city-poem (39–48), for example, the poet begins by describing the city in a single couplet ('This city is pregnant, Cyrnus, and I am afraid lest...'), whereas Solon devotes two couplets to his city (1–4). Both poets place the word πόλις in the nominative case in the first line, and then in the fifth they use the same word in the accusative case in the same *sedes* before the bucolic diaeresis. They then go on to discuss the city's citizens and leaders. The Theognidean poet does so

---

[21] Adkins (1985, ad loc.) notes the odd placement of the μέν, in line 1 between the preposition and its object, which focuses our attention on the contrast between Zeus' intention and those of the citizens themselves (αὐτοὶ δέ).

[22] Mülke (2002) 90–91.

[23] Tedeschi (1995, 34–39) treats both as part of the same tradition of symposiastic songs on political topics.

in a single couplet (2–3: ἀστοὶ μὲν ... ἡγεμόνες δέ), while Solon again doubles the length of his description, giving a couplet each to the ἀστοὶ (5–6) and the ἡγεμόνων (7–8). Solon also makes a boast that Athens will never be destroyed (1: ἡμετέρη δὲ πόλις ... οὔποτ' ὀλεῖται) that is somewhat similar in its wording and fragility to the wishful Theognidean assertion at 'Never yet ... have noble men destroyed a city' (44: οὐδεμίαν πω ... ἀγαθοὶ πόλιν ὤλεσαν ἄνδρες)—indeed both poets go on to imagine just this kind of destruction under the current circumstances.[24] And both, finally, end their stanzas by stressing with similar phrases (Solon 4.10: δαιτὸς ἐν ἡσυχίη and Theognidea 48: πολλῇ ἐν ἡσυχῇ) the civic calm that is at stake if the citizens and their leaders continue on the same dangerous path.

Such parallels in content, language and stanzaic structure suggest that all three of these city-poems reflect a generic form of political elegy, one that takes for granted a pessimistic outlook for the continued survival of the city, while at the same time allows for radically different diagnoses of the cause. Thus the first Theognidean poem (39–48) asserts that the citizens (41: ἀστοί) are good, but the leaders (41: ἡγέμονες) are bad, whereas in the second poem (53–62) the citizens (53: λαοί and 61: ἀστοί) are to blame, because they are now drawn from a different class of people, who in former times dwelt in the rural areas clothed 'in tattered goat-skins'. And although Solon blames 'the citizens themselves' (5–6: ἀστοί) for their foolishness and love of money, he emphasizes the culpability of the leaders (7: ἡγέμονες), by devoting two couplets, not just one, to their faults and ending with two powerful charges—of hybris and excess (κόρος)—that resonate widely with traditional Greek ideas about human self-destruction. Thus if we are to label the first Theognidean city poem as vaguely 'democratic' and the second 'oligarchic' in its outlook, this Solonic contribution seems (as he represents himself in some of his other poems) to fall somewhere in between: critical of both factions but tilting more of his ire towards the political elite in Athens.[25] Solon's city-poem is, of course, just the

24 Irwin (2005) 227.
25 Nagy (1985) 42–46. Tedeschi (1995, 35–38) thinks that the first Theognidean poem (he does not discuss the second) represents an aristocratic ideology and Solon 4 a democratic one, and Irwin (2005, 226 n. 61) suggests that we should think of 'sympotic capping games.'

opening salvo in a much longer poem that seems to be composed in stanzas and that goes on to dissect Athens' political problems in much greater detail and then to describe the benefits of good rule (*Eunomia*).[26]

4.3. A FRAGMENT OF A THEOGNIDEAN CHAIN

The remains of another interactive sympotic performance seem to survive at *Theognidea* 467–96 (= Evenus 8a), a long fragment which scholars usually take to be a single poem.[27] They have not, however, appreciated the fact that these thirty verses separate fairly easily into three stanzas. The first runs as follows (467–76):

μηδένα τῶνδ' ἀέκοντα μένειν κατέρυκε παρ' ἡμῖν,
μηδὲ θύραζε κέλευ' οὐκ ἐθέλοντ' ἰέναι·
μηδ' εὕδοντ' ἐπέγειρε, Σιμωνίδη, ὅντιν' ἂν ἡμῶν
470   θωρηχθέντ' οἴνῳ μαλθακὸς ὕπνος ἕλῃ,
μηδὲ τὸν ἀγρυπνέοντα κέλευ' ἀέκοντα καθεύδειν.
πᾶν γὰρ ἀναγκαῖον χρῆμ' ἀνιηρὸν ἔφυ.
τῷ πίνειν δ' ἐθέλοντι παρασταδὸν οἰνοχοείτω·
οὐ πάσας νύκτας γίνεται ἁβρὰ παθεῖν.
475   αὐτὰρ ἐγώ μέτρον γὰρ ἔχω μελιηδέος οἴνου
ὕπνου λυσικάκου μνήσομαι οἴκαδ' ἰών.

Don't hold back anyone of these so that he remain with us against his will, don't tell anyone to depart who does not want to, don't waken from his sleep, Simonides, anyone of us who, fortified with wine, has been overcome by gentle sleep, and don't tell one who's wide awake to sleep against his will. All force is disagreeable. And let (a slave) stand by and pour wine for him who wants to drink; it's not possible to have a good time every night. But I'll

---

[26] For a full discussion, see the end of the previous chapter and Appendix II.

[27] See e.g. Harrison (1902, 116) for the *communis opinio* at the turn of the last century ('most scholars have thought it to be a complete elegy'), and the more recent assessments ad loc. of van Groningen (1966), West (1992) and Gerber (1999). But others have worried that lines 493–96 at the very close of the poem seem to contradict views taken earlier; see e.g. Garzya (1958) ad loc. Since Aristotle twice attributes line 472 to Evenus of Paros, many scholars think that this poem was composed by him, but the problem is complicated by the fact that there were apparently two 5th-cent. Parian poets of this name, presumably grandfather and grandson. For discussion, see Bowra (1934), Carrière (1975) 160–62, and the introduction to Ch. 6.

go home—I've had my limit of honey-sweet wine—and I'll take thought for sleep that brings release from ills.

In these ten verses the speaker addresses five imperatives to Simonides in his role as symposiarch or host and gives him advice about what he should and should not do with regard to the guests at his apparently late-night party. In addition to the imperatives, other deictic markers, such as the vocative and the specific references to 'these men here' (467) and to 'us' (467 and 470) give the vivid impression that we are present at the symposium.[28] These four couplets of exhortation are followed by a single summary verse expressing the intention of the speaker (emphatically introduced with αὐτὰρ ἐγώ) to go home and sleep it off (85–86). This is, in short, a good example of the four-plus-one configuration of a single-stanza poem that we have seen before in the *Theognidea*, but here in reversed form: a series of exhortations capped by a single meditation. The poet also frames the stanza with some ring-composition. He sets up, for example, one of the main themes of the poem—knowing when its time to drink up and go home—by repeating the verb 'to go' at the very end of the first and last pentameters (468: θύραζε . . . ἰέναι and 476: οἴκαδ᾽ ἰών) and he knits the body of the stanza together formally by focusing on the willingness or unwillingness of the individual symposiast in a clever pattern of repetition and alternation: ἀέκοντα μένειν (467), θύραζε . . . οὐκ ἐθέλοντ᾽ ἰέναι (468), ἀέκοντα καθεύδειν (471) and τῷ πίνειν δ᾽ ἐθέλοντι (473). These ten lines, then, seem to be a neatly composed and well-balanced stanza.

The fragment continues on for twenty more verses (477–96):

> ἥκω δ᾽ ὡς οἶνος χαριέστατος ἀνδρὶ πεπόσθαι·
> οὔτε τι γὰρ νήφων οὔτε λίην μεθύων·
> ὃς δ᾽ ἂν ὑπερβάλλῃ πόσιος μέτρον, οὐκέτι κεῖνος
> τῆς αὐτοῦ γλώσσης καρτερὸς οὐδὲ νόου·   480
> μυθεῖται δ᾽ ἀπάλαμνα, τὰ νήφοσι γίνεται αἰσχρά,
> αἰδεῖται δ᾽ ἔρδων οὐδέν, ὅταν μεθύῃ,
> τὸ πρὶν ἐὼν σώφρων, τότε νήπιος. ἀλλὰ σὺ ταῦτα
> γινώσκων μὴ πῖν᾽ οἶνον ὑπερβολάδην,
> ἀλλ᾽ ἢ πρὶν μεθύειν ὑπανίστασο—μή σε βιάσθω   485
> γαστὴρ ὥστε κακὸν λάτριν ἐφημέριον—

---

[28] Pellizer (1990, 179–80) suggests that this kind of *deixis* is typical of sympotic poetry *tout court*.

ἢ παρεὼν μὴ πῖνε. σὺ δ᾽ "ἔγχεε" τοῦτο μάταιον
κωτίλλεις αἰεί· τοὔνεκά τοι μεθύεις·
ἡ μὲν γὰρ φέρεται φιλοτήσιος, ἡ δὲ πρόκειται,
490   τὴν δὲ θεοῖς σπένδεις, τὴν δ᾽ ἐπὶ χειρὸς ἔχεις·
ἀρνεῖσθαι δ᾽ οὐκ οἶδας. ἀνίκητος δέ τοι οὗτος,
ὃς πολλὰς πίνων μή τι μάταιον ἐρεῖ.
ὑμεῖς δ᾽ εὖ μυθεῖσθε παρὰ κρητῆρι μένοντες,
ἀλλήλων ἔριδας δὴν ἀπερυκόμενοι,
495   εἰς τὸ μέσον φωνεῦντες ὁμῶς ἑνὶ καὶ συνάπασιν·
χοὔτως συμπόσιον γίνεται οὐκ ἄχαρι.

I've reached the stage where the consumption of wine is most pleasant for a
man, since I am neither sober nor too drunk. Whoever exceeds his limit of
drink is no longer in command of his tongue or his mind; he says wild
things, which are disgraceful in the eyes of the sober, and he's not ashamed of
anything he does when he's drunk. Formerly he was sensible, but then he's a
fool. Aware of this, don't drink wine to excess, but either rise before you're
drunk—don't let your belly overpower you as if you were a wretched hired
help for the day—

or stay without drinking. But you say 'fill it up!' This is always your idle
chatter; that's why you get drunk. One cup is a toast to friendship, another is
set before you, another you offer as a libation to the gods, another you have
as a penalty, and you don't know how to say no. That man is truly the
champion who after drinking many cups will say nothing foolish. If you stay
by the mixing bowl, make good conversation, long avoiding quarrels with
one another and speaking openly to one and all alike. In this way a
symposium turns out to be not half bad.

The first of these two stanzas (477–86) takes up a related sympotic
theme, but it differs from the one just discussed: the contrast between
sobriety/wisdom and drunkenness/foolishness, a commonplace in
sympotic discourse.[29] There is no more talk here of sleeping or
waking, or of willingness and unwillingness. The verb 'to be drunk'
appears at the end of the first and third pentameters (478 and 482)
and before the caesura of the fifth (485), and in the first instance it is
contrasted directly with the verb 'to be sober', with which it shares a
medial rhyme (478): (νήφων . . . μεθύων). The relationship between
wisdom and sobriety is also key to the verbal echo between the

[29] Pellizer (1990) 177–95.

second and fourth couplets, where the summary command in the latter, 'because you recognize these facts, don't drink wine *excessively*' (483–84: μὴ πῖν'...ὑπερβολάδην) recalls and echoes the general rule stated in the former (479–80): 'whoever *exceeds* (ὑπερβάλλῃ) his limit of drink, no longer has command of his tongue or mind.' This five-couplet section also exhibits the A–B–A structure discussed in Chapter 2. It begins with the speaker's boast that he is neither sober nor drunk (A), then gives examples of the evils of inebriation (B), and closes with an exhortation to avoid excessive drinking or leave the party (A).

Lines 477–86 cannot, of course, be a stanza in the sense that I use the term in this study—at least not in the form they have been transmitted—because the poet overruns the boundary at the end of it with a disjunction that begins at the end of one stanza (485: ἀλλ' ἢ... ὑπανίστασο) and ends at the start of the next (487: ἢ παρεὼν μὴ πῖνε). Independent textual evidence from Athenaeus suggests, however, that these stanzas were once disconnected from one another. He preserves a version of the second stanza that differs significantly from the Theognidean one in the first and last couplets, that is, precisely where it joins the stanzas that precede and follow.[30] In the case of the first couplet, modern editors like West have, in fact, adopted Athenaeus' text as the superior version:[31]

ἥκω δ' ὡς οἶνος χαριέστατος ἀνδρὶ πεπόσθαι
οὔτε τι γὰρ νήφων οὔτε λίην μεθύων

More importantly for this study, however, West rightly prefers Athenaeus' ἥκω at the start of the verse, instead of ἥξω, on the grounds that the future tense in the Theognidean manuscripts arises from the mistaken impression of a later scribe that this verb refers to an 'arrival' back home that is promised at the end of the previous stanza. In short, the Theognidean version assumes that the second stanza is a

---

[30] Athenaeus 428c–d. West (1992) prints, for example, Athenaeus' νήφων...μεθύων, instead of the Theognidean νήφω...μεθύω because it avoids the elision after νήφω. See Carrière (1975) 160–62 for discussion. Stobaeus 3.18.13 quotes the five-folder without the first couplet, but this would be consistent with his practice of editing out the personal and particular, since the first couplet has a first-person verb 'I will come'. For Stobaeus' methods, see Campbell (1984).
[31] West (1974) 155.

part of the same poem as the first. Athenaeus' version of the final couplet, moreover, differs in precisely the same way, for it leaves off the beginning of the disjunction (485: ἀλλ' ἤ) that ties the two final stanzas together in the Theognidean version:

ἀλλ ἤ πρὶν μεθύειν ὑπανίστασο   (*Theognidea* 485)

('... but either rise before you're drunk')

πρὶν μεθύειν ἄρξῃ δ' ἀπανίστασο   (Athenaeus 10.428d)

('But before you begin to get drunk, get up')

In other words, Athenaeus' version of these five couplets was designed to stand independently from the other two and probably circulated as a separate five-couplet poem,[32] whereas the variants in the Theognidean version are apparently generated by a scribe or performer, who thought that all three stanzas were part of a single, continuous poem.

The question arises then: did Athenaeus or his source extract the stanza from some version in the *Theognidea* and then rework the first and last couplet so it could stand independently? Or did a scribe copying the *Theognidea* 'correct' the opening and closing verses of the stanza so they fit together as a continuous poem? The latter of these two hypotheses seems more likely, because the opening lines of the last stanza suggest that it, too, was designed from the start as a separate poem. In the first place, it shifts the theme once again, this time from drunkenness to the foolish talk generated by it. And in a nice bit of ring-composition the poet insists that this is usually a two-way relationship: at the start of the stanza he berates the addressee (487–88): 'But you say 'Fill it up!' This is always your idle chatter (τοῦτο μάταιον κωτίλλεις αἰεί); that's why you get drunk.' Later on at lines 491–92, however, he implies that foolish talk only starts after a man is drunk: 'That man is truly a champion, who after drinking many cups will not say anything foolish (μή τι μάταιον ἐρεῖ).'[33] The final command to the whole group (ὑμεῖς) to speak well, if they remain at the party (παρὰ κρητῆρι μένοντες), likewise recalls the first couplet, which began: 'Or if you stay (παρεὼν), don't drink!'

---

32 So Carrière (1975) 160–62.   33 West (1974) 155.

The third stanza ends, moreover, with a simple declarative sentence that begins with a demonstrative adverb (496): 'And in this way (χοὕτως) a symposium turns out to be not without charm.' We have, in fact, seen this kind of pentameter conclusion before, in Mimnermus:

οὕτως ἀργαλέον γῆρας ἔθηκε θεός (Mimnermus 1.10)

χοὕτως συμπόσιον γίνεται οὐκ ἄχαρι. (*Theognidea* 496)

This last stanza, like the first, is mainly hortatory with a strong focus on the audience, first invoked as a single person with a possible drinking problem (487: σύ), but then in the last two couplets as a larger group (493: ὑμεῖς), a change that is a bit jarring. There are, however some good parallels among the archaic stanzas discussed earlier. Archilochus 13 begins with an address to a single man named Pericles (1) but ends with a second-person plural imperative (10: τλῆτε),[34] and the final stanza of Tyrtaeus 11 begins with a series of single, third-person imperatives ('but let him strike the enemy, etc.') but then closes, as this Theognidean stanza does, with a quatrain that addresses a group of men (ὑμεῖς) and advises them with a second-person plural imperative (35–38).

Most scholars believe that *Theognidea* 467–96 is a complete poem, but as we have seen there is something peculiar and unsatisfying about the way these stanzas are linked together. Although they all share the same setting (a symposium) and give advice about sympotic decorum, the assumed status and personality of the speaker and the addressee seems to change. In the first, the speaker, who is about to leave the party and go home, seems to be speaking to Simonides as symposiarch. In the second stanza, however, the speaker boasts of his own ability to strike the correct balance between sobriety and drunkenness, and warns the addressee not to drink to excess, but rather to stand up and leave before he gets drunk. This tone here—of a close but annoyed friend—is at odds with the tone of the first stanza, in which the advice to the symposiarch is more polite and assumes that he is in control of himself and the party. The third stanza is more in line with the second, but in this case the opening command to stay and refrain from drinking seems to challenge the command at the end of the previous stanza to leave the party. And when we add to these discontinuities the

---

[34] West (1974) 16; see Section 2.1 above for discussion.

evidence that Athenaeus knew a stand-alone version of the middle stanza, it hardly seems rash to suggest (i) that they were, in fact, originally composed as separate elegiac contributions to a symposium, much like the single five-couplet poems from Elephantine and by Ion of Chios; and (ii) that in their sequence we might have evidence for how such sympotic poems responded to each other.

There is, then, sufficient evidence to suggest that the kind of *catena symposiale* often envisaged by scholars for ancient elegy was paced by recurring contributions of single five-couplet stanzas. Indeed, it would certainly fit the egalitarian ethos of the symposium, if each singer were limited ahead of time to the same number of verses. It would also serve another practical purpose: as one person was singing his five-couplet portion of the chain, his companions could calculate how soon they themselves needed to be ready to perform their own contributions. This scenario would also fit the case of the hexametrical *skolia* preserved on papyrus, which as we saw earlier were all four verses in length. If the five-couplet stanza was, moreover, the working unit in elegiac performances of this type, then we might surmise that many of the individual stanzas analysed in Chapter 2 may have been composed for precisely this kind of setting, especially those in the A–B–A form or those that have four couplets of meditation followed by one of exhortation, that is: stanzas that seem to encompass a full elegiac thought or movement. The two-stanza seal-poem at the start of the 'Cyrnus Book', on the other hand, suggests that when symposiasts singing to the tune of an *aulos* 'took up' the elegiac song in turn, they might on some occasions— presumably at the direction of the symposiarch—have sung a pair of five-folders, one of meditation followed by a second of exhortation. As we saw at the end of Chapter 2, Mimnermus 2 may also preserve the remains of a pair of elegiac stanzas, the second of which was also apparently designed to explain (11: γάρ) the sentiments of the first. Imagining paired stanzas as a single contribution also makes good sense and by the same logic, since these are the two essential parts of an elegiac poem and if individual symposiasts were required to register a full elegiac opinion in the span of a single turn—a likely assumption—they could just as well have performed a two-stanza contribution, one to explain and speculate and another to give advice.

5

Improvisation

We can detect another kind of polyphony in the extant fragments
of archaic elegy, one that evolves over long stretches of time as
one generation re-performs and improvises upon the favorite elegiac
songs of the past.[1] It seems clear, for example, that fourth-century
Athenians informally recited the elegiac verses of Tyrtaeus, Solon,
and 'Theognis' at their symposia, apparently in a context that
allowed for improvisation.[2] And since a number of the extant fragments of archaic elegy survive only as quotations in the texts of
fourth-century Athenian writers, it is unavoidable that we ask
whether these fragments record an earlier—perhaps even original—
archaic performance (memorized carefully over the intervening centuries) or whether they reflect a more recent improvisation upon a
traditional poem in private symposia, a venue which presumably
would allow adaptations over time, while preserving the general

---

[1] I use the terms 're-performance' and 'improvisation' interchangeably to refer to
the later and often creative performances of a traditional song or poem, following the
lead of e.g. Herington (1985) 5–7 (the re-performance of Alcman in Sparta), Nagy
(1985) 34–36 ('Theognis' in Megara) and Kurke (1991) 5 n. 17 (Pindar in Athens).
Collins (2004, x–xi) defines 'improvisation' as 'the recomposition of both traditional
and invented material at the level of diction, formulae, phrases, and so forth,
rearranged in a novel way during a live performance'.

[2] See e.g. Young (1964) 311–12, and Herington (1985) 48–50, on the reperformance of Tyrtaeus in Sparta and Athens; Rösler (1980) 87–89, on the reperformance
of 'Theognis'; and Henderson (1982) 25, and Lardinois (2006) 17–22, for Solon.
Allen (1993) 59–60, suggests that the version of Mimnermus 5 recorded at *Theognidea* 1020–22 represents a later reperformance of that poem. The recent realization
that there were in antiquity two different versions of the end of Sappho 58 suggests
that her poetry was also reperformed and improvised in symposia; see Gronewald
and Daniel (2004) and Lardinois (2006) 24 n. 23.

content of the poem and the persona of the archaic personality.[3] This is a complex question. In some cases, for example, when Demosthenes asks a court official to 'take and read' Solon 4, it seems likely that he had access to a written text of the poem.[4] And indeed, this is something we might expect in fourth-century Athens for the text of a famous elegy composed by such an important culture hero. But even in the case of Solon we find significant variations in the texts of his fragments. The second line of Solon 22a, for example, is preserved in one source in a more archaic and Ionic version, but also by Aristotle, who in his *Rhetoric* seems to quote (probably from memory) a more prosaic, Attic version.[5] The situation is perhaps less obvious, however, in the case of Tyrtaeus, a Spartan poet popular in private Athenian symposia of the classical period, a time and place where there was presumably less pressure or desire to recite a written or closely memorized text and more incentive to update and revise the poetry to reflect new historical and social circumstances.[6] At this point, then, a second question arises: can we find evidence for this kind of creative re-performance or improvisation in the extant corpus of Greek elegy?

[3] See esp. Nagy (1985, 34–36), who argues that 'Theognis represents a cumulative synthesis of Megarean poetic traditions' from the end of the 7th cent. to the second Persian invasion in 480. Nagy (1990*b*, 52–54) frames his discussion even more widely by claiming that 'various types of archaic poetry, such as the elegiac tradition preserved by Theognis, make their bid for Panhellenic status considerably later than Homeric and Hesiodic poetry' and that in the case of the *Theognidea* this is accomplished by 'on-going recomposition' of a sort that is parallel in its effect to the oral recomposition of epic poetry.

[4] Demosthenes 19.254; see Henderson (1982) 24–25, Bowie (1997) 55, MacDowell (2000), and Appendix II below. Whether Demosthenes was correct in believing that Solon 4 was actually composed by the historical Solon, is another matter, for which see Lardinois (2006). Regarding the question of an official Athenian text or a formal Alexandrian edition, we should probably understand that as in the case of the Attic tragedians, the former became the basis for the latter. Indeed, Dirk Obbink reminds me that the lists of Solon's works in Diogenes Laertius and the *Suda* imply a schema of division that was favoured in Alexandrian editions and that the grammarians and lexicographers who quote Solon must have had some standard edition to cite from.

[5] Lardinois (2006) 21–22.

[6] Indeed, there is even evidence that in their desire to make Tyrtaeus their own, Athenians in the classical period invented out of whole cloth the legend that the poet was in fact originally an Athenian who had gone to Sparta to help out during a crisis. See Lefkowitz (1981) 38–39.

In the past, aside from a few rare cases of blatant internal disagreement or outright anachronism, scholars have had few analytical tools for teasing out different historical layers of performance and re-performance. A good example is the so-called doublets (nearly verbatim repetitions of couplets) in the *Theognidea*. Nineteenth-century textual critics had traditionally argued that these doublets represented different scribal selections from a no longer extant and much larger elegiac corpus of gnomological sayings,[7] but in recent years another hypothesis has steadily evolved, namely that these doublets represent chronologically different phases of a centuries-long tradition of performance.[8] Take, for example, yet another version of the Theognidean city-poem discussed in the previous chapter (*Theognidea* 1081–82b):[9]

Κύρνε, κύει πόλις ἥδε, δέδοικα δὲ μὴ τέκῃ ἄνδρα
ὑβριστήν, χαλεπῆς ἡγεμόνα στάσιος·
ἀστοὶ μὲν γὰρ ἔθ᾽ οἵδε σαόφρονες, ἡγεμόνες δὲ
τετράφαται πολλὴν εἰς κακότητα πεσεῖν.

Cyrnus, this city is pregnant and I am afraid she will give birth to a man who commits wanton outrage, a leader of grievous strife. These townsmen are still of sound mind, but their leaders have changed and fallen into the depths of depravity.

These two couplets are, of course, identical to the opening verses of the first city-poem discussed in the previous chapter (*Theognidea* 39–42), with one crucial change in the first pentameter: the version that appears near the beginning of the 'Cyrnus Book' describes the object of fear as a man 'who will set right our wicked outrage' (40: εὐθυντῆρα κακῆς ὕβριος ἡμετέρης), while this version speaks of a man 'who commits wanton outrage, a leader of grievous strife' (1082: ὑβριστήν, χαλεπῆς ἡγεμόνα στάσιος). The composer of this later version, in short, has removed the description of a potential tyrant, who might rise up as a cure for the hybris of the oligarchs, and has replaced it with one of a man who himself will be the perpetrator—not the regulator—of hybris.[10]

[7] West (1974, 40–61) gives an excellent summary of this scholarly tradition.

[8] See e.g. Reitzenstein (1893) 60–65, Rösler (1980) 77–91, esp. 86–89, and Nagy (1985) 48–51.

[9] Reitzenstein (1893) 61–62, West (1974) 67–71, and Nagy (1985) 45–46.

[10] Nagy (1985) 45–46.

The first city-poem (49–38) seems, then, to have generated at least two different forms of elegiac reaction: the second city-poem (53–62), which follows it closely in the 'Cyrnus Book', and the verses quoted above, which appear much further on in the collection (1081–82b) and preserve the first four lines of it nearly verbatim. These differing reactions, I suggest, neatly illustrate the contrast between poetry produced by a communal performance, which encourages antagonistic responses and corrections, and poetry produced at a much later date, which is perhaps equally antagonistic but seems more derivative or aligned with a more or less carefully memorized text. Recall how the composer of the second city-poem (53–62) creatively echoes the language and form of the first two couplets of the first city-poem (i.e. the same parts repeated at 1081–82b), without ever quoting either of them precisely. He also mirrors the overall form of the first city-poem: a full elegiac stanza with four couplets of meditation and a final one of exhortation. He seems, in short, to been a poet fully aware of the technique of stanzaic composition, who challenges the political ideas and matches the creativity of the first poet by composing a clever and poetically brilliant riposte. The second reaction (1081–82b), on the other hand, seems to have been an improvisation by a poet who re-performs and perhaps updates in minimal (but potentially significant ways) a partially memorized version of what we must imagine to have been a popular poem,[11] but one whose version was nevertheless memorable, since it, too, was eventually written down and drawn into the Theognidean corpus.

Scholars interested in elegiac re-performance have generally limited their inquiry to doublets like these on the grounds that they alone provide the comparative data—a before and after snapshot, if you will—for this change from archaic oral composition to classical improvisation. I suggest, however, that knowledge of the various internal and external features of the five-couplet stanza will allow us occasionally to identify traces of such re-performances and improvisations in our extant texts. This is possible primarily because the stanza along with the musical accompaniment of the *aulos* seems

---

[11] Nagy (1985, 45–46), for instance, suggests that this poet has a more 'Solonian stance', a term he borrows from Donlan.

to disappear from elegiac compositions sometime during the fifth century and thus provides us with an analytical tool, a kind of literary carbon-14 dating if you will, by which we can observe both the original stanzaic architecture and at the same time see to what degree it has decayed. In the best cases we can observe in a single text evidence of both stages of elegiac performance, an earlier one in which the boundaries of individual stanzas are strictly observed and a later one in which they are neglected. A striking example is found at *Theognidea* 699–718:[12]

πλήθει δ' ἀνθρώπων ἀρετὴ μία γίνεται ἥδε,
  πλουτεῖν· τῶν δ' ἄλλων οὐδὲν ἄρ' ἦν ὄφελος, 700
οὐδ' εἰ σωφροσύνην μὲν ἔχοις Ῥαδαμάνθυος αὐτοῦ,
  πλείονα δ' εἰδείης Σισύφου Αἰολίδεω,

ὅς τε καὶ ἐξ Ἀΐδεω πολυϊδρίῃσιν ἀνῆλθεν
  πείσας Περσεφόνην αἱμυλίοισι λόγοις,
ἥ τε βροτοῖς παρέχει λήθην βλάπτουσα νόοιο— 705
  ἄλλος δ' οὔπώ τις τοῦτό γ' ἐπεφράσατο,
ὅντινα δὴ θανάτοιο μέλαν νέφος ἀμφικαλύψῃ,
  ἔλθῃ δ' ἐς σκιερὸν χῶρον ἀποφθιμένων,
κυανέας τε πύλας παραμείψεται, αἵ τε θανόντων
  ψυχὰς εἴργουσιν καίπερ ἀναινομένας· 710
ἀλλ' ἄρα κἀκεῖθεν πάλιν ἤλυθε Σίσυφος ἥρως
  ἐς φάος ἠελίου σφῇσι πολυφροσύναις—

οὐδ' εἰ ψεύδεα μὲν ποιοῖς ἐτύμοισιν ὁμοῖα,
  γλῶσσαν ἔχων ἀγαθὴν Νέστορος ἀντιθέου,
ὠκύτερος δ' εἴησθα πόδας ταχεῶν Ἁρπυιῶν 715
  καὶ παίδων Βορέω, τῶν ἄφαρ εἰσὶ πόδες.
ἀλλὰ χρὴ πάντας γνώμην ταύτην καταθέσθαι,
  ὡς πλοῦτος πλείστην πᾶσιν ἔχει δύναμιν.

For the majority of people this alone is best: wealth. Nothing else after all is of use, not even if you have the good judgement of Rhadamanthys himself or know more than Sisyphus, son of Aeolus,

who by his wits came up even from Hades, after persuading with wily words Persephone who impairs the mind of mortals and brings them into forgetfulness. No one else has ever yet contrived this, once death's dark cloud has enveloped him and he has come to the shadowy place of the dead and

---

12 Much of what follows first appeared as Faraone (2005*a*) 253–56.

passed the black gates which hold back the souls of the dead, for all their protestations. But even from there the hero Sisyphus returned to the light of the sun by his cleverness.

(Nothing else is of use), not even if you compose lies that are like the truth, with the eloquent tongue of godlike Nestor, and were faster of foot than the swift Harpies, and the fleet-footed sons of Boreas. No, everyone should store up this thought, that for all people wealth has the greatest power.

The isolated section in the middle of this poem contains a digression on Sisyphus' legendary journey to the underworld. The trigger for this narrative is, of course, the passing mention of the hero in the catalogue that surrounds it. This inserted narrative seems to be, in fact, yet another kind of elegiac set-piece, similar to the stanzaic priamel and prayer discussed in Chapter 2: it is precisely five couplets long and framed by the repeated description of the hero's successful return from Hades, each time stressing his great cleverness (703: ἐξ Ἀΐδεω πολυϊδρίῃσιν ἀνῆλθεν and 711–12: κἀκεῖθεν πάλιν ἦλθε... σφῇσι πολυφροσύναις).[13]

Commentators have observed that all twenty verses work extremely well as an independent poem, beginning and ending with the assertion that to humankind wealth is the greatest thing (700: πλουτεῖν and 718: πλοῦτος).[14] Carrière points out, however, that, if we remove the digression on Sisyphus, the remaining five couplets work even better as a concise and well-ordered priamel:[15]

> πλήθει δ᾽ ἀνθρώπων ἀρετὴ μία γίνεται ἥδε,
>   πλουτεῖν· τῶν δ᾽ ἄλλων οὐδὲν ἄρ᾽ ἦν ὄφελος, (700)
> οὐδ᾽ εἰ σωφροσύνην μὲν ἔχοις Ῥαδαμάνθυος αὐτοῦ,
>   πλείονα δ᾽ εἰδείης Σισύφου Αἰολίδεω,
> οὐδ᾽ εἰ ψεύδεα μὲν ποιοῖς ἐτύμοισιν ὁμοῖα,
>   γλῶσσαν ἔχων ἀγαθὴν Νέστορος ἀντιθέου,
> ὠκύτερος δ᾽ εἴησθα πόδας ταχεῶν Ἁρπυιῶν (715)
>   καὶ παίδων Βορέω, τῶν ἄφαρ εἰσὶ πόδες.
> ἀλλὰ χρὴ πάντας γνώμην ταύτην καταθέσθαι,
>   ὡς πλοῦτος πλείστην πᾶσιν ἔχει δύναμιν.

---

[13] In Appendix I, I suggest that Mimnermus 12, which narrates the journey of the sun after he disappears from the sky, probably preserves another stanza-long digression of this sort.

[14] See e.g. Hudson-Williams (1910) ad loc., Race (1982) 67–68, and Henderson (1983) 86–88.

[15] Carrière (1962) 59.

For the majority of people this alone is best: wealth. Nothing else after all is of use, not even if you have the good judgement of Rhadamanthys himself or know more than Sisyphus, son of Aeolus, not even if you compose lies that are like the truth, with the eloquent tongue of godlike Nestor, and were faster of foot than the swift Harpies, and the fleet-footed sons of Boreas. No, everyone should store up this thought, that for all people wealth has the greatest power.

This 'original version' of the poem begins with a general statement ('Nothing else is useful'), and then offers us—as in the first stanza of Tyrtaeus 12—four mythic examples of natural gifts that are inferior to wealth: the wisdom of Rhadamanthys, the knowledge of Sisyphus, the eloquence of Nestor and the swiftness of the Harpies and the Boreads. And, like Tyrtaeus 12, this catalogue repeats (albeit here only twice) the same phrase οὐδ᾽ εἰ ... μὲν ... δὲ at the beginning of different hexameters, allots one example for each verse or couplet, with regular punctuation at verse-end, and features the penthemimeral caesura in four of its five hexameters. Its rhetorical shape, on the other hand, conforms to another Theognidean pattern of composition for single-stanza poems: four couplets of description followed by one of exhortation to a certain kind of mental activity, in this case to 'store up the thought' that wealth is best.

The verses that surround the digression on Sisyphus (699–702 and 713–18) were, in short, originally designed as a continuous single-stanza poem. I would suggest, therefore, that at some later point in time another performer inserted into this catalogue the digression on Sisyphus, which is itself a finely wrought stanza. Or to put it another way: this second performer combined two perfectly good elegiac stanzas into a single poem, but did so in a manner that suggests he was somewhat ignorant or careless of stanzaic technique, because he creates a ten-couplet poem with no internal boundary between the fifth and sixth couplet. This later poet was not untalented, of course, since he adapted the original catalogue and produced a new and different poem of high quality. Such a poem, moreover, would probably be an acceptable contribution to a sympotic performance that required a ten-couplet composition rather than a five-couplet one. A difficulty in the syntax suggests, however, that this improvised version of the priamel was an imperfect one, for the second protasis (713–15) has been moved so far from its apodosis in the first couplet,

that it is difficult to recall its syntactical relation.[16] Carrière noted all
of this quite carefully, and decided that the digression on Sisyphus
was a later scribal interpolation.[17] But the apparent constraints on
the compositional process—the poet uses full stanzas as his building
blocks and creates a pleasing ten-couplet poem—suggest instead a
case of creative re-performance, in which a later poet orally improvised an elegiac poem, by combining two elegiac set-pieces—a catalogue and a mythological digression—with great industry and
cleverness, but apparently without full understanding of or regard
for archaic technique.

Tyrtaeus 12, the longest of the poet's extant fragments, displays a
similarly rich stratigraphy with regard to its performance history.[18]
Unlike Tyrtaeus 10 and 11 it is—with the exception of the very last
couplet—entirely devoted to reflection and meditation, and thus seems
more like a fragment of Solon or the *Theognidea* than of early martial
elegy. In fact until relatively recently many scholars even doubted its
authenticity and argued that it was entirely or partly a composition of
the late archaic or classical age.[19] Although I see no problem with the
idea that Tyrtaeus composed an entirely meditative elegy, this old
controversy over authenticity does, in fact, highlight some important
stylistic inconsistencies in the fragment that suggest it, too, can provide
a glimpse of two performances, an earlier composition by stanzas in the
archaic period and a later, freer improvisation in classical times. One
can with relative ease divide the first twenty lines of Tyrtaeus 12 into

---

[16] In the translation given above, for example, Gerber (1999, loc. cit.) is forced to
enclose 705–12 in dashes to indicate the discontinuity and then reiterate the syntax of
the catalogue after the digression by inserting a parenthetical phrase ('Nothing else is
of use') to remind the reader of the wider construction.

[17] Carrière (1962) 59 and 116–17. Van Groningen (1966, 278–79), on the
other hand, thinks that all ten couplets were composed by the same poet. The
digression is, however, so inessential to the catalogue, that when Barron and Easterling (1989, 102) quote and discuss a translation of these verses, they leave out the
Sisyphus section entirely, without mentioning it and without any detriment to their
discussion.

[18] Much of this argument appeared earlier as Faraone (2006) 34–46.

[19] The fragment is preserved in Stobaeus in two sections: verses 1–14 appear in
4.10.1 and the remainder of the fragment in 4.10.6. Plato quotes and/or paraphrases
lines 1–20 at *Laws* 629a–30b and lines 1–12 at *Laws* 660e–661a. See Gerber (1970) 75,
for bibliography and the current agreement on its authenticity.

two elegiac stanzas distinguished primarily on the grounds of theme and formal structure:[20]

οὔτ' ἂν μνησαίμην οὔτ' ἐν λόγῳ ἄνδρα τιθείμην
οὔτε ποδῶν ἀρετῆς οὔτε παλαιμοσύνης,
οὐδ' εἰ Κυκλώπων μὲν ἔχοι μέγεθός τε βίην τε,
νικῴη δὲ θέων Θρηΐκιον Βορέην,
οὐδ' εἰ Τιθωνοῖο φυὴν χαριέστερος εἴη,   5
πλουτοίη δὲ Μίδεω καὶ Κινύρεω μάλιον,
οὐδ' εἰ Τανταλίδεω Πέλοπος βασιλεύτερος εἴη,
γλῶσσαν δ' Ἀδρήστου μειλιχόγηρυν ἔχοι,
οὐδ' εἰ πᾶσαν ἔχοι δόξαν πλὴν θούριδος ἀλκῆς·
οὐ γὰρ ἀνὴρ ἀγαθὸς γίνεται ἐν πολέμῳ   10

εἰ μὴ τετλαίη μὲν ὁρῶν φόνον αἱματόεντα,
καὶ δηίων ὀρέγοιτ' ἐγγύθεν ἱστάμενος.
ἥδ' ἀρετή, τόδ' ἄεθλον ἐν ἀνθρώποισιν ἄριστον
κάλλιστόν τε φέρειν γίνεται ἀνδρὶ νέῳ.
ξυνὸν δ' ἐσθλὸν τοῦτο πόληΐ τε παντί τε δήμῳ,   15
ὅστις ἀνὴρ διαβὰς ἐν προμάχοισι μένῃ
νωλεμέως, αἰσχρῆς δὲ φυγῆς ἐπὶ πάγχυ λάθηται,
ψυχὴν καὶ θυμὸν τλήμονα παρθέμενος,
θαρσύνῃ δ' ἔπεσιν τὸν πλησίον ἄνδρα παρεστώς·
οὗτος ἀνὴρ ἀγαθὸς γίνεται ἐν πολέμῳ.   20

I would not mention or take account of a man for his prowess in running or in wrestling, not even if he had the size and strength of the Cyclopes and outstripped Thracian Boreas in the race, nor if he were more handsome than Tithonus in form and richer than Midas and Cinyras, nor if he were more kingly then Pelops, son of Tantalus, and had a tongue that spoke as winningly as Adrastus, nor if he had a reputation for everything save furious valour. For no man is good in war

unless he can endure the sight of bloody slaughter and, standing close, can lunge at the enemy. This is excellence, this the best human prize and the fairest for a young man to win. This is a common benefit for the state and all the people, whenever a man with firm stance among the front ranks never ceases to hold his ground, is utterly unmindful of shameful flight, risking his life and displaying a steadfast spirit, and standing by the man next to him speaks encouragingly. This man is good in war.

---

[20] Weil (1862, 9) and Fränkel (1975, 339 n. 8) both pointed out that the first twenty lines of the poem are divided into two equal parts, which end in similar declarations at lines 10 and 20. For scholars who note that the first ten lines form a unit, see Ch. 2, n. 44.

These stanzas contrast two different kinds of men: the first describes those who have talents that fall short of the excellence necessary for war, whereas the second focuses—with the possible exception of the first couplet (a problem to which I will return)—on the best kind of fighting man. The contrast between these two sections, moreover, is signaled in the final pentameter of each stanza by the kind of formal response we have seen before in Tyrtaeus:[21]

οὐ γὰρ ἀνὴρ ἀγαθὸς γίνεται ἐν πολέμῳ (10)

οὗτος ἀνὴρ ἀγαθὸς γίνεται ἐν πολέμῳ. (20)

As in the other cases of elegiac responsion discussed above, the nearly identical structure and wording serves well to highlight the differences in content: these verses describe diametrically opposed kinds of men, the first unskilled in warfare and the second skillful. And in addition to their diverse content, the poet creates a striking formal contrast between these two stanzas. As we saw earlier in Section 2.3, he designed the first stanza as an independently coherent priamel, which sums up a list of potentially desirable human skills or traits only to reject them all as insufficient for the task of war: 'I would not take account of him, . . . not even if he had a reputation for everything except furious valor.'[22] What we expect in the final pentameter of this priamel, however, is some kind of summary explanation for Tyrtaeus' opinion, e.g.: 'for *such* a man is not good in war', an expectation that is doubly warranted by the wording of the responding final pentameter of the next stanza (20), which as we saw makes the opposite claim: 'For *this* (οὗτος) man is good in war.'

But in fact the fragment, as it has been transmitted in the manuscripts of Stobaeus, provides no summary statement at all and line 10 spills over unimpeded into a conditional apodosis at the start of the second stanza. This necessary overrun of the stanzaic boundary is, in fact, unparalleled among the longer fragments of Tyrtaeus, but Weil found nothing amiss here, because he modeled his idea of the

[21] Plato (*Laws* 629a–30b) paraphrases lines 1–20 (see n. 28 below) and presumably he understood them to be a complete poem or rhetorical unit. Weil (1862, 9) notes that lines 10 and 20 both stand at the end of five-couplet 'strophes'. Others have noted the closely parallel language: Jaeger (1966, 125–26), for instance, calls them 'a beautiful archaic feature', while Campbell (1967, ad loc.) and Fowler (1987, 82) remark on the 'verbal echo.'

[22] Race (1982) 57–59 ('one of the best known priamels') and Adkins (1985) 74.

repeating five-couplet unit on the strophe of choral poetry, where sentences occasionally do run over the end of a strophe.[23] Additional oddities in the second stanza of Tyrtaeus 12 suggest, however, that an earlier boundary between these two stanzas has been obscured by a later re-performance.[24] Indeed, the content of the first couplet (11–12: endurance of the sight of slaughter and lunging at the enemy) fits well at the start of a stanza devoted to a description of the man who is good at war, but only if we ignore the negation μὴ at the beginning of line 11. The standard interpretation of the stanza, moreover, (as illustrated by the text and translation of Gerber given above) ignores entirely the contrast between the deictic pronouns in line 13 (ἥδ' ... τόδ') and the following τοῦτο in line 15, and explains the μέν in line 11, as an early example of μέν ... καί, even though such a construction is uncertain in Homer and extremely rare in early elegy.[25]

If, however, we ignore the μὴ in line 11 and the period that modern editors place at the end of line 12, a neat chiastic structure emerges for the second stanza, one that contrasts (with the δέ in line 15 answering the μέν in line 11) the personal glory that a young man gains for himself as an individual (ἀνδρὶ νέῳ at the end of line 14) with the common good that he provides to the entire state (πόλῃί τε παντί τε δήμῳ at the end of line 15). I suggest that the syntax of this hypothetical and presumably earlier version of the second stanza was organized as follows:

Protasis A: 'If, on the one hand (μέν), he can endure the sight (of slaughter) and standing close lunge at the enemy...'

Apodosis A: 'then, this is bravery, this is a prize (ἥδ' ἀρετή, τόδ' ἄεθλον) ... best for a young man'

[23] Weil (1862, 10) points out that Pindar often runs a grammatical construction over the junction between two strophes, citing as an example the overrun boundary between the first strophe and antistrophe of *Pythian* 4. This is also true for the stanzas of Sappho and Alcaeus; see Slings (1991).

[24] We have, in fact, encountered in the last chapter two cases of apparently overrun stanzaic boundaries: (i) at the end of the first Theognidean city poem (line 48; see Chapter 4.2 for discussion) and (ii) between the last two stanzas of a putative poem (467–96) about when to stop drinking, where the Theognidean version overruns the boundary, but the one preserved by Athenaeus does not (see Section 4.3).

[25] For the last, see ad loc. Campbell (1967), Prato (1968) and Gerber (1970), who all cite Denniston (1954) 374. But Denniston himself is diffident about the early use, e.g. 'Homeric examples are not conclusive, as in them μέν may be purely emphatic', and he cites Tyrtaeus 12.11–12 as his only example from elegy.

Apodosis B: 'but on the other hand (δέ), this thing (τοῦτο, i.e. another thing, to be contrasted with the preceding ἥδ' ... τόδ') is a common good (ξυνὸν ἐσθλὸν) for both the city and the people,'

Protasis B: 'if someone stands fast and remains among the fore-fighters (ὅστις ἀνὴρ διαβὰς ἐν προμάχοισι μένῃ)'

In this hypothetical reconstruction of an earlier version of Tyrtaeus 12.11–20 the poet praises and contrasts both the personal glory of charging—presumably single-handed—into battle against the enemy, as well as the communal virtue of holding one's place in the traditional hoplite formation and thereby preserving the collective safety of the army and the city. And he does so by making precisely the same contrast between offensive and defensive warfare—and indeed using some of the same language—that we saw earlier in the balanced responsion of the pair of stanzas at the end of Tyrtaeus 11.[26]

That the second stanza once began, as I have suggested, with the protasis of a condition is made more probable by Tyrtaeus' practice elsewhere at the start of stanzas:[27]

εἰ δ' οὕτως ἀνδρός τοι ἀλωμένου οὐδεμί᾿ ὥρη
γίνεται οὔτ᾿ αἰδὼς οὔτ᾿ ὀπίσω γένεος,
θυμῷ γῆς πέρι τῆσδε μαχώμεθα... (Tyrtaeus 10. 11–13)

But if there is no regard or respect for a man who wanders thus, nor yet for his family after him, let us fight...

35 εἰ δὲ φύγῃ μὲν κῆρα τανηλεγέος θανάτοιο,
νικήσας δ' αἰχμῆς ἀγλαὸν εὖχος ἕλῃ,
πάντες μιν τιμῶσιν... (Tyrtaeus 12.35–37)

And if he escapes the doom of death that brings long sorrow and by his victory makes good his spear's splendid boast, he is honoured by all...

---

[26] Thus the type of fighter who provides a common good for the city is described in Tyrtaeus 12:16 as: ὅστις ἀνὴρ διαβὰς ἐν προμάχοισι μένῃ (recall how Tyrtaeus 11.21 introduces the defensive fighter: ἀλλά τις εὖ διαβὰς μενέτω), and the one who gains glory for himself as (12.12): δηίων ὀρέγοιτ᾿ ἐγγύθεν ἱστάμενος (recall the offensive fighter in Tyrtaeus 11.29: ἀλλά τις ἐγγὺς ἰὼν αὐτοσχεδὸν ... δήϊον ἄνδρ᾿ ἑλέτω).

[27] See also the beginning of the second stanza of Tyrtaeus 11 (discussed above in Section 3.2), where 'those who dare' (οἳ μὲν γὰρ τολμῶσι, cf. 12.11 εἰ ... τετλαίη μὲν) are contrasted with the frightened men in line 14 (τρεσσάντων δ' ἀνδρῶν).

I shall discuss the second example below in more detail, but for the present I would stress the fact that within the rather small corpus of the longer Tyrtaean fragments we find two good parallels for a stanza beginning with a conditional prodosis that is framed in a single couplet and then followed by its main sentence. But there are no parallels for a sentence overrunning an obvious stanzaic boundary, as the received text of Tyrtaeus 12 demands after line 10.

This putative earlier design of Tyrtaeus 12, then, makes much better sense of the μέν . . . δέ construction and the contrasting pronouns (ἥδ' . . . τόδ' followed by τοῦτο), and also takes into account the change in construction and content between the two stanzas. The first stanza, as we saw earlier in Section 2.3, is a complete priamel dense with mythological allusions to the Cyclopes, Boreas, and others, which is so artfully constructed that were it stripped of its final couplet, we would have no idea that it is part of a martial elegy. The second stanza of Tyrtaeus 12, on the other hand, is more typical of martial elegy, with its detailed references to hoplite warfare and the Tyrtaean distinction between a soldier's offensive and defensive capabilities. I should stress the fact, however, that since Plato clearly knew a version of the fragment that overran the stanzaic border between lines 10 and 11,[28] this putative earlier version of the second stanza was probably not altered by scribal lapse, but rather by the creativity of some re-performer in the classical period, who perhaps recalled the gist of the first two stanzas from memory (he preserves, for example, the responsion at lines 10 and 20), but without full appreciation of the stanzaic boundary after line 10.

In the second half of Tyrtaeus 12 we encounter more evidence for this kind of improvisation, in this case, at the internal border between a pair of coordinated stanzas. The poet continues to describe the excellent fighter and the fame that accrues to him, but this praise appears in three distinct sections, the first and last of which seem to be complete five-couplet stanzas (12. 21–44):[29]

[28] Plato twice paraphrases or quotes lines from Tyrtaeus 12.1–20 and then offers a close paraphrase of lines 11–12 as Stobaeus reports them, once in the plural οἳ μὴ τολμήσωσιν μὲν ὁρᾶν φόνον αἱματόεντα, | καὶ δηίων ὀρέγοιντ' ἐγγύθεν ἱστάμενοι (*Laws* 629e) and once in the singular δηίων τοιοῦτος ὢν [= the just man] ὀρέγοιτ' ἐγγύθεν ἱστάμενος, ἄδικος δὲ ὢν μήτε τολμῷ ὁρῶν φόνον αἱματόεντα (*Laws* 660e).

[29] Although they both divide up the fragment differently, Jaeger (1966, 122–23) agrees that line 35 begins a new section of the poem and Fowler (1987, 82) thinks that the second half of the poem begins at line 21.

αἶψα δὲ δυσμενέων ἀνδρῶν ἔτρεψε φάλαγγας
τρηχείας· σπουδῇ δ' ἔσχεθε κῦμα μάχης,
αὐτὸς δ' ἐν προμάχοισι πεσὼν φίλον ὤλεσε θυμόν,
ἄστυ τε καὶ λαοὺς καὶ πατέρ' εὐκλεΐσας,
25   πολλὰ διὰ στέρνοιο καὶ ἀσπίδος ὀμφαλοέσσης
καὶ διὰ θώρηκος πρόσθεν ἐληλαμένος.
τὸν δ' ὀλοφύρονται μὲν ὁμῶς νέοι ἠδὲ γέροντες,
ἀργαλέῳ δὲ πόθῳ πᾶσα κέκηδε πόλις,
καὶ τύμβος καὶ παῖδες ἐν ἀνθρώποις ἀρίσημοι
30   καὶ παίδων παῖδες καὶ γένος ἐξοπίσω·
οὐδέ ποτε κλέος ἐσθλὸν ἀπόλλυται οὐδ' ὄνομ' αὐτοῦ,
ἀλλ' ὑπὸ γῆς περ ἐὼν γίνεται ἀθάνατος,
ὅντιν' ἀριστεύοντα μένοντά τε μαρνάμενόν τε
γῆς πέρι καὶ παίδων θοῦρος Ἄρης ὀλέσῃ.
35   εἰ δὲ φύγῃ μὲν κῆρα τανηλεγέος θανάτοιο,
νικήσας δ' αἰχμῆς ἀγλαὸν εὖχος ἕλῃ,
πάντες μιν τιμῶσιν, ὁμῶς νέοι ἠδὲ παλαιοί,
πολλὰ δὲ τερπνὰ παθὼν ἔρχεται εἰς Ἀΐδην,
γηράσκων δ' ἀστοῖσι μεταπρέπει, οὐδέ τις αὐτὸν
40   βλάπτειν οὔτ' αἰδοῦς οὔτε δίκης ἐθέλει,
πάντες δ' ἐν θώκοισιν ὁμῶς νέοι οἵ τε κατ' αὐτὸν
εἴκουσ' ἐκ χώρης οἵ τε παλαιότεροι.
ταύτης νῦν τις ἀνὴρ ἀρετῆς εἰς ἄκρον ἱκέσθαι
πειράσθω θυμῷ μή μεθιεὶς πολέμου.

He quickly routs the bristling ranks of the enemy and by his zeal stems the tide of battle. And if he falls among the front ranks, pierced many times through his breast and bossed shield and corselet from the front, he loses his own dear life but brings glory to his city, to his people, and to his father. Young and old alike mourn him, all the city is distressed by the painful loss, and his tomb and children are pointed out among the people, and his children's children and his line after them.

Never do his name and good fame perish, but even though he is beneath the earth he is immortal, whoever it is that furious Ares slays as he displays his prowess by standing fast and fighting for land and children.

And if he escapes the doom of death that brings long sorrow and by his victory makes good his spear's splendid boast, he is honoured by all, young and old alike, and many are the joys he experiences before he goes to Hades, and in his old age he stands out among the townsmen; no one seeks to deprive him of respect and his just rights, but all men at the benches yield their place to him, the young, those of his own age, and the elders. Let everyone strive now with all his heart to reach the pinnacle of this excellence, with no slackening in war.

If for the moment we ignore the four-line section in the middle, we find a coordinated pair of five-couplet stanzas, which describe in two different scenarios the honours that await the heroic warrior.[30] In the first, the citizens mourn the soldier who falls fighting bravely on the field of battle (21–26) and they give honour to his children and tomb (27–30), whereas in the second, they honour and give deference even in old age (37–42) to the brave warrior who returns home alive (35–36). Tyrtaeus then ends this final stanza with the only exhortation in the entire fragment (43–44): 'let each man try to reach the pinnacle of *this* excellence.'

Tyrtaeus highlights the parallel themes of these two stanzas by a elaborate triple responsion of a similar half-hexameter, which describes the actions of 'the young and old alike', a common Greek periphrasis for 'everyone':

> τὸν δ' ὀλοφύρονται μὲν ὁμῶς νέοι ἠδὲ γέροντες (27)
>
> πάντες μιν τιμῶσιν, ὁμῶς νέοι ἠδὲ παλαιοί (37)
>
> πάντες δ' ἐν θώκοισιν ὁμῶς νέοι οἵ τε κατ' αὐτὸν (41–42)
> εἴκουσ' ἐκ χώρης οἵ τε παλαιότεροι.

Some scholars have argued that these repetitions are the signs of inferior poetry or scribal doublets,[31] but their regular placement in the stanzaic architecture of the fragment suggests otherwise. Indeed, the third repetition at line 41 performs the same kind of double duty that we saw in the variations on the phrase ἐνὶ προμάχοισι πεσόντα in lines 1, 21, and 30 of Tyrtaeus 10: it creates a kind of echoing ring-composition between the second and fourth couplets of its own stanza (37: πάντες μιν τιμῶσιν, ὁμῶς νέοι, 41: πάντες δ' ἐν θώκοισιν ὁμῶς νέοι), but at the same time it also looks back to the end of line 27, with which it stands in perfect parallel, each being the fourth hexameter of its own stanza. This triple responsion, moreover, throws into relief the significant words in the first half of each verse,

---

[30] So Fowler (1987, 82).

[31] Van Groningen (1966, 354–56), for example, believed that the transmitted text preserves and conflates two different versions of the end of the poem.

which directly contrast the different treatment of the heroic soldiers: they mourn the one who dies in battle (27: τὸν δ' ὀλοφύρονται), whereas they honour and yield place to the brave warrior who survives (37: μιν τιμῶσιν and 41: ἐν θώκοισιν ... εἴκουσ').

But how, then, do we explain the quatrain (31–34) that I have isolated above between these two stanzas?

> οὐδέ ποτε κλέος ἐσθλὸν ἀπόλλυται οὐδ' ὄνομ' αὐτοῦ,
> ἀλλ' ὑπὸ γῆς περ ἐὼν γίνεται ἀθάνατος,
> ὅντιν' ἀριστεύοντα μένοντά τε μαρνάμενόν τε
> γῆς πέρι καὶ παίδων θοῦρος Ἄρης ὀλέσῃ.

Never do his name and good fame perish, but even though he is beneath the earth he is immortal, whoever it is that furious Ares slays as he displays his prowess by standing fast and fighting for land and children.

Since these four verses can be removed from Tyrtaeus 12 without the slightest disruption to the syntax or logic of the surrounding verses, Weil simply dismissed them without argument as a scribal interpolation from another poem,[32] and in the early twentieth-century controversy over the authenticity of Tyrtaeus 12, these lines were, in fact, suspected by some as a later fifth-century insertion into an original archaic composition.[33] Indeed, the idea of post-mortem deification ('he is immortal') is typical of the epinician odes of Pindar,[34] the epitaphs of Simonides,[35] or the spirited poem at the end of the Theognidean 'Cyrnus Book',[36] but are otherwise completely unparalleled in the extant military elegy of the early archaic period, which instead promises personal honour and civic or familial safety as the sole rewards for bravery. The language here is, in fact,

[32] Weil (1862) 10.   [33] See e.g. Jacoby (1918) 35–36

[34] Tarditi (1982) 272–74. See Faraone (2002) for the idea in Pindar that κλέος can conquer death. Day (1989, 24 n. 61) notes how Pindar sometimes 'quotes' epigrams or epitaphic *topoi* in his epinician odes.

[35] Tarditi (1982) 273. See e.g. the end of Simonides *Epigram* no. 9 (Page) 'by dying they did not die, since Arete by granting them *kudos*, leads them up from Hades'. The word ἀθάνατος in elegy always refers to the gods, except in this passage; see the index in West (1992) s.v. Loraux (1986, 113–15) shows that the immortality-theme in Athenian epitaphs is a *topos* of the post-Persian-War period. Jaeger (1966, 135–36), in fact, concedes the similarities between the quatrain and the epigram for the Athenians who died at Potidaea, but claims that the 5th-cent. poet is imitating Tyrtaeus.

[36] See e.g. *Theognidea* 237–54, the remains of two-stanza poem that uses the language of immortal fame to predict the effect of elegiac poetry.

that of eulogy, not elegy, and close parallels with the form[37] and vocabulary[38] of late sixth- and fifth-century epitaphs suggest that these two couplets do indeed reflect the work of a poet of the classical period, who at the end of the third stanza—prompted no doubt by the mention of the warrior's tomb in line 29—added a fairly standard form of elegiac epitaph while re-performing this presumably well-known poem of Tyrtaeus.

But regardless of the source of this extraneous quatrain, my argument rests ultimately on the analysis of the wider stanzaic architecture of Tyrtaeus 12, which in its earlier manifestation could not have included the quatrain, any more than it could have included the present version of lines 10–12, which overruns the boundary between the first and second stanzas. The structure of this earlier, hypothetical version can be summarized as follows:

[10 lines]   Priamel and disparagement of various non-fighters
[10 lines]   Description and praise of the ideal fighter that begins
               with a conditional protasis: 'But if he dares to...'
[10 lines]   Description of honours given to dead warrior.
[10 lines]   Description of honours given to living warrior, that
               begins with a conditional protasis: But if he escapes....'

Whereas Tyrtaeus 10 and 11.1–20 were composed in paired stanzas that alternate between exhortation and meditation (the latter usually introduced by $\gamma \acute{\alpha} \rho$), this fragment is entirely meditative (save the final couplet) and carefully organized as a pair of diptychs, the first of which contrasts two kinds of men (brave fighters and the rest) and the second the two kinds of glory that await the heroic fighter. These

---

[37] Tyrtaeus 12.33–34 employs the 'laudatory relative clause', which Day (1989, 18–19) describes as a 'distinct linguistic feature of encomium'. As an example, he cites and discusses in detail an Athenian epitaph for a man named Croesus 'whom rushing Ares once destroyed among the fore-fighters' ($\mathring{o}\nu$ $\pi o \tau$' $\grave{\epsilon}\nu \iota$ $\pi \rho o \mu \acute{\alpha} \chi o \iota s$ $\mathring{\omega} \lambda \epsilon \sigma \epsilon$ $\theta o \hat{\upsilon} \rho o s$ $\mathring{A} \rho \eta s$), which can be compared with Tyrtaeus' $\mathring{o}\nu \tau \iota \nu$'... $\theta o \hat{\upsilon} \rho o s$ $\mathring{A} \rho \eta s$ $\mathring{o} \lambda \acute{\epsilon} \sigma$'. For text and discussion, see Friedlander and Hoffleit (1948) no. 82.

[38] Most of the words in the second couplet have epitaphic parallels. A 6th-cent. Corcyrean tombstone, for instance, describes how 'Ares destroyed this man as he fought... and displayed the highest valour' ($\tau \acute{o} \nu \delta \epsilon$ $\mathring{\omega} \lambda \epsilon \sigma \epsilon \nu$ $\mathring{A} \rho \eta s$ $\beta \alpha \rho \nu \acute{\alpha} \mu \epsilon \nu o \nu$... $\mathring{a} \rho \iota \sigma \tau \epsilon \acute{\upsilon} o \nu \tau \alpha$); see Friedlander and Hoffleit (1948) 29–30, for bibliography and discussion. And an Acarnanian epitaph of similar date speaks of Procleidas, who died 'while fighting for his own land' ($\pi \epsilon \rho \grave{\iota}$ $\tau \hat{a} s$ $\alpha \mathring{\upsilon} \tau \hat{\omega}$ $\gamma \hat{a} s$ ... $\beta \alpha \rho \nu \acute{\alpha} \mu \epsilon \nu o s$); see Friedlander and Hoffleit (1948) no. 64.

are precisely the kind of coordinated stanzas that we saw at work in the catalogues in Solon 13.43–62 and Solon 27.[39]

There are signs, moreover, that the earlier version of these four stanzas was designed as a single poem or as a continuous and coherent four-stanza section of an even larger one. The final couplet, as was noted earlier, contains the only exhortation in the fragment (43–44):

> ταύτης νῦν τις ἀνὴρ ἀρετῆς εἰς ἄκρον ἱκέσθαι
> πειράσθω θυμῷ μὴ μεθιεὶς πολέμου.

Let everyone strive now with all his heart to reach the pinnacle of this excellence, with no slackening in war.

Within the confines of its own stanza this couplet displays what I have been calling the traditional 'Theognidean' pattern of four couplets of meditation followed by a single one of exhortation. But this same couplet also brings closure to the entire fragment. The focus on a generic 'everyman' here and the mention of 'this excellence' (ταύτης ... ἀρετῆς) recalls the very first line of the fragment, where the poet lists the other possible types of ἀρετή he ultimately rejects: 'I would not mention or take account of a man (ἄνδρα) for his excellence (ἀρετή) in running or in wrestling, not even if...' There are, moreover, some broader parallels in the fragment between the hypothetically reconstructed second stanza of Tyrtaeus 12 and its fourth stanza: both begin with conditional protases bounded by a single couplet (12.11: εἰ ... τετλαίη μὲν ... and 12.35: εἰ δὲ φύγῃ μὲν ...) and end with a single couplet that summarizes the content of the stanza with initial pronominal adjectives of the sort we have seen often at the end of single-stanza poems in the *Theognidea*: οὗτος (12.20) and ταύτης (12.43). Finally, in the context of a martial elegy it seems worthy of note that the final word in three of the four stanzas is 'war' (10: γίνεται ἐν πολέμῳ, 20: γίνεται ἐν πολέμῳ, and 44: μὴ μεθιεὶς πολέμου), a word that is significantly placed within the structure of the fragment, since it appears at the end of these three stanzas, but nowhere else in the fragment.[40]

Moreover, the stanzaic architecture of Tyrtaeus 12 allows us to observe that the 'mistakes' in the extant version of the fragment all occur at the internal boundary that divides the two stanzas of a

[39] As we saw in Sections 2.3 and 3.2.
[40] I noted in Ch. 3, n. 23 that the same word appears at the end of the damaged stanza that precedes the final stanza of Callinus 1.

thematically and structurally coordinated pair: (i) between the first and second stanzas (lines 10–12), where the final sentence of the first overruns the boundary; and (ii) at the juncture of the second pair of stanzas, where the generic epitaph intrudes. I suggest that neither deviation is a case of scribal misbehaviour or error, but rather evidence for at least two performances of Tyrtaeus 12, an earlier one by a presumably archaic poet who sang a poem of at least four stanzas arranged in coordinated and responding pairs, and a later performance by another poet, who seems less aware of or interested in the constraints of stanzaic composition. And because the overrun boundary shows up twice in the Platonic paraphrases of the poem and because the extraneous quatrain seems so strongly influenced by the language and rhetoric of fifth-century epitaphs, it seems prudent to date these modifications to a re-performance sometime in the late fifth or early fourth century. This second poet is not to be despised. The fact that he improvises only at stanzaic borders suggests that he is still performing in a traditional manner using elegiac stanzas as his basic building blocks. Indeed, he places the extraneous quatrain neatly at the boundary between two stanzas and appropriately after the mention of the warrior's tomb, cleverly producing a generic epitaph by placing the genitive pronoun αὐτοῦ in the first line, where one usually finds the name of the deceased in the genitive case. Weil blamed scribes for these two violations of stanzaic composition in Tyrtaeus 12. His assumption of scribal misbehaviour is, of course, typical of his generation, and indeed nearly a half-century later, in the aftermath of the powerful arguments of Schwartz and Verrall that *all* of the fragments in the Tyrtaean corpus may have been later forgeries, Wilamowitz and others made similar suggestions about the inauthenticity of parts of Tyrtaeus 12 (including the quatrain), in order to provide a middle ground between the factions: they hypothesized the existence of a fourth-century BCE Athenian manuscript of the Tyrtaean corpus, which contained—like the Hesiodic corpus and the *Theognidea*—authentic archaic verses side-by-side with later interpolations and doublets.[41] My argument, therefore, that Tyrtaeus 12 is a chronologically composite text has much in common

---

[41] See Wilamowitz (1900) 96–118, esp. 96–97 and 111–12, and (1913) 257, where he declared: 'Solche Kunst kann mann erst der Sophistenzeit zutrauen.' Jacoby (1918, 31–42) dates it to the time of Simonides. See Prato (1968) 8*-20* and Gerber (1997) 104–5 for the current consensus on the authenticity of most of the fragments.

with those of Weil and Wilamowitz, but only if we dismiss their anxiety about 'authenticity' and replace their notion of an Ur-text fixed in classical times with more current notions of a fluid tradition of archaic oral composition and then classical improvisation.[42]

I have argued that the received text of Tyrtaeus 12, when examined in the light of its stanzaic architecture, reveals at least two different moments of performance: a hypothetically more orderly and therefore presumably earlier version that closely follows the 'rules' for stanzaic construction, and a less orderly and presumably later version that was known to Plato and which also survives in the manuscripts of Stobaeus. At the heart of my formulation lies the assumption that knowledge or at least appreciation of an originally archaic feature of elegy (the responding stanza) weakens during the fifth century, probably at the same time that elegiac performances begin to lose their musical orientation. We have seen, however, a range of causes for the degeneration of these earlier archaic songs. The apparent loss of a couplet from the third stanza of Tyrtaeus 11, for example, could have been the result of a scribal or an oral mistake, and because we lack any pre-Hellenistic evidence for the text (it is preserved only in Stobaeus), it is natural to suspect (as Weil did) that the anthologist himself or the scribes that copied his manuscripts are to blame.[43] In the case of the quatrain inserted between the final two stanzas of Tyrtaeus 12, we also have evidence for a later change: it stands completely outside of the stanzaic architecture of the fragment. But because it is redolent of the language of fifth-century eulogy and is set neatly between the stanzaic boundaries of the earlier poem, I have followed the suggestion of Jacoby and others that the addition was made during the classical period, but probably not—as they would

Tyrtaeus 12, despite Jaeger's spirited defence in 1938 (= Jaeger [1966]), still has its detractors, who wish to eject it from the corpus by redating it to a later period, e.g. Fränkel (1975, 337–38), who treats the author as a contemporary of Xenophanes, and Tarditi (1982, 274–75), who believes it must have been composed shortly before Pindar's *Pythian* 10.

[42] Indeed, in recent years scholars have argued in a similar vein that the composite nature of the *Hesiodea* and the *Theognidea*—i.e. the comparanda of Wilamowitz and Jacoby—are also probably the product of oral performance over time, rather than scribal mistakes, see e.g. Nagy (1990*a*, 36–47) for the former and (1985) for the latter.

[43] For recent and growing concern about the accuracy of excerption and attribution in Stobaeus' *Florilegium*, see Campbell (1984) and Sider (2001*b*) 272–80.

have it—by the hand of a scribe tampering with an early manuscript of Tyrtaeus' poems, but rather during an oral re-performance by another poet improvising at a symposium in a wealthy house in Athens.

Most interesting, however, is the case of the overrun stanza in the first half of Tyrtaeus 12, where the poet ignores the stanzaic boundary but nonetheless retains the contrastive content of the two stanzas and their responding final pentameters ('he is not good/good in war'). The hypothetically earlier version preserves the boundary between the stanzas, expresses more succinctly the contrast between the them, and makes better sense of the overall syntax of the second stanza. Here, because there seems to be a more rigidly stanzaic and perhaps poetically superior version, I have suggested that my hypothetical version is an earlier one and that the surviving text stems from a later re-performance of the poem. Unlike the case of the inserted quatrain, however, this later re-performance shows enough deference to stanzaic structure and responsion to merit, perhaps, a more subtle designation as a 'multiform of a performance tradition'.[44] In this case it is impossible to say for certain which of the two performances is the 'original', 'prior', or even 'superior' composition. Indeed, it is easy enough to imagine that both versions coexisted in the repertoire of Tyrtaean performance in the classical period and even earlier, but because we do not have among the ten extant Tyrtaean stanzas another example of an overrun stanzaic border, we cannot tell if the more creative and innovative of the elegiac poets were themselves beginning to push at the boundaries of the stanzas even in the late archaic period. But regardless of whether we explain this tension between the surviving text and its underlying stanzaic structure as evidence for mounting carelessness or for an imaginative and creative tension within an implied traditional model, we have seen how Weil's theory of responding elegiac stanzas adds enormously to our knowledge of both the synchronic form of early Greek elegy and the diachronic variations it encompassed.

[44] Nagy (1996) 151–52.

6

Innovation and Archaism

In addition to re-performing and improvising upon the archaic repertoire, Greeks continued to compose original elegiac poetry down to the beginning of the fourth century, just as new epic poems were still being composed, even while the rhapsodes performed and to some degree improvised the traditional favourites.[1] This is, of course, a crucial period of transition, during which elegy apparently becomes detached from its musical origins and interest in the techniques of stanzaic design—at least among the amateur performers in private symposia—seems to decline. Unfortunately not much survives of the original elegiac compositions of the classical age. Among the recently discovered fragments of Simonides' elegies, for example, a short section of his long narrative poem on the battle of Plataea tantalizingly suggests some knowledge of the elegiac stanza, but in the end it is too damaged to provide any hard evidence.[2] The two symposiarch-poems

---

[1] Collins (2004) 179–92.

[2] Fragment 11, the only substantial remnant of Simonides' poem on Plataea, straddles the end of the hymnic introduction and the beginning of the historical narrative proper, and at this point of transition (line 19) there is some evidence of a boundary between two elegiac stanzas (lines 9–18 and 19–28), but the badly tattered papyrus does not inspire confidence. If we rely on the restored text and translation by West as printed in the 'Appendix' to Sider (2001a, 27–29), Simonides seems to set up an important comparison in the final quatrains of each stanza—both introduced by a relative pronoun at or near the start of the fourth hexameter (15: οἷσιν and 25: οἳ)—that speak of and implicitly compare the fame of the fighters at Troy and those at Plataea. We see this same pattern of responding quatrains in the middle stanzas of Solon 4 (see Appendix II). Another possible instance of response might be the placement of the word ἀ]νθρώπων before the midline dieresis of the final pentameter of the second stanza (28), where it responds to and contrasts with the word ἡμ]ιθέων in precisely the same position in the putative first stanza (18)—a responsion, which compliments the warriors at Plataea by comparing them with the legendary heroes at Troy, but at the same time underscores the difference between demigods like Achilles and mortals like Pausanias.

discussed in Chapter 4 (Adespota 27 and Ion of Chios 27) are both
probably fifth-century compositions and are stanzaic in construction,
but since they were composed on a traditional theme, one suspects that
they may not have been original poems in the sense required here, but
rather improvisations of sympotic set-pieces handed down from earlier
times. Indeed, Ion 26, the only other long elegiac fragment of the Chian
poet, does not seem to be composed in stanzas, and the same is true
for the two long fragments of Critias (2 and 6), which date to the end of
the fifth century and, like the formless Hellenistic catalogue poem of
Hermesianax, show no sign of stanzaic architecture. We will probably
never know, unfortunately, how many fifth-century elegiac compositions lie still unrecognized in the *Theognidea*, but the shadowy existence
there of some stanzaic poems of Evenus of Paros is suggestive. Scholars
have long argued over the precise date of this poet, some thinking that
he is the Evenus mentioned by Plato as a contemporary of Socrates, and
others suggesting that he is the grandfather of this man and therefore
a younger contemporary of Simonides.[3] The evidence for stanzaic
design in these fragments is encouraging, but not conclusive. We have
seen that two of the three Theognidean poems assigned to the Parian
poet, the Ganymede poem (= Evenus 8c), and the first stanza of the
Theognidean chain discussed at the end of Chapter 4 (= Evenus 8a)
were composed in elegiac stanzas for sympotic performances,[4] but
since the third, the problematic 'ship of state' poem (Evenus 8b),
shows little sign of stanzaic construction, it is tricky to generalize
about Evenus' elegiac practices.

[3] Bowra (1934) relying on the testimony of Eratosthenes suggested that there were
two poets, grandfather and grandson, and that Evenus the elder reached his *floruit* in
460 BCE. Garzya (1963, 75–90), however, concludes that there was in fact only one
pre-Hellenistic poet named Evenus and that all of the surviving fragments are the
work of Socrates' peer.

[4] *Theognidea* 1341–50 (= Evenus 8c), the lovely Ganymede-poem, is discussed in
Section 2.1. As we saw there, it is exactly five-couplets long, has an A–B–A thematic
design and an obvious ring-composition in its first and last couplets. It begins,
moreover, like many Theognidean stanzas, with four couplets of meditation and
ends with a single line of exhortation ('So don't be astonished, Simonides,....').
Theognidea 467–96 (= Evenus 8a) were also composed as three stanzas for sympotic
performance, but as I argued in Section 4.3, they are probably by more than one
author. Since the first ten verses address Simonides and are partly quoted (in a slightly
different version) by Aristotle as a poem by Evenus, the first stanza is probably a
poem of his.

This overall paucity of evidence for later elegiac stanzas is particularly frustrating when we find a late archaic or classical poet composing a type or style of stanzaic elegy that differs markedly in form or genre from what came before, and we are faced with a difficult, but interesting question: do these differences result from self-conscious innovation or do they simply represent anomalous or poorly attested local traditions that co-existed from the start with the other kinds of elegy discussed in this volume, but rarely survive in the extant corpus? I treat here two rather different cases. First are the two long fragments of Xenophanes, which both seem designed (as Weil noted a century and a half ago) as pairs of traditional stanzas, with one important exception: Xenophanes' stanzas are six couplets in length, rather than the usual five. The second case involves the curious lament sung in elegiac couplets near the beginning of Euripides' *Andromache*, a tragic song that sits at the centre of a long debate about the alleged existence of an old but difficult-to-document tradition of threnodic elegy among the Peloponnesian Greeks.

6.1. THE SIX-COUPLET STANZAS OF XENOPHANES

Xenophanes of Colophon is best known perhaps as a maverick pre-Socratic philosopher who wrote poems in hexametrical verse about the gods and natural phenomena. His attacks on traditional Greek religion and his 'scientific' outlook mark him as a member of the Ionian tradition, although like many of his generation he fled his hometown when the Medes overran the Anatolian coast in the late 540s and spent the rest of his adult life in Magna Graecia. He died around 470 BCE.[5] Of the nine extant fragments of his elegiac poetry, only two are longer than three couplets. Both Xenophanes 1 and 2 are preserved by the second-sophistic author Athenaeus, and are characteristically philosophical in their critique of contemporary Greek *mores*, including the widespread popularity of Homer and Hesiod and the near worship of successful athletes. It must be stressed, however, that his views on poetry were specially informed, since he himself was a poet and rhapsode by calling.[6]

[5] Gerber (1997) 129–30.   [6] Collins (2004) 147–52.

Xenophanes 1 takes aim at contemporary sympotic behaviour and seems to have been composed, like the Tyrtaean and Theognidean poems discussed in Section 3.1, as a pair of alternating stanzas, the first purely descriptive and the second paraenetic:[7]

νῦν γὰρ δὴ ζάπεδον καθαρὸν καὶ χεῖρες ἁπάντων
  καὶ κύλικες· πλεκτοὺς δ᾽ ἀμφιτιθεῖ στεφάνους,
ἄλλος δ᾽ εὐῶδες μύρον ἐν φιάλῃ παρατείνει·
  κρητὴρ δ᾽ ἕστηκεν μεστὸς ἐυφροσύνης·
ἄλλος δ᾽ οἶνος ἑτοῖμος, ὃς οὔποτέ φησι προδώσειν,   5
  μείλιχος ἐν κεράμοις, ἄνθεος ὀζόμενος·
ἐν δὲ μέσοις ἁγνὴν ὀδμὴν λιβανωτὸς ἵησιν,
  ψυχρὸν δ᾽ ἐστὶν ὕδωρ καὶ γλυκὺ καὶ καθαρόν·
πάρκεινται δ᾽ ἄρτοι ξανθοὶ γεραρή τε τράπεζα
  τυροῦ καὶ μέλιτος πίονος ἀχθομένη·   10
βωμὸς δ᾽ ἄνθεσιν ἂν τὸ μέσον πάντῃ πεπύκασται,
  μολπὴ δ᾽ ἀμφὶς ἔχει δώματα καὶ θαλίη.

χρὴ δὲ πρῶτον μὲν θεὸν ὑμνεῖν εὔφρονας ἄνδρας
  εὐφήμοις μύθοις καὶ καθαροῖσι λόγοις,
σπείσαντάς τε καὶ εὐξαμένους τὰ δίκαια δύνασθαι   15
  πρήσσειν—ταῦτα γὰρ ὦν ἐστι προχειρότερον,
οὐχ ὕβρεις—· πίνειν δ᾽ ὁπόσον κεν ἔχων ἀφίκοιο
  οἴκαδ᾽ ἄνευ προπόλου μὴ πάνυ γηραλέος.
ἀνδρῶν δ᾽ αἰνεῖν τοῦτον ὃς ἐσθλὰ πιὼν ἀναφαίνει,
  ὡς ᾖ μνημοσύνη καὶ τόνος ἀμφ᾽ ἀρετῆς,   20
οὔ τι μάχας διέπειν Τιτήνων οὐδὲ Γιγάντων
  οὐδὲ ⟨τι⟩ Κενταύρων, πλάσμα⟨τα⟩ τῶν προτέρων,
ἢ στάσιας σφεδανάς—τοῖς οὐδὲν χρηστὸν ἔνεστιν—
  θ⟨εῶ⟩ν ⟨δὲ⟩ προμηθείην αἰὲν ἔχειν ἀγαθήν.

For now the floor is clean and clean the hands of everyone and the cups; (one servant) places woven garlands round (the heads of the guests), and another offers sweet-smelling perfume in a saucer; the mixing-bowl stands filled with good cheer; on hand is additional wine, which promises never to run out, mellow in its jars and fragrant with its bouquet; in the middle incense sends forth its pure and holy aroma and there is water, cool, sweet, and clear; nearby are set golden-brown loaves and a magnificent table laden with cheese and thick honey; in the center an altar is covered all over with flowers, and song and festivity pervade the room.

---

[7] Quoted by Athenaeus 11.462c.

For men of good cheer it is meet first to hymn the god with reverent tales
and pure words, after pouring libations and praying for the ability to do
what is right—for in truth this is a more obvious thing to do, not deeds of
violence; it is meet to drink as much as you can hold and come home
without an attendant unless you are very old, and to praise that man who
after drinking reveals noble thoughts, so that there is a recollection of and
striving for excellence; it is not meet to make an array of the wars of the
Titans or Giants or Centaurs, creations of our predecessors, or violent
factions—there is nothing useful in them; and it is meet always to have a
good regard for the gods.

As many scholars have noted, this fragment splits quite easily (as
indicated above) into equal sections, each six couplets long.[8] In the
first half Xenophanes describes in some detail the preparations for a
feast. We expect a continuous description of the activities of the
servants, but after describing the placement of the garlands and
perfume, the subjects of the main verbs become the tableware and
the food themselves, which are oddly anthropomorphized, for example, the mixing bowl 'full of good cheer' and the wine that 'promises never to run out.' The stanza, in fact, vaguely takes the shape of an
elegiac catalogue of servile objects, both material and human, with its
end-stopped lines, penthemimeral caesurae and the initial iteration of
the pronoun ἄλλος at the start of the second and third couplet.

The second half of the poem is, however, different and clearly
designed as a new section. Whereas the first stanza was purely descriptive, this one is filled with advice using the formula of χρή plus
the infinitive. It falls into three equal parts: the first pair of couplets
stresses the preliminary religious rites of the symposium (13–16); the
second suggests rules about excessive drinking and proper conversation (17–20); and the third castigates, as a counter-example, poor
choices for sympotic discourse (mythological battles and tales of
strife) and then closes with advice to respect the gods (21–24). This
second stanza, therefore, begins and ends with the gods, and indeed,

---

[8] Weil (1862, 7–8), for example, suggested in passing that Xenophanes composed
the fragment as six-couplet 'strophes'. For the consensus on the rhetorical division of
the fragment into two equal halves, see e.g. Gerber (1970) 243, Adkins (1985) 177,
Marcovich (1978) 1–12, and Lesher (1992) 50–51. They all follow Bowra (1938) in
believing that we do not have the beginning of the poem, on the grounds that a poem
cannot start with νῦν γὰρ δή. The discussion of Xenophanes 1 that follows appeared
earlier in Faraone (2005*a*) 330–333.

the word θεόν in the first line (13) is echoed by θεῶν in the last (24). A threat of violence, however, hangs over this stanza: the participants are asked to pray for the ability to do just things rather than acts of ὕβρις (17) and they are prohibited from reciting tales about battles (21) or violent factions (23). These three words are, in fact, placed emphatically at the beginning of the third, fifth and sixth hexameters, in the first and last case enjambed: οὐχ ὕβρεις ... οὔ τι μάχας ... ἢ στάσιας σφενδανάς.[9] The effect is, I think, to emphasize greatly the prohibitions: 'no violence, no fighting, no factions!'

Although the poet is pushing an agenda very different from the martial elegists discussed in Section 3.1, the architecture of Xenophanes 1 is familiar in its alternation between quiet reflection and advice:

[1–12] Meditation on the sympotic setting introduced by γάρ
(indicative, mainly predicate sentences)

[13–24] Encouragement to good behaviour at the symposium
(χρή + the infinitive)

The initial stanza is entirely descriptive and may have originally provided some kind of explanation for something that preceded, for it begins with γάρ, like nearly all of the meditative stanzas discussed earlier. In the second stanza, however, Xenophanes gives advice about proper sympotic behaviour, using χρή followed by seven infinitives, syntax that distinguishes it quite dramatically from the first stanza, which contains no infinitives. There is, however, a curious calm about this second stanza, especially when we compare it to the stanzas of exhortation in the Tyrtaean corpus: there are no deictic references to the scene, no explicit references to an audience and the subjects of the infinitives are the somewhat generic 'men of good cheer' who appear at the end of line 13. There is no doubt that Xenophanes does alternate between a purely descriptive first stanza, and a second stanza of advice about good behaviour, but the tone is more philosophical and one wonders if the poet has taken the traditional elegiac form of alternating stanzas and subtly adapted it to a purely meditative composition.[10]

---

[9] Marcovich (1978) 13.

[10] Andre Lardinois suggests to me that the construction χρή plus the infinitive with a generic subject should be regarded as a general gnomic expression, comparable to

Xenophanes, like Tyrtaeus, has composed his alternating stanzas as fit companions for each other. In the first couplet of the second stanza (13–14), for example, he echoes in parallel position the qualitative language used in the first two couplets of the first stanza, translating notions of purity and goodliness from the concrete, physical world of the sympotic table to the more abstract realm of human behaviour. The exhortation to pure words (14: καθαροῖσι λόγοις) matches, for instance, the description of the clean floor, hands and cups in the first line (1: ζάπεδον καθαρὸν καὶ χεῖρες ἁπάντων | καὶ κύλικες),[11] just as the 'men of *good* cheer' and the 'stories of *good* omen' (13–14: εὔφρονας ἄνδρας and εὐφήμοις μύθοις) recall the '*good*-smelling perfume' and the 'mixing bowl filled with *good* cheer' in the second couplet of the fragment (3–4: εὐῶδες μύρον and κρητήρ . . . μεστὸς ἐυφροσύνης). Xenophanes also places internal pentameter-rhymes in a significant pattern that suggests both symmetry and closure in the second stanza. One appears at the start of the second stanza (14: μύθοις . . . λόγοις) and two at the very end (22: Κενταύρων . . . προτέρων and 24: προμηθείην . . . ἀγαθήν), that is: at the same relative points in his six-couplet stanza—the first, penultimate and final pentameters—that Callinus placed the pentameter rhymes in his sole surviving five-couplet stanza. If scholars are accurate in their shared sense of closure at the end of Callinus 1 (see the end of Section 3.1), we might speculate that the triple rhymes here in the second stanza of Xenophanes 1 also point to the end of an elegiac poem composed of alternating stanzas of meditation and exhortation.[12]

Xenophanes 2, the only other substantial elegiac fragment of the poet, also seems to have been composed as two six-couplet stanzas. Like Solon 27, it is designed as a pair of coordinated stanzas, employs

those, for example, that we find in the meditative passages of Tyrtaeus, e.g. 'It is noble (καλόν) for the young man to die among the fore-fighters'. See Lardinois (1995) 78–79.

[11] Campbell (1983, 40) notes that the repetition of the adjective καθαρός 'contributes to the pleasing balance between the two twelve-line sections of our poem: the preparations for the symposium are to be matched in beauty and order by the songs and stories'.

[12] There is also a pentameter rhyme in the first couplet of the first stanza, which—given its position parallel to the rhyme in the first couplet of the second stanza—may be designed to stress even more the contrast between the physical objects in the first half of the poem (2: πλεκτοὺς . . . στεφάνους) and the prescribed human speech that is the general focus of the second (14: μύθοις . . . λόγοις).

the techniques of elegiac catalogues, and it is apparently missing, again like Solon 27, a couplet from its second stanza:[13]

ἀλλ' εἰ μὲν ταχυτῆτι ποδῶν νίκην τις ἄροιτο
ἢ πενταθλεύων, ἔνθα Διὸς τέμενος
πὰρ Πίσαο ῥοῆς ἐν Ὀλυμπίῃ, εἴτε παλαίων
ἢ καὶ πυκτοσύνην ἀλγινόεσσαν ἔχων
εἴτε τὸ δεινὸν ἄεθλον ὃ παγκράτιον καλέουσιν,   5
ἀστοῖσίν κ' εἴη κυδρότερος προσορᾶν,
καί κε προεδρίην φανερὴν ἐν ἀγῶσιν ἄροιτο,
καί κεν σῖτ' εἴη δημοσίων κτεάνων
ἐκ πόλεως, καὶ δῶρον ὅ οἱ κειμήλιον εἴη—
εἴτε καὶ ἵπποισιν, ταῦτά κε πάντα λάχοι,   10
οὐκ ἐὼν ἄξιος ὥσπερ ἐγώ· ῥώμης γὰρ ἀμείνων
ἀνδρῶν ἠδ' ἵππων ἡμετέρη σοφίη.

ἀλλ' εἰκῇ μάλα τοῦτο νομίζεται, οὐδὲ δίκαιον
προκρίνειν ῥώμην τῆς ἀγαθῆς σοφίης·
οὔτε γὰρ εἰ πύκτης ἀγαθὸς λαοῖσι μετείη   15
οὔτ' εἰ πενταθλεῖν οὔτε παλαισμοσύνην,
οὐδὲ μὲν εἰ ταχυτῆτι ποδῶν, τόπερ ἐστὶ πρότιμον,
ῥώμης ὅσσ' ἀνδρῶν ἔργ' ἐν ἀγῶνι πέλει,
τούνεκεν ἂν δὴ μᾶλλον ἐν εὐνομίῃ πόλις εἴη·
σμικρὸν δ' ἄν τι πόλει χάρμα γένοιτ' ἐπὶ τῷ,   20
εἴ τις ἀεθλεύων νικῷ Πίσαο παρ' ὄχθας·
οὐ γὰρ πιαίνει ταῦτα μυχοὺς πόλεως.

But if someone were to gain a victory by the swiftness of his feet or in the pentathlon, where there is the precinct of Zeus by Pisa's stream in Olympia, or in wrestling or engaging in painful boxing or in that terrible contest which they call the pancratium, he would have greater renown (than others) in the eyes of his townsmen, he would gain a conspicuous front seat at the games, he would have food from the public store granted by the city, and a gift which would be a treasure for him—or if (he were to gain a victory) even with his horses, he would obtain all these things, although he is not as deserving as I. For my expertise is better than the strength of men or horses.

But this custom is quite irrational and it is not right to give strength precedence over good expertise. For neither if there were a good boxer among the people nor one good at the pentathlon or in wrestling or again

[13] Quoted by Athenaeus 10.413c–414b. Like most commentators, Campbell (1967, 337) and Adkins (1985, ad loc.) believe that this fragment is a complete poem and that the first twelve verses are a complete unit. Weil (1862, 8) suggested in passing the argument that I shall make in detail below, namely that Xenophanes

in the swiftness of his feet, the most honoured of the deeds of human strength in the contest, would there for that reason be better law and order in the city. Little would be the city's joy, if one were to win while contending by the banks of Pisa; for this does not fatten the city's treasury.

The two sections of this fragment are clearly designed to mirror one another. In form they both contain catalogues, which discuss the civic value of various athletic victors in a complicated double series of conditional sentences. The regularity of a formal catalogue is enhanced, as we have seen before in Section 2.3, by reiterated words or phrases—εἴτε in the first stanza and various forms of οὔτ' εἰ in the second—usually placed at the beginning of a couplet or verse.[14] In the first stanza, after listing the athletic events in a series of four conditional protases, the poet gives a delayed series of matching apodoses (lines 6–9) that culminate in line 10: 'or if he (should gain victory) with his horses, too, he would obtain all of these prizes.' Xenophanes might have, in fact, stopped here and ended up with a coherent five-couplet catalogue, but he presses on and undermines it entirely with a single concessive participial phrase: 'although he is not deserving as I', followed by an explanation: 'For my expertise (σοφίη) is better than the strength of men or horses.' As in the first ten lines of Tyrtaeus 12, then, in the first half of Xenophanes 2 a coherent stanza coincides exactly with the boundaries of a priamel.

In the second half of this fragment, Xenophanes explains why, precisely, his σοφίη—his talent as a skilled poet and adviser to the city—is more important than the strength of athletes. He does so by carefully 'mirroring' the list given in the first half, a chiastic feature of elegiac composition that we saw in much smaller scale in the first ten verses of Mimnermus 2 (see Section 2.1).[15] This is especially obvious

originally designed this fragment as a pair of six-couplet stanzas, but then at some point later in time it lost a couplet from the second one.

[14] In the first half of the fragment Xenophanes repeats the conditional particle four times—ἀλλ' εἰ μέν (1), εἴτε (3, at the bucolic caesura), εἴτε (5) and εἴτε (10)—but in the second half he switches to the 'not even if' form used in Tyrtaeus 12 and the Theognidean Sisyphus poem: οὔτε γὰρ εἰ (15), οὔτ' εἰ (16), and οὐδὲ μὲν εἰ (17).

[15] Adkins (1985, 188–89) notes the chiastic ring-composition in the second listing of these four events and suggests (p. 194) that lines 13–22 create a 'mirror image' of the first twelve verses. Race (1982, 62) also discusses this 'mirroring effect' of the two parts pointing out how 'Xenophanes lists individual events (15–18), this time in the negative, in more or less reverse order.'

in the way that Xenophanes begins the second stanza by summarizing the content of the final couplet of the first, again in the negative, ending both couplets in parallel constructions that compare 'strength' (ῥώμη) unfavorably with 'expertise' (σοφίη), a word which stands as the last word of both:

> οὐκ ἐὼν ἄξιος ὥσπερ ἐγώ· ῥώμης γὰρ ἀμείνων
> ἀνδρῶν ἠδ᾽ ἵππων ἡμετέρη σοφίη. (11–12)

... although he is not as deserving as I. For my expertise is better than the strength of men or horses.

> ἀλλ᾽ εἰκῇ μάλα τοῦτο νομίζεται, οὐδὲ δίκαιον
> προκρίνειν ῥώμην τῆς ἀγαθῆς σοφίης· (13–14)

But this custom is quite irrational and it is not right to give strength precedence over good expertise.

The first stanza, then, concludes with a simple statement of fact and the second one begins by reiterating this fact and then explaining why this should not be the case.

This process of mirroring continues in a series of negative protases ('For not even if...') that list almost all of the same athletic events, but in an order that is (with one minor exception) reversed from the first:[16]

FIRST STANZA	SECOND STANZA
Four events bundled in a single quatrain:	[horses: before line 15?]
swiftness of feet (1: ταχυτῆτι ποδῶν)	[pancratium before line 15?]
pentathlon (2: πενταθλεύων)	
wrestling (3: παλαίων)	*Four events bundled in a single*
boxing (4: πυκτοσύνην)	*quatrain:*
	boxer (15: πύκτης)
	pentathlon (16: πενταθλεῖν)
	wrestling (16: παλαισμοσύνην)
pancratium (5: παγκράτιον)	swiftness of feet (17: ταχυτῆτι
horses (10: ἵπποισιν)	ποδῶν)

---

[16] Perfect *chiasmos* is spoiled by the absence of the horses and pancratium in the second half, and because in line 16 the pentathlon precedes wrestling.

The poet, finally, frames these two stanzas as a coordinated pair and caps this overarching chiastic design with close verbal repetitions at the very beginning and the very end of the fragment. His description of the foot-racing in the first couplet (1: ἀλλ' εἰ μὲν ταχυτῆτι ποδῶν), for instance, is recalled at the end of the reversed list of athletic events in the second stanza, where the phrase 'swiftness of feet' appears likewise in a conditional protasis and in the same *sedes* of the hexameter (17: οὐδὲ μὲν εἰ ταχυτῆτι ποδῶν). The generic description in the final couplet of an athletic victor who 'might win by the banks of the river Pisa' (21–22: εἴ τις ... νικῷ Πίσαο παρ' ὄχθας) likewise echoes closely the description at the very start of the fragment of the man who 'might seize victory... by the streams of the river Pisa' (1–3: εἰ μὲν ... νίκην τις ἄροιτο | ... πὰρ Πίσαο ῥοῆς).[17]

Weil suggested in passing that a couplet was missing from the second half of this fragment, but he did not venture to say precisely from where. Given the almost perfectly chiastic structure of the two stanzas illustrated above, one might have expected the poet to mention horse- or chariot-racing and the pancratium before line 15 (where I have placed them in square brackets in the outline above).[18] The manner and order in which Xenophanes lists the events also suggest that the lacuna occurred here. As he moves through the first list he emphasizes heavier and more brutal contests that successively require more raw power and violence, ending with 'painful' boxing and 'the terrible contest they call the pancratium', whose descriptions each take up an entire verse.[19] Given the crescendo of emphasis here, it is hard to understand why he would leave out the pancratium in the reversed list in the second half of the poem. The absence of the horses in the second stanza is equally puzzling. The phrasing at the end of the list in the second stanza (18: ῥώμης ὄσσ' ἀνδρῶν) clearly recalls that in the summary flourish at the end of first section (12–13: ῥώμης ... | ἀνδρῶν ἠδ' ἵππων), which contrasts Xenophanes' poetic skills with the power of both men and beasts. Because of the reversed order of events, it makes sense, perhaps that the horses might not be mentioned in the summation at line 18, but

---

[17] Adkins (1985) 188–89.
[18] Adkins (1985, 195) notes this absence without comment.
[19] Race (1982) 61.

why have they disappeared from the second stanza entirely? Indeed, given the emphasis on them in the first stanza (10: ἵπποισιν echoed by 12: ἵππων in the same *sedes*), the absence of the horses, along with the differently, but nonetheless equally, highlighted pancratium is odd. The incomplete chiastic structure charted above, the fact that Xenophanes uses a pair of six-couplet stanzas in his only other extant fragment of appreciable size, and the disappearance of two of the more important athletic events (pancratium and horses) from the second stanza all suggest, therefore, that a couplet mentioning these two events once stood before line 15.[20] We should not be surprised, of course, that this lost couplet somehow disappeared from the text of Athenaeus (our only source for Xenophanes 2), for this lacuna was undoubtedly encouraged, as in the second stanza of Solon 27, by the end-stopped couplets and the anaphora at the beginnings of individual verses in this section of the poem (15–17: οὔτε γὰρ εἰ . . . οὔτε εἰ . . . οὐδὲ μὲν εἰ). Once again the apparent popularity of monotonous and rigidly regular elegiac catalogues cannot be stressed enough, despite their sometimes mind-numbing effect on the modern reader.

It would appear, then, that Xenophanes 1 and 2 were both carefully designed as coordinated pairs of stanzas that display in a masterly manner the same techniques of responsion, ring-composition and stanzaic design that we have seen in the fragments of other archaic elegiac poets. It is difficult, however, to explain the anomalous length of his stanzas. It may, of course, simply be the case that Xenophanes composed his elegies in an alternate tradition of six-couplet stanzas

---

[20] The γὰρ at the start of line 15 must have stood originally at the start of the missing line, not here. We can, moreover, make this reconstruction more precise by noting the careful manner in which Xenophanes groups the various events. As indicated in the outline of the poem presented on p. 123, he bundles the first four events of the first stanza into a quatrain that begins with εἰ μὲν (1–4), to which he adds the fifth and sixth events in single verses, each introduced by reiterating the condition twice more at the start of a new verse, εἴτε (5, the pancratium) and εἴτε (10, the horse races). In the second stanza he bundles together the same four events into a single quatrain (15–18), but here, because the order is reversed, he places the quatrain towards the end of the stanza. A strictly symmetrical composition would require that the single couplet that has dropped out of our text before line 15 probably allotted the hexameter to the horses and the pentameter to the pancratium, and that each of these two verses began with the some version of the phrase (οὔτ᾽ εἰ) that is reiterated at the start of the first three lines of the quatrain.

that was, perhaps, native to Colophon and other eastern Greek cities, but then perished under Persian occupation. There are signs, however, that this iconoclastic philosopher, whose lifetime bridges the archaic and classical periods and whose hexametrical fragments provide a withering critique of traditional religious beliefs and of traditional hexametrical poetry, may have extended his innovative and somewhat belligerent attitude into the arena of elegiac poetics as well. There is, for example, the curious fact mentioned earlier that the first stanza of Xenophanes 2 may play on the audience's expectation of the end of the traditional five-couplet stanza: the first five couplets provide a full catalogue of athletic victories and their rewards and, if the poet had stopped at the end of the fifth couplet, the list would be fully comprehensible and vaguely complimentary. With the addition of the sixth couplet, however, Xenophanes turns the stanza into a priamel, which dismisses athletic competition entirely and the system of evaluation that lies behind its popularity. The poet, in short, may have added even more dramatic power to the final turnabout of the priamel by upsetting as well the traditional expectation of closure at the end of the fifth couplet. Since Xenophanes' poems were apparently popular in antiquity, we should also ask why his innovation did not catch on, for there are only a few other possible examples of six-couplet stanzas, most of them in the later parts of the *Theognidea*.[21] Since the Cynic philosopher Crates penned a six-couplet parody of the opening lines of Solon 13, that also has a clear stanzaic design, one wonders whether the six-couplet stanza may have had some special but limited appeal among philosophers who tried to imitate Xenophanes in his role as an elegiac social critic.[22] Parallel developments in Renaissance poetry suggest that

---

[21] Among the elegiac couplets collected in West (1992), I find only three other possible examples of six-couplet stanzas: *Theognidea* 197–208 (which like Crates' poem imitates Solon 13), 511–22 and 1283–94.

[22] Fragment 1 (Bergk), quoted in full by Linforth (1919) 228. I thank Ted Courtney for pointing it out to me. The poem has lost a hexameter after line 4, but because it is a fairly close line-by-line parody of the first seven lines of Solon 13, we can be fairly certain that the entire poem was only six couplets long. It does show, however, a few signs of stanzaic architecture. Like Solon's poem, it is a prayer to the Muses that opens with a two-line invocation of them and closes by repeating their name along with Hermes. The final pentameter, moreover, has an internal rhyme that contrasts δαπάναις τρυφεραῖς with ἀρεταῖς ὁσίαις.

limits in the size of stanzas were dictated on the one side by the need for a form long enough for an extended meditation in a single stanza, but not so long as to lose its felt connection with the shorter stanzas of song. In the realm of archaic Greek elegy, then, both five-couplet and the six-couplet stanzas would have filled these requirements.

6.2. EURIPIDES *ANDROMACHE* 103–116 AND THE TRADITION OF ELEGIAC LAMENT

In the opening scene of Euripides' *Andromache*, the enslaved heroine converses with her former maid—and now fellow slave—and tells of her plans to seek asylum from her cruel mistress Hermione by sitting as a suppliant at the altar of Thetis. After the servant departs, Andromache speaking in iambic trimeters declares that 'with laments and groans and tears' (92: θρήνοισι καὶ γόοισι καὶ δακρύμασιν) she will unfold before heaven the three causes of her sorrow (97–99): her (lost) native city (πόλιν πατρῴαν), her dead husband Hector (τὸν θανόντα Ἕκτορα), and her subsequent enslavement (δούλειον ἦμαρ). She then switches to elegiac couplets and sings a solo lament in the Doric dialect (103–16):[23]

> Ἰλίῳ αἰπεινᾷ Πάρις οὐ γάμον ἀλλά τιν' ἄταν,
>   ἀγάγετ' εὐναίαν εἰς θαλάμους Ἑλέναν·
> ἇς ἕνεκ', ὦ Τροία, δορὶ καὶ πυρὶ δηιάλωτον   105
>   εἷλέ σ' ὁ χιλιόναυς Ἑλλάδος ὀξὺς Ἄρης
> καὶ τὸν ἐμὸν μελέας πόσιν Ἕκτορα, τὸν περὶ τείχη
>   εἷλκυσε διφρεύων παῖς ἁλίας Θέτιδος·
> αὐτὰ δ' ἐκ θαλάμων ἀγόμαν ἐπὶ θῖνα θαλάσσας,
>   δουλοσύναν στυγερὰν ἀμφιβαλοῦσα κάρᾳ.   110
> πολλὰ δὲ δάκρυά μοι κατέβα χροός, ἁνίκ' ἔλειπον
>   ἄστυ τε καὶ θαλάμους καὶ πόσιν ἐν κονίαις.
> ὤμοι ἐγὼ μελέα, τί μ' ἐχρῆν ἔτι φέγγος ὁρᾶσθαι
>   Ἑρμιόνας δούλαν; ἇς ὕπο τειρομένα
> πρὸς τόδ' ἄγαλμα θεᾶς ἱκέτις περὶ χεῖρε βαλοῦσα   115
>   τάκομαι ὡς πετρίνα πιδακόεσσα λιβάς.

[23] I give the text and translation of Kovacs (1995) ad loc.

For lofty Troy it was not as bride but as mad ruin that Paris brought Helen into his bedchamber! For her sake the keen warcraft of Greece, its ships a thousand strong, captured you, O Troy, sacked with fire and sword, and killed Hector, husband of my unlucky self! The son of the sea goddess Thetis dragged him behind his chariot as he rode about the walls. I myself was led off from my chamber to the seashore, wrapping hateful slavery as a covering for my head. Many were the tears that rolled down my cheeks when I left city and home and husband lying in the dust!

Oh, unhappy me, why should I look on the light as Hermione's slave? Oppressed by her I have come as suppliant to this statue of the goddess and thrown my arms around it, melting in tears like some gushing spring high up on a cliff.

Page stresses the important fact that these lines were most likely sung (not recited) to the accompaniment of the *aulos* and that this mode of performance explains why the metre of these verses is regular and smooth, with dactyls predominating and a consistent penthemimeral caesura in all seven hexameters, features which would allow the performer to sing along more easily to the repeated and invariable melody of the *aulos*.[24] We find, in fact, the same phenomenon in early English poetry, where stanzaic poems set to music have a more regular structure and rhythm than those recited without music.[25] We saw near the start of this study (Section 2.1) that the notion of a single repeated couplet-long melodic line did not make much sense for the vigorously enjambed and rhythmically complicated stanzas of Archilochus and Mimnermus, but perhaps here, in the context of a traditional lament, it was more appropriate to adapt the more staid and regular line-by-line compositional technique that we have hitherto associated primarily with the elegiac catalogue (see Section 2.3).

Indeed, scholars have long debated the precise genre of Andromache's song. In the 1930s Page and then Bowra argued that, despite the obvious influence of Homeric language in some places, these Euripidean verses preserve evidence for a rare and archaic genre of Peloponnesian lament that also shows up sporadically in some fifth-century epitaphs and eventually even in Callimachus' elegiac *Hymn*

---

[24] Page (1936) 221 and Allan (2000) 56. On auletic accompaniment of archaic elegy in general, see Ch. 1.
[25] Herrnstein-Smith (1968) 57–62.

to Athena, which was also composed in the Doric dialect.[26] Page also suggested that the late fifth-century use of the word ἔλεγος to mean 'sung lament' also pointed to this older tradition. By this account, then, Andromache's song is an indirect but valuable literary witness to an archaic form of threnodic elegy sung in the Doric dialect. Page's thesis was vigorously attacked by a number of scholars, who argued among other things that the classical use of ἔλεγος to mean 'threnody' was not a survival of an older archaic term, but rather a fifth-century invention generated by Athenians interested in etymology and the history of music, who perhaps noted the growing popularity of elegiac couplets in epitaphs and provided the word ἔλεγος with a faulty etymology.[27] In terms of the question laid out at the start of this chapter, then, the dissidents generally argue that Andromache's lament is a fifth-century innovation generated by a fictive etymology,[28] whereas Page and his followers see it as an archaistic composition based on some real, albeit distant, knowledge of Peloponnesian laments.

In what follows I shall argue, in fact, that Andromache's lament displays sure signs of stanzaic design and that this fact adds to the recent and growing consensus that Page was probably correct in seeing her song as a literary survival.[29] What are, then, the signs of stanzaic structure in Andromache's lament? Page noted long ago that the first five couplets have what he termed an 'inward symmetry' of

[26] Page (1936) and Bowra (1938) 86–88. The latter adds other examples of this putative genre from epitaphs (e.g. for the Athenian dead at Coronea and Chaeronea) and from the lament of Chariclea in Callimachus' *Hymn to Athena* 85–94.

[27] Although others had questioned Page's thesis earlier—e.g. Friedländer and Hoffleit (1948) 66, Rosenmeyer (1969) 225–26, and Gentili (1967) 52–64—the combined arguments of Bulloch (1985, 32–34), who is mainly concerned to detach Callimachus' *Hymn to Athena* from this tradition, and Bowie (1986, 22–27) appear to have been more successful. Their critique has a number of supporters, e.g. Fowler (1987) 86–87 and 98, and Bartól (1993) 53–54. Harvey (1955, 170–72), Ford (1985, 111), and Bowie (1986, 22) all suggest, however, that there was some kind of vague generic connection between Andromache's lament, poems of consolation (not lament) and the more reflective fragments of archaic elegy, for example, Archilochus 13.

[28] See e.g. Rosenmeyer (1969) 225–26: 'The scholar-poet Euripides in the *Andromache* wrote a piece in elegiac couplets that was designed to invoke the shades of the early ἔλεγος of whose form he himself had no inkling.'

[29] Both Page (1936, 215) and Bowie (1986, 23) rightly note, however, that the Doric dialect of Andromache's lament does not prove anything by itself, since nearly all tragic song was sung in this dialect.

their own and were designed rhetorically as a complete unit that covers all three items that Andromache promised she would sing about in lines 97–99, devoting in the manner of a catalogue a single internal couplet to each:[30] her city (105–6, with Troy named in the hexameter), her husband (107–8, with Hector likewise mentioned by name) and herself (109–10, with an emphatically placed αὐτά at the beginning of the hexameter). The final couplet, moreover, neatly sums up the content the stanza: 'Many were the tears that rolled down my cheeks, when I left my city, my home and my husband lying in the dust.' And when Andromache uses the word θαλάμους in the final pentameter of the stanza (112), she recalls the appearance of this same word twice in the preceding lines, where she had with much pathos described in similar language the ruinous marriage of Helen (106: ἀγάγετ᾽ ... εἰς θαλάμους Ἑλέναν) and the undoing of her own (109: αὐτὰ δ᾽ ἐκ θαλάμων ἀγόμαν).[31]

There can, I think, be little doubt that Euripides composed these five couplets as a complete unit, in which Andromache recalls a moment in the past on a beach in Phrygia when she first lamented the fall of Troy, the death of her husband and her sorrowful new status as a slave. She does, however, have more to say about her current misery, which according to the background to Euripides' plot, has recently been exacerbated by the jealously of her mistress Hermione. And indeed, the two couplets that follow this first stanza are rhythmically and stylistically more agitated,[32] shifting our attention away from the distant scene of her former lament on the Trojan shore to her present and troubling circumstance as a suppliant before a shrine of the goddess Thetis in Thessaly where the play is set. There are, moreover, signs that Euripides designed these additional verses to respond to those in the first stanza. At the beginning of this second

---

[30] Page (1936) 217: 'The poem consists of fourteen lines; of the first ten the Past, of the last four the Present is the subject. The first ten lines have their own inward symmetry.'

[31] Page (1936) 219.

[32] Page (1936) 217: 'Then in the last four lines a conclusion is formed by a remarkable break in style and rhythm. Hitherto all of the couplets have been complete in themselves and there has been no heavy punctuation within a couplet; in the twelfth line the pentameter is abruptly broken into two equal portions, and the pentameter's sentence runs over into the following hexameter. All of the other pentameters end with nouns; the twelfth line ends with a participle.'

section of her song Andromache picks up some of the language of the first—ὤμοι ἐγὼ μελέα (112) recalls τὸν ἐμὸν μελέας πόσιν (107) and δούλαν (113) echoes δουλοσύναν (110)—and she emphasizes the baneful presence of her new tormentor Hermione, the daughter of Menelaus, placing her in a position at the start of this second section that is neatly parallel to that of another Spartan woman, the one who destroyed Troy: Ἑλέναν· | ἇς ἕνεκ᾽ (104–5) and Ἑρμιόνας ... ἇς ὕπο (114).[33]

What, then, are we to make of the length of Andromache's lament? On the one hand, given the apparent fifth-century trend toward elegiac composition without stanzas, one would not expect to find any stanzas at all in a play produced sometime in the 420s. It would be convenient, of course, to suggest that we have simply lost the last three couplets of the second stanza, but we are not dealing as before with an archaic fragment, transmitted orally through the shifting shoals of re-performance and improvisation, and then dismembered and anthologized in later antiquity by excerpters and learned *deipnosophistai*. Unlike the fragments of archaic elegy, these elegiac verses have been transmitted to us in a relatively stable manuscript tradition, and the manuscripts and the scholia give no hint that any additional verses have been lost at this point. There may be, however, a dramaturgical explanation for the truncated second stanza, for the entrance of the chorus at the end of the lament is plainly unexpected. This is suggested by the fact that Andromache does not, as is so often the case in tragedy, acknowledge their arrival before they speak.[34] One might argue, then, that Andromache is interrupted in the midst of her song and never gets to finish her second stanza, a fact that could be made obvious to the audience in the staging of the action, but which would not necessarily show up in the text of the play. A second and more complicated possibility is that the chorus themselves actually take up and finish her lament, when they sing three epodic verses of increasing length, each beginning with a dactylic hexameter identical in shape to those sung by Andromache.[35] In

---

[33] Page (1936) 218.   [34] Allan (2000) 199.

[35] Allan (2000) 200: 'the opening hexameter of their dactylo-iambic song smoothes the transition from Andromache's elegiacs to their own view of events.' See also Willink (2001) 724–25.

either case, however, Andromache seems to sing an elegiac lament that she never finishes, for if she had, we would expect some detailed complaints about the abuse she has more recently endured at Hermione's hands. This suggestion of missing content is, moreover, strongly supported by the hallmarks of stanzaic composition discussed above: the extraordinary cohesiveness, both thematic and stylistic, of the first five couplets and the stark difference between them and the verses that follow.

Euripides, then, seems to have composed the beginning of a plaintive elegy in stanzas that the chorus cuts short for dramatic purposes. But does it constitute a formal lament? Andromache does mention her tears in both parts of her song, both those shed at Troy (111) and those she is shedding as she sings (116). The second passage, moreover, includes the first-person verb τάκομαι, a feature that is (as we shall see) suggestive of threnodic verse. It is true, however, that—with the exception of the apostrophe to Troy in the third line—Andromache's description of the scene of her first lament is oddly distanced and indeed it has been suggested that the first stanza of her song was a complimentary nod toward a famous Argive poem that narrated the destruction of Troy.[36] The initial stanza in Andromache's lament might, therefore, reflect the traditional stanzaic techniques of elegiac narrative poetry, rather than those of lament. References to past injuries and mourning are not, however, uncommon in Greek laments, especially when used (as they are here) to foreground present misfortunes.[37] Therefore, to ascertain fully the threnodic character of Andromache's song, we must bring in some early comparanda.

The study of elegy's relationship to lament has, in fact, been given new impetus in recent years by the discovery of some elegiac fragments of Simonides (most notably the newly reconstructed fragment

---

[36] Bowie (2001, 52–53) suggests that Euripides may have been paying a compliment to *The Fall of Troy*, a famous and lengthy poem by Sacadas of Argos, a poem that Bowie suggests was composed in elegiac couplets. Given the hints that the *Andromache* may have itself been performed in Argos, this suggestion is worth considering. Sacadas' poem is, however, entirely lost and the argument that it was composed in elegiac couplets rests on an emendation of Athenaeus 13.610c; see Page (1936) 228 n. 1.

[37] In the lament for Hector in *Iliad* 24, for example, Hecuba narrates the previous deaths of her other sons. See Alexiou (2002) 132–33 and (for a modern Greek parallel) Holst-Warhaft (1992) 51–52.

22), which support the notion of a threnodic genre of elegy,[38] and the ongoing publication of early metrical epitaphs, which use verbs of lamentation and thereby illustrate the convention of 'the anonymous first-person mourner'.[39] Such discoveries have encouraged some scholars to revive older suggestions that these brief elegiac inscriptions were excerpts from longer funerary dirges,[40] and others to reinsert Callimachus' *Hymn to Athena* back into this threnodic tradition—as Bowra had originally suggested.[41] The recent discovery in Ambracia of a mid-sixth-century BCE polyandrion has perhaps given the greatest impetus to this ongoing revival of Page's hypothesis. Its coping stones were engraved in the Corinthian alphabet with an elegiac epitaph that honours two Corinthian envoys and their Ambracian companions, who were all apparently killed in an ambush.[42] The length of this text has amazed scholars, when they compare it to the typically one- or two-couplet epitaphs of the late archaic period.[43] In the context of this study, however, its length sparks a different kind of interest, for the poem was originally five couplets long:[44]

---

[38] Allan (2000) 55–57, Aloni (2001) 90–91, and Yatromanolakis (2001) 211–12 and 219–20. Mace (2001) argues that Simonides 22 is erotic rather than threnodic.

[39] Lewis (1987), for example, on the heels of Bowie (1986) immediately brought new epigraphical data to bear on the question, and soon after Day (1989, 25–28) noted further signs of threnodic elegy in a number of late-archaic epigrams. See Cassio (1994) and Kowerski (2005, 115–19) for summation and still more examples. For 'the anonymous first-person mourner' (Lewis' coinage) see Cassio ibid. 107–8. I should note, however, that Page (1936, 211–14) maintained that there were two distinct genres: Ionic epitaphs and Doric laments. Recent discoveries, especially the long Doric epitaph from Ambracia (see below), suggest he was wrong to do so.

[40] See e.g. Wilamowitz (1913) 211–12 (songs at the funeral banquet) and Friedländer and Hoffleit (1948) 65–67 (elegiac lament at the tomb), who are followed by Raubitschek (1967) 7–9.

[41] Hunter (1992) 22.

[42] See Bousquet (1992), whose text is printed in *SEG* XLI 540. I use the improved text of D'Alessio (1995). For the important ramifications of this text, with regard to the relationship between elegy and lament, see Cassio (1994). I thank Julia Lougovava for bringing this inscription to my attention.

[43] Cassio (1994, 103 n. 3), for example, quotes West (1974) 2: 'Before the Persian Wars it is unusual to find an epigram more than four lines long.'

[44] The inscription originally ran across the uppermost of the polyandrion's façade. One block is missing, resulting in the lacuna at lines 4–5. The final couplet was apparently inscribed in a different hand, but probably at or near the same time as the first four. All commentators understand the final couplet to be part of the original poem.

ἄνδρας [τ]ούσδ᾽ [ἐ]σθλοὺς ὀλοφύρομαι, οἷσι Πυραιβῶν
παῖδες ἐμητίσαντ᾽ ἀ[λι]γινόεντα φόνον
ἀνγε[λ]ίαν μετιόντας ἀπ᾽ εὐρυχόρο[ιο Κορίνθου]
[.   .   .   .   .   .   .]
5   [.   .   .   .   .   .   .]
πατρίδ᾽ ἀν᾽ ἱμερτὰν πένθος ἔθαλλε τότε.
τώδε δ᾽ ἀπ᾽ Ἀνπρακίας, Ναυσίστρατον, αὐτὰ παθόντε,
Καλλίταν τ᾽ Ἀίδα δῶμα μέλαν κατέχει.
καὶ μὰν Ἀραθθίωνα καὶ Εὔξενον ἴστε, πολῖται,
ὡς μετὰ τῶνδ᾽ ἀνδρῶν Κὰρ ἔκιχεν θανάτου.

I lament these brave men, for whom the children of the Puraiboi devised painful slaughter as they (i.e. the dead men) were accompanying an embassy from Corinth of the wide dancing-floor...

... throughout our lovely fatherland grief kept welling up then. These two men from Ambracia, Nausistratos and Callites, the black house of Hades holds, because they suffered the same fate. And also know, fellow citizens, that the demon of death overtook Arathion and Euxenos along with these men.

Like the Megarian epitaph that catalogued those killed during the Persian War (Section 2.3) these verses are not great poetry, but they do give us important new insights into the genre of elegiac epitaph in the late archaic period. Indeed, in addition to the five-couplet frame, this poem conforms in other ways to the genre of archaic elegy. The poet, for instance, speaks in the first-person (1: ὀλοφύρομαι) and addresses the citizens of Ambracia (7: πολῖται), much the same as Solon or Tyrtaeus claim to speak to the assembled citizens or soldiers of their respective cities.[45] The poet, moreover, has in his own workmanlike way constructed a solid elegiac stanza. The poem is framed by deictic references to 'these men here' (1: ἄνδρας [τ]ούσδ᾽ and 10: μετὰ τῶνδ᾽ ἀνδρῶν), that is: to the dead men honoured by the inscription and (most likely) depicted by statues on top of the tomb.[46] And like the Megarian epitaph, this inscription, after invoking the whole group, separates them into three different subsections—assuming that the names of the Corinthian dead appeared in the lost

[45] Cassio (1994) 108–14.
[46] Cassio (1994, 103–4) notes another curious fact, similar perhaps to the occasional use of rhyming pentameters at the start and finish of elegiac stanzas (e.g. the final stanza of Callinus 1 as discussed in Section 3.1): the prosody of the first couplet is matched syllable for syllable with that of the final couplet.

couplet—with probably two men to each section. Although this poet does not provide, as the Megarian one does, a full summary at the end of the poem, he nonetheless manages to bring it to closure by recalling the entire group in the final pentameter (10: μετὰ τῶνδ' ἀνδρῶν).

This inscription is, finally, helpful for assessing the relationship between elegy and lament in the archaic period.[47] The poet says explicitly that he 'mourns' (1: ὀλοφύρομαι) the men honoured by the tomb and that throughout the land 'grief kept welling up' (1: πένθος ἔθαλλε). We have, of course, already seen both of these features—the performative verb and the past perspective on grief—in Andromache's lament. The public context of the Ambracian epitaph, moreover, also recalls Archilochus 13 (discussed in Section 2.1), in which the poet addresses his friend Pericles in a similar context of civic mourning. That five-couplet fragment began:

> κήδεα μὲν στονόεντα, Περίκλεες, οὔτέ τις ἀστῶν
> μεμφόμενος θαλίῃς τέρψεται οὐδὲ πόλις·
> τοίους γὰρ κατὰ κῦμα πολυφλοίσβοιο θαλάσσης
> ἔκλυσεν, οἰδαλέους δ' ἀμφ' ὀδύνης ἔχομεν
> πνεύμονας.

There will be no disapproval of our mourning and lamentation, Pericles, when any citizen or even state takes pleasure in festivities, since such fine men did the wave of the loud-roaring sea wash over, and our lungs are swollen from pain.

Here, too, we find a past perspective on the disaster (3–4: τοίους γὰρ κατὰ κῦμα . . . ἔκλυσεν) combined with emphatic references to the ongoing grief in the city (1: κήδεα μὲν στονόεντα and 4–5: οἰδαλέους δ' . . . πνεύμονας). In the past some scholars have, in fact, adduced this fragment, along with Andromache's song, as evidence that elegiac poets composed formal laments, and indeed a biographical tradition mentioned earlier in Section 2.1 suggests that this fragment was part of a longer composition triggered by the death of the poet's brother-in-law in some major disaster at sea.[48] The epitaph for the Ambracian ambassadors and their escorts has understandably rekindled interest in Page's theory about a Peloponnesian genre of threnodic elegy, and rightly so

---

[47] As Cassio (1994) stresses.   [48] Fera (1990) 20–23.

for it is clearly a first-person lament composed in elegiac couplets.[49] For the purposes of this study, however, it suffices to add this: the fact that the Ambracian epitaph and the first ten verses of Andromache's lament are composed as elegiac stanzas in the Doric dialect lends greater heft to Page's argument that the Euripidean song somehow reflects an older, archaic tradition of Peloponnesian lamentations.[50]

I suggest that Euripides, when he has Andromache begin her lament with a stanza composed in the archaic fashion, does so in order to distance himself and his audience from it in two ways. Writing as he is in the last quarter of the fifth century, he perhaps considered this lament appropriately old-fashioned for the Homeric heroine who famously laments in the *Iliad*. But I suggest that in this song he also reveals his interest in the exotic musical and religious traditions of the other Greek states, just as he does, for example, in the wild maenadic songs of the *Bacchae*. Andromache's lament, then, is both archaistic and exotic, but it probably reflects some knowledge that Euripides and presumably some of his audience had of this epichoric tradition. Or to put it another way: if Euripides' exotic songs in the *Bacchae* can be useful, albeit heavily dramatized, sources for the history of Bacchic song, why shouldn't the same be true for Andromache's lament at Sparta? Finally, as was mentioned in passing earlier, we find the same collocation of poetic and ethnic features in Callimachus' *Hymn to Athena*, an elegiac poem composed in Doric and set in the city of Argos.[51] The fictive speaker of the poem, moreover, is a priestess or female cult official who uses a series of four elegiac stanzas in her preliminary address to other female worshippers and the goddess.[52] Scholars sometimes adduce

---

[49] Cassio (1994).

[50] Page (1936) 226–28. Although the Doric cast of Andromache's lament can easily be dismissed as a tragic convention (see n. 29), it may indeed have a special point, given the fact that the plot is set in Sparta and that the play itself may have been performed in Argos.

[51] Bulloch (1985) 3–13.

[52] In Faraone (forthcoming–*a*) I argue that Callimachus, at the beginning of the *Bath of Athena*, composes a series of five-couplet stanzas in part to establish order in a complicated sequence of invocations and commands, during which the narrator first addresses a group of Argive maidens, who are about to transport and wash the Palladion, and then the goddess herself embodied in her statue within the temple. Three of these stanzas begin with verse-initial imperatives that seem to be designed as a triple responsion: ὦ ἴτ' Ἀχαιιάδες (13); ἔξιθ' Ἀθαναία (33); and ἔξιθ' Ἀθαναία (43).

Callimachus' hymn as evidence for Doric lament, on the grounds that it contains a short lament by Teiresias' mother at lines 85–95. But given the brevity of the mother's response and the fact that ancient Greek laments and hymns seem to share the same tripartite structure,[53] it seems more prudent to suggest a broader generic connection: namely that in the Peloponnese elegiac couplets sung in stanzas were used by women for a number of ritual purposes, including lament and hymns.

We have seen, then, that knowledge of stanzaic technique, once it is disconnected from musical accompaniment and singing in the fifth century, seems to fade and then disappear, among those composing new songs as well as those reperforming old ones. There are, however, scattered hints that some poets were self-consciously aware of its archaic form as well as its ongoing demise. Xenophanes, a poet who probably survived down until the 470s, apparently innovates when he uses traditional compositional techniques with what seems to be a unique six-couplet stanza. The results are impressive but as far as we can tell he has few followers. He seems to play, moreover, on his audience's expectation of a traditional five-couplet stanza to enhance the dramatic end of the priamel in the first stanza of Xenophanes 1. In Andromache's interrupted lament, on the other hand, Euripides probably reflects an earlier and otherwise nearly invisible tradition of Peloponnesian threnody, sung in elegiac stanzas and in the Doric dialect to the tune of an *aulos*. The evidence of the Ambracian epitaph suggests that this tradition of elegiac lament survived in stanzaic form at least down to the mid-sixth century and probably even further, perhaps because in the typically conservative context of a funeral or burial it was the last to be disconnected from its musical accompaniment or ritual setting.

[53] See Alexiou (2002) 131–34 for the common features of lament and hymn.

7

Revival

In the Hellenistic period poets often compose elegiac verse, not only in the popular miniaturist form known as 'epigram', but also in longer genres, such as hymns, epinicia, and historical narratives. They seem to do so, however, after a significant hiatus in elegiac production in the middle of the fourth century, a hiatus that serves as a convenient caesura between the orally composed and improvised elegies of the archaic and classical periods and the written and self-consciously literary poems of the Hellenistic period, which begin to appear in at the end of the fourth century, for example, the famous (lost) elegiac *Hymn to Demeter* by Philetas of Cos.[1] Not surprisingly elegiac stanzas do not appear often in Hellenistic poems and when they do show up it is often in a context of self-conscious archaism or pseudepigraphy.[2] Callimachus provides us with the best information about the reception of archaic elegy in the Hellenistic period. His *Hymn to Athena*, as was mentioned at the end of the previous chapter, seems to provide evidence that, like threnodic elegy, cult hymns were perhaps once sung in elegiac stanzas by women in the Peloponnese.[3] In this mimetic hymn, not at all unlike Euripides, Callimachus places his stanzas in the mouth of a priestess of Athena at Argos in a manner that is either archaizing or exoticizing or some

---

[1] See e.g. West (1974) 1: 'The first quarter of the fourth century BC saw an almost drying up of elegy in the classical sense ... the last quarter saw the vigorous, but self-conscious revival that heralded the Alexandrian Age.'

[2] See Faraone (forthcoming–*b*) for a study of a series of five-couplet epigrams that poets in the late classical and Hellenistic period tried to pass off as Simonidean or that they composed as anachronistic epitaphs for the poets of old.

[3] See Ch. 6, n. 52.

mixture of both.[4] In the 'Prologue' to his *Aetia*, however, Callimachus steps away from the mimetic mask and addresses us directly as a practising poet, who openly discusses the best style for contemporary elegiac poetry. Although scholars have in the past focused mainly on the content of the 'Prologue' with its many allusions to the poetry of the past,[5] I hope to show that its poetic form and stanzaic architecture are themselves equally compelling programmatic 'statements' about elegiac poetry. Or to put it another way: Callimachus, not surprisingly, practises what he preaches in the 'Prologue'. Ignoring, therefore, the long and sometimes contentious debates over its content, I focus instead on how Callimachus designed his 'Prologue' as a sequence of four closely responding five-couplet stanzas in a way that imitates and thereby praises the kind of elegiac design he thought best.

At the start of the fragment Callimachus responds vigorously to critics who fault him for refusing to write a long and continuous elegiac poem about the deeds of kings or mythical heroes:[6]

πολλάκ]ι μοι Τελχῖνες ἐπιτρύζουσιν ἀοιδῇ,
νήιδες οἳ Μούσης οὐκ ἐγένοντο φίλοι,
εἵνεκεν οὐχ ἓν ἄεισμα διηνεκὲς ἢ βασιλ[ήων
.....]ας ἐν πολλαῖς ἤνυσα χιλιάσιν

---

[4] There are in fact precious few comparanda for a hymn composed in elegiac couplets (and stanzas) in the Doric dialect, so we cannot know if Callimachus was reflecting a contemporaneous, but otherwise unknown Peloponesian cult practice, an archaic one, or neither. See Faraone (forthcoming–*a*).

[5] Our appreciation of the uniquely elegiac stance of the 'Prologue' was in the past hampered by the long-standing but erroneous view that Callimachus was discussing the genre of hexametrical epic or poetry in general. In recent years, however, scholars have come to the sensible consensus that the arguments and the content of the 'Prologue' are mainly concerned with a popular but unfortunately lost genre of 'repetitive "catalogue elegy," of the kind most familiar to us from the fragments of Hermesianax and Phanocles, but clearest for Callimachus' generation in the *Lydê* of Antimachus'. See Cameron (1995) 277–89, who provides a detailed argument for this view.

[6] I give the text and (with some minor changes; for example I translate παῖς as 'boy' not 'child', for reasons that will become apparent) the translation of Acosta-Hughes and Stephens (2002), which reflects the most recent consensus—Fantuzzi and Hunter (2004, 67–68) and Asper (2004), for example, offer a nearly identical text, differing only rarely in the placement of brackets and the addition or subtraction of one or two conjectured words in the lacunae. Pfeiffer (1949), Massimilla (1996), and Asper (2004) print two additional and very fragmentary lines (numbered 39–40) that they suggest are part of the 'Prologue'—a question that I address below.

5   ἦ.....].ους ἥρωας, ἔπος δ' ἐπὶ τυτθὸν ἐλ[
      παῖς ἅτε, τῶν δ' ἐτέων ἡ δεκὰς οὐκ ὀλίγη
      ......].[.]και Τε[λ]χῖσιν ἐγὼ τόδε· "φῦλον α[
      ......] τήκ[ειν] ἧπαρ ἐπιστάμενον,
      ......]..ρεην[ὀλ]ιγόστιχος·· ἀλλὰ καθέλκει

10   .... πολὺ τὴν μακρὴν ὄμπνια Θεσμοφόρο[ς··
      τοῖν δὲ] δυοῖν Μίμνερμος ὅτι γλυκύς, αἱ κατὰ λεπτόν
      ῥήσεις], ἡ μεγάλη δ' οὐκ ἐδίδαξε γυνή.
      .....]ον ἐπὶ Θρήϊκας ἀπ' Αἰγύπτοιο [πέτοιτο
      αἵματ]ι Πυγμαίων ἡδο μένη [γ]έρα[νος,

15   Μασσαγέται καὶ μακρὸν ὀϊστεύοιεν ἐπ' ἄνδρα
      Μῆδον]· ἀ[ηδονίδες] δ' ὧδε μελιχρ[ό]τεραι.
      ἔλλετε Βασκανίης ὀλοὸν γένος·· αὖθι δὲ τέχνη
      κρίνετε,] μὴ σχοίνῳ Περσίδι τὴν σοφίην··
      μηδ' ἀπ' ἐμεῦ διφᾶτε μέγα ψοφέουσαν ἀοιδήν

20   τίκτεσθαι·· βροντᾶ]ν οὐκ ἐμόν, ἀλλὰ Διός."

Often the Telchines croak at my song, fools, no friends of the Muse, because I did not complete one continuous poem on kings [...] in many thousands of lines [or...]heroes, but my tale little by little [I...] like a boy, though the ten-count of my years is not small. To the Telchines I [say] this: '... tribe, knowing how to waste your liver... few-lined, but bountiful Demeter drags down (i.e. outweighs) by far the long [lady?].

And of the two, the slender verses taught that Mimnermus is sweet, not the large lady. [...] may the crane, rejoicing in the Pygmies' blood, fly [...] against the Thracians from Egypt, and may the Massagetae shoot at their man, the Mede, from afar. So are nightingales sweeter. Be gone, Envy's baneful race. And in turn judge poetry by its art, not by the Persian chain, nor ask me to produce a loud-sounding song. To thunder is not mine, but Zeus'.'

Although the loss of the beginning and end of nearly every verse sorely limits our ability to trace the organization of these verses, signs of stanzaic design do remain. The last line quoted here, for example, marks an important boundary within the 'Prologue', because (as we shall see) in the next couplet Callimachus moves from his argument against the Telchines to a chronologically earlier scene of Apollonian advice (lines 21–29, discussed below).[7] There are, moreover, internal signs that these first ten couplets were composed as a complete unit.

---

[7] Massimilla (1996) ad loc.

It is not an accident, for example, that they are framed by echoing references at the end of the first and last hexameters to different kinds of song (in both cases the final word in the verse is ἀοιδή):[8] (i) the Callimachean type that the Telchines complain about (1: πολλάκ]ι μοι Τελχῖνες ἐπιτρύζουσιν ἀοιδῇ); and (ii) the 'loud-sounding song' that the Telchines prefer and demand of him (19: μηδ᾽ ἀπ᾽ ἐμεῦ διφᾶτε μέγα ψοφέουσαν ἀοιδήν). We can see, moreover, by the parallel placement of the personal pronouns at the start of the second foot (μοι and -μεῦ) and by the echoing sounds at verse-end (-ουσιν ἀοιδῇ and -ουσαν ἀοιδήν) that Callimachus composed these lines in ring-composition to formally mark the start and finish of the first half of the 'Prologue'.

The especially lacunose state of lines 4–10 precludes any certainty, but there are also hints that Callimachus composed these first twenty lines of the 'Prologue' as a coordinated pair of stanzas, with the second responding in its structure and thematic development to the first. Each stanza begins, for example, with metrically equivalent names, each placed before the feminine caesura of the first hexameter of the stanza: the Telchines (Callimachus' arch-enemies) in line 1 and Mimnermus (an important Callimachean model) in line 11. Each stanza also ends with the name of a deity, whose superiority over a mortal is emphasized: Thesmophorian Demeter is far superior to the 'long [lady?]' (9–10), and the power to thunder belongs to Zeus and not Callimachus (20). Here, too, we find parallels in the word placement, sound, and sense of the two pentameters: the spondaic-shaped words describing the poetic style that Callimachus deems inferior (μακρὴν and βροντᾶ]ν) both end with long 'a' sounds and sit before the midline diaeresis.

The penultimate couplets in each stanza, moreover, refer to the Telchines as a tribal group prone to jealousy and the evil-eye (7–8): 'To the Telchines I say this: tribe... who knows how to waste your liver' (φῦλον ... τήκ[ειν] ἧπαρ ἐπιστάμενον)—a conventional description of the envious[9]—and 'Be gone, Envy's baneful race.

---

[8] Hopkinson (1988) ad loc.

[9] On the idea that envy or those who cast evil eye (βασκανία) destroy themselves (and especially their livers), see Dunbabin and Dickie (1983, 15–16), who also note that: 'the verb most commonly used in Greek of the wasting effect of φθόνος is τήκειν' citing Theocritus 5.12–13 and 6.26–27.

And in turn judge poetry by its art' (17–18: ἔλλετε Βασκανίης ὀλοὸν γένος· αὖθι δὲ τέχνῃ | [κρίνετε]...σοφίην). There seems to be, moreover, a number of sly references to technical skills here. The Telchines, whose practical knowledge (8: ἐπιστάμενον) seems to be limited to jealousy and the evil-eye, are contrasted in the parallel section of the next stanza with the poetic σοφίη of Callimachus (18), which can be judged by its skill (17: τέχνῃ).[10] These thematic parallels are even more obvious in the second and third couplets, where the poet begins by describing or alluding to the grandiose themes he eschews— the deeds of kings or heroes in the first stanza (3–5) and the long-distance flight of exotic African cranes and Massagetan arrows in the second (13–15)—but ends with a diminutive counter-image that sums up his own poetic practice: a boy (5–6) and a nightingale (16).

Modern readers might find the use of such parallel themes to be rigid or redundant—just as nineteenth-century scholars once suspected the paired stanzas at the end of Tyrtaeus 11 and 12 to be scribal doublets—but we have seen how such redundancy is an important feature of archaic elegy and usually augurs some subtle, but significant contrast between the stanzas, such as that between defensive and offensive warfare in the second half of Tyrtaeus 11 or the development of the body and that of the mind in Solon 27. The damage to the papyrus in the first stanza of the 'Prologue' make it more difficult to observe such distinctions, but it is striking that in the second stanza Callimachus refers to five different foreign peoples by name or adjective (Thracians, Pygmies, Massagetae, Medes and Persians), whom he aligns with the wrong kind of poets, the Telchines, who are themselves called 'the baneful γένος of Envy'.[11] In the geography of Callimachean aesthetics, therefore, the envious Telchines are persistently aligned with barbarians who traditionally live outside of the civilized Greek world. There are, however, no references to such foreigners in the first stanza, nor for that matter anywhere else in the 'Prologue' outside of this stanza.

[10] For σοφίη as a somewhat coded word for elegiac poetry or technique, see Xenophanes 2.11–14 (Section 6.1) and the participle σοφιζομένῳ at the start of the Theognidean 'Seal Poem' (19), for which see the end of Section 3.1.

[11] All these terms refer to people rather than places. Callimachus also mentions the land of Egypt, which given the poet's position in the Ptolemaic court, probably does not refer invidiously to the Egyptian people as a race, but simply to the territory, understood as the last stopping point on the cranes' annual journey out of Africa.

The second half of the 'Prologue' is much better preserved and shows greater signs of stanzaic design:

καὶ γὰρ ὅτε πρώτιστον ἐμοῖς ἐπὶ δέλτον ἔθηκα
γούνασιν, Ἀ[πό]λλων εἶπεν ὅ μοι Λύκιος··
" ......]... ἀοιδέ, τὸ μὲν θύος ὅττι πάχιστον
θρέψαι, τὴ]ν Μοῦσαν δ' ὠγαθὲ λεπταλέην··
πρὸς δέ σε] καὶ τόδ' ἄνωγα, τὰ μὴ πατέουσιν ἅμαξαι   25
τὰ στείβειν, ἑτέρων ἴχνια μὴ καθ' ὁμά
δίφρον ἐλᾶν μηδ' οἷμον ἀνὰ πλατύν, ἀλλὰ κελεύθους
ἀτρίπτο]υ ς, εἰ καὶ στεινοτέρην ἐλάσεις."

τῷ πιθόμη]ν·· ἐνὶ τοῖς γὰρ ἀείδομεν οἳ λιγὺν ἦχον
τέττιγος, θ]όρυβον δ' οὐκ ἐφίλησαν ὄνων.   30
θηρὶ μὲν οὐατόεντι πανείκελον ὀγκήσαιτο
ἄλλος, ἐγ]ὼ δ' εἴην οὐλ[α]χύς, ὁ πτερόεις,
ἆ πάντως, ἵνα γῆρας ἵνα δρόσον ἦν μὲν ἀείδω
πρώκιον ἐκ δίης ἠέρος εἶδαρ ἔδων,
αὖθι τὸ δ' ἐκδύοιμι, τό μοι βάρος ὅσσον ἔπεστι   35
τριγλώχιν ὀλοῷ νῆσος ἐπ' Ἐγκελάδῳ.
...... Μοῦσαι γὰρ ὅσους ἴδον ὄμματι παῖδας
μὴ λοξῷ, πολιοὺς οὐκ ἀπέθεντο φίλους.

For when, for the very first time I placed my tablet on my knees, Lycian Apollo enjoined me thus: '... singer, raise your victim to be as fat as possible but, my good man, your Muse to be slender. And I bid you this, go there, where wagons do not pass; do not drive your chariot along the same ways as others, nor along the broad path, but the untrodden roads, although you will drive a narrower route.'

I obeyed him, for we sing among those who love the clear sound of the cicada, not the din of asses. Let another bray like a long-eared beast; I would be the small, the winged one, ah truly, that I may sing feeding upon the moisture, the morning dew from the divine air, and that in turn I may shed old age, which is a weight upon me, like his tricorn island upon destructive Enceladus. [...] for whom the Muses look upon with favor as youths, these they do not abandon as friends when they are old.

Line 29 marks a firm boundary between Apollo's advice (lines 21–28)[12] and the lyrical verses that follow, in which Callimachus resumes his role as narrator ('I obeyed him ...') and apparently

[12] This eight-line section is not, of course, a complete five-couplet stanza; see below for discussion of the missing couplet.

launches into the kind of song Apollo recommends ('for we sing...'). This embedded song, as it turns out, is precisely five couplets in length and of all the stanzas in the 'Prologue', it displays the greatest level of internal organization, undoubtedly because it is the best preserved. Like most meditative stanzas, it begins with γὰρ and describes or expresses hopes about Callimachus' own poetic preferences and destiny in a style much like the Theognidean seal-poem (discussed in Section 3.1), where the poet in a similarly self-conscious manner discusses his own poetry and the prospective fame of Cyrnus, the object of his song. And since Callimachus places this meditation on the heels of a section devoted entirely to Apollonian advice, it seems that here, as in many of the extant longer fragments of elegy, we have a stanza of exhortation followed by a stanza of meditation introduced by γὰρ.

These last five couplets of the 'Prologue' also show formal signs of internal coherence and closure. The final two couplets, for example, are end-stopped and both have internal rhymes in their pentameters (ὀλοῷ ...Ἐγκελάδῳ and πολιούς ... φίλους), much like the final two couplets of Callinus 1 and Xenophanes 1. Callimachus, moreover, frames this final stanza with references to φιλία at the beginning and end:

τῷ πιθόμη]ν· ἐνὶ τοῖς γὰρ ἀείδομεν οἳ λιγὺν ἦχον
τέττιγος, θ]όρυβον δ' οὐκ ἐφίλησαν ὄνων. (30)

.... Μοῦσαι γὰρ ὅσους ἴδον ὄθματι παῖδας
μὴ λοξῷ, πολιοὺς οὐκ ἀπέθεντο φίλους. (38)

Callimachus underscores the ring-composition here by the close similarities in syntactical form and word placement in the couplet: both sentences begin at the same point in the hexameter (in the middle of the second foot) after a short phrase or sentence, and both provide explanations (with γάρ appearing in the same *sedes*) that justify Callimachus' aesthetic stance. The words placed before γάρ, moreover, bring the Muses (37: Μοῦσαι γὰρ) in parallel with those discriminating poets or listeners with whom Callimachus associates himself (29: ἐνὶ τοῖς γὰρ ἀείδομεν). The pentameters of these couplets also have a similar structure: they both begin with an enjambed spondaic word (τέττιγος) or phrase (μὴ λοξῷ) and end with a similarly composed *hemiepes* that (as we saw earlier) makes negative assertions about φιλία (30: θ]όρυβον δ᾽ οὐκ ἐφίλησαν ὄνων and 38: πολιοὺς οὐκ ἀπέθεντο φίλους). Callimachus, therefore, has composed the final five couplets of the 'Prologue' as a meditative stanza of the archaic type in which the poet both describes and (I suggest) self-consciously demonstrates his own skill in singing the kind of elegiac poetry that he and his Muses love.

There are, moreover, plentiful signs that Callimachus has crafted, as Tyrtaeus did in Fragment 12, this fourth and final stanza of the 'Prologue' in close parallel to the second stanza, where as we saw he names Mimnermus as a model elegist and describes in qualitative and comparative terms the superiority of that poet's shorter poems.[13] The couplet at the beginning of the fourth stanza, for example, echoes the programmatic content, verse structure and the syntax of the first couplet of the second stanza:

> τοῖν δὲ] δυοῖν Μίμνερμος ὅτι γλυκύς, αἱ κατὰ λεπτὸν
> ῥήσεις], ἡ μεγάλη δ᾽ οὐκ ἐδίδαξε γυνή.

(11–12, start of 2nd stanza)

> τῷ πιθόμη]ν· ἐνὶ τοῖς γὰρ ἀείδομεν οἳ λιγὺν ἦχον
> τέττιγος, θ]όρυβον δ᾽ οὐκ ἐφίλησαν ὄνων.

(29–30, start of 4th stanza)

In both couplets similarly constructed phrases (αἱ κατὰ λεπτὸν | ῥήσεις and οἳ λιγὺν ἦχον | τέττιγος) begin at the bucolic diaeresis with a description of the approved Callimachean style, in each case using adjectives ('slender' and 'clear') of programmatic importance.[14] These sentences then end in the pentameter with identically

---

[13] The Florentine scholia clearly suggest that the shorter poetry of Philetas, like the shorter poems of Mimnermus, were equally praised by Callimachus in this section of the fragment; see e.g. Cameron (1995) 302–38, Allen (1993) 146–56, and Fantuzzi and Hunter (2004) 61–71, for the ongoing debate over these allusions. But since we cannot actually see explicit references to Philetas in the surviving text of the 'Prologue' and since few verses of Philetas survive antiquity, it seems more productive to concentrate on Mimnermus.

[14] Fantuzzi and Hunter (2004) 72. The phrase that bridges lines 11–12, αἱ κατὰ λεπτὸν | ῥήσεις, has been restored from the London scholia, which reads αἱ κατὰ λεπτ(όν). Luppe (1997) has, however, recently challenged this reading—he is followed by Asper (2004) ad loc.—on the grounds that the 'Prologue' papyrus cannot accommodate all of these letters. He suggests restoring αἱ ἀπαλαί τοι (or μέν) | νήνιες, which preserves the same rhythm, but uses an adjective (ἀπαλός) that is admittedly far less programmatic.

formulated and situated negative sentences that dismiss the poetry of his rivals (ἡ μεγάλη δ᾽ οὐκ ἐδίδαξε γυνή and θ]όρυβον δ᾽ οὐκ ἐφίλησαν ὄνων). Because of this shared syntax and word placement, moreover, both pentameters isolate a word before the diaeresis, which is programmatically significant: they describe the inferior kind of poetry, 'large' (μεγάλη) and 'din' (θόρυβος)—the same pattern, in fact, that we saw in the final pentameters of the first two stanzas, where two other words describing bad poetry (10: μακρὴν and 20: βροντᾶ]ν) likewise fall before the midline diaeresis. More importantly, both couplets make similarly articulated comparisons between the two kinds of poetry, by delaying the main verb to the second part of the sentence: 'the slender verses, not the grand lady, teach' and 'those, who the clear sound of the cicada, not the din of asses, love'. Thus Callimachus uses a structural kind of responsion, more similar to that of Solon or the Theognidean seal-poem than to the nearly verbatim verse-end responsion of Tyrtaeus, to align and compare the Mimnerman poetics praised at the start of the second stanza with the poetic style he professes and enacts at the beginning of the fourth.

The rest of the final stanza of the 'Prologue', in fact, underscores the poet's special Mimnerman inspiration. In it Callimachus takes up the typically Mimnerman theme of the inequities of old age (γῆρας), which now weighs him down (33–36),[15] and he deploys the cicada as a model for the ageing poet who sings clear, light verses, an image that may recall a description of Tithonus that seems to have appeared in Mimnermus' famous poem *Nanno*: 'He (i.e. Zeus) gave Tithonus

---

[15] See e.g. Mimnermus 1.6 and 10, 2.6, 4.2, and 5.3. See Hunter (2001) on the theme of old age here. Some scholars, e.g. Hopkinson (1988, 97), think Callimachus is echoing Euripides' *Heracles Furens*, where the chorus of old men does indeed go through the same sequence that we find here. They start by complaining that old age lies upon their head 'heavier than the crags of Aetna' (638–42, beginning of first strophe) and then (673–77, start of second strophe) predict happily that they will never stop singing and honouring the Muses. Garzya (1963, 171–73) has shown, however, that Euripides himself is probably borrowing from Mimnermus here and it seems much more likely (given the elegiac context of Callimachus' verses and the mention of Mimnermus earlier) that both Euripides and Callimachus are alluding to a lost Mimnerman original. For Euripides' apparent fondness for paraphrasing older elegiac poets, see, for example, the fragment from his lost *Erechtheus* (Fragment 362 [Nauck]) that imitates the opening lines of Solon 13 and (as Athenaeus himself notes at 10.413c–f) a passage from his *Autolycus* (Fragment 282 [Nauck]) that borrows heavily from Xenophanes 2.

an everlasting evil, old age, which is more terrible than even woeful death.'[16] Callimachus, of course, contradicts Mimnermus, who in his extant verses at least, everywhere laments the fact that once a man has become old he is no longer attractive to anyone (see further discussion below). Callimachus playfully asserts to the contrary—presumably with the same elegiac licence that also prompted Solon to correct Mimnermus on a similar point—that the Muses, at least, do not turn their affectionate gaze away from a poet, once they have 'loved' him as a youth,[17] a playfully erotic theme that also alludes to the myth of Tithonus, especially the version that casts the young man in the role of a singer.[18]

The papyrus that preserves the 'Prologue' has one additional and very fragmentary couplet after line 38 that is usually and rightly ignored in most scholarly discussions.[19] The most telling argument against their inclusion in the 'Prologue' proper is the strong sense of

[16] Mimnermus 4: Τιθωνῷ μὲν ἔδωκε ἔχειν κακὸν ἄφθιτον ⟨--⟩ | γῆρας, ὃ καὶ θανάτου ῥίγιον ἀργαλέου. The connection between Tithonus and the cicada is apparently a later one and probably unknown to Mimnermus. But Callimachus could very well have known about it. See the discussion of Allen (1993) 54–55.

[17] Most commentators have not, I think, fully appreciated the erotic potential of these lines, because they imagine (plausibly enough) that in the scene with Apollo, the poet (with writing tablet on his knees) as a mere child learning his letters. See, e.g. Acosta-Hughes and Stephens (2002) 240, who translate παῖδας in line 37 as 'children' and try to connect it with a wider sequence of images (including the dictation scene with Apollo) that juxtapose childhood and old age, beginning with the simile in line 6 ('like a child [παῖς]'). The simile, however, reports the uncharitable assessment of the Telchines, not the poet's own, and the scene with Apollo is surely meant to recall the first time Callimachus attempted to write a poem (i.e. as a youth), not the first time he was learning his alphabet (i.e. as a child). The god, after all, addresses the poet as 'singer' (23: ἀοιδέ) and then 'my good man' (24: ὠγαθέ), neither of which suggest childhood. Those who see a reference to children also ignore the positive reference to Mimnerman verse in line 11, in whose poetry the word παῖς always means an attractive young man (e.g. twice in Mimnermus 1). An erotic reading, moreover, utilizes the full potential of the underlying reference in the closing lines of the 'Prologue' to the myth of the passion of Eos and Tithonus, in which another female goddess (i.e. like the Muses) falls in love with an attractive younger mortal and abducts him as her consort, albeit only to abandon him in fact when he is old and infirm. See Crane (1986) for an excellent discussion (esp. pp. 269–70).

[18] See *LIMC* 'Eos' nos. 135–94 and 268–72 for a series of red-figured vases that depict Eos pursuing or flying off with a lyre-holding youth.

[19] See e.g. Acosta-Hughes and Stephens (2002, 244–46) and Fantuzzi and Hunter (2004, 67–68), who quote and discuss 1–38 as a single unit or Trypanis (1958, 8–9), who ignores lines 39–40 entirely. The consensus that the poet composed lines 37–38 as the conclusion to the 'Prologue' is further strengthened by the fact that these two

closure that one gets in the verses that precede, especially in the boast
in lines 37–38, which (like the last couplet of Tyrtaeus 12) recalls in a
rather pointed way the first couplet of the four-stanza sequence, in
which the poet claims that the 'Telchines' are *not* the friends of the
Muses:[20]

$$Πολλάκ]ι μοι \ Tελχῖνες \ ἐπιτρύζουσιν \ ἀοιδῆι$$
$$νήιδε]ς, οἳ \ \overline{Mούσης} \ οὐκ \ ἐγένοντο \ φίλοι \quad (2)$$

$$.......... \ \overline{Mοῦσαι} \ γὰρ \ \underline{ὅσους} \ ἴδον \ ὄθματι \ παῖδας$$
$$μὴ \ λοξῷ, \ πολιοὺς \ \underline{οὐκ \ ἀπέθεντο \ φίλους} \quad (38)$$

The echo of the theme of friendship with the Muses in these two
hemiepe—οὐκ ἐγένοντο φίλοι (2) and οὐκ ἀπέθεντο φίλους (38)—
powerfully contrasts (as elegiac responsion so often does) the different relationships that Callimachus and the Telchines have with these
goddesses. Line 38, moreover, also recalls (as we saw earlier) the first
pentameter of its own stanza, a couplet that is also directly concerned
with φιλία (30: θ]όρυβον δ' οὐκ ἐφίλησαν ὄνων). This triple responsion
is, of course, similar to, albeit more subtle than, the thrice-repeated
phrase 'fallen among the fore-fighters' in Tyrtaeus 10 or the three
versions of 'the young and old alike' in the final two stanzas of
Tyrtaeus 12.

Each of these interlocked responsions of the 'Prologue' fall at the
beginning or end of a stanza, and they are, as we might expect of
Callimachus, extremely sophisticated, combining as they do, two
different, but related schemes, both formulated around a negative
statement that takes up the second half of a pentameter: three are
concerned with φιλία (lines 2, 30, and 38), while three (12, 20, and
30) dismiss the rhythmically isolated and aesthetically loaded words
(discussed earlier) that describe the rejected style of poetry:

lines were apparently better known in antiquity than all of the other verses of the
'Prologue,' suggesting that they appeared in a significant position, either first or last
lines of a poem or of an important section of a longer poem. They are cited by the
scholia vetera to Hesiod's *Theogony* (at line 81) and they seem to have been particularly important to Callimachus himself, who at the end of his *Epigram* 29, seems to
quote them as a kind of *sphragis* to recall his most famous poetic achievement, much
the same way as Vergil recalls the first lines of his famous *Eclogues* at the end of the
Georgics. See Faraone (1986) for discussion.

[20] Hopkinson (1988) 97.

οἳ Μούσης οὐκ ἐγένοντο φίλοι (2 = start of 1st stanza)

μεγάλη δ' οὐκ ἐδίδαξε γυνή (12 = start of 2nd stanza)

βροντᾶ]ν οὐκ ἐμόν, ἀλλὰ Διός (20 = end of 2nd stanza)

θ]όρυβον δ' οὐκ ἐφίλησαν ὄνων (30 = start of 4th stanza)

πολιοὺς οὐκ ἀπέθεντο φίλους (38 = end of 4th stanza)

The pattern is quite persistent here, with οὐκ appearing in the same position followed in every case but one by a four-syllable aorist verb. The syntactic, programmatic and thematic connections between these five pentameters, each placed in the first or last couplet of a stanza, are dazzling, especially when we recall that the second and fourth stanzas (which each begin and end with one of these responding verses) are themselves also closely aligned by references, both explicit and implicit, to Mimnerman poetry or technique. I should stress again, however, that these Callimachean responsions are subtler than the Tyrtaean ones, because although they involve a repetition of key ideas and terms (e.g. friendship or affection) and the use of the same syntax (οὐκ followed by a third-person, four-syllable aorist verb) they never repeat verbatim any phrase or word, with the exception of the negation οὐκ.

From the responsions charted above and the overall stanzaic design sketched earlier we can, I suggest, draw two inferences about the received text of Callimachus' 'Prologue': (i) the fragmentary last couplet preserved on the papyrus (lines 39–40) marks the beginning of the next section of the 'Prologue' or of the *Aetia* proper; and (ii) a single couplet has dropped out of the third stanza. This leaves us with the following scheme:

[1–10] Callimachus' argument with and reply to the Telchines (part 1)
[11–20] Callimachus' argument with and reply to the Telchines (part 2)
[21–28] Apollo's exhortation to the best poetry (missing one couplet)
[29–38] Callimachus' meditation (beginning with γὰρ) on Mimnerman song

The primary rationale for suspecting that a couplet has gone missing from the third stanza is, of course, the same as in Solon 27 or Tyrtaeus 11.21–28: the overarching structure of the 'Prologue' and especially the persistent fivefold responsion of the negated phrases (all beginning with οὐκ) at the start and finish of most of the stanzas. There is, moreover, no formal conclusion to Apollo's speech in the surviving papyrus text, although the broad scholarly support for the restoration of the transitional phrase τῷ πιθόμη]ν ('and I obeyed him') at the beginning of line 31 reveals the expectation that there should be one. The accepted restoration is quite possible, but I suggest that it is *a priori* more likely that Callimachus concluded Apollo's commands with a now-missing couplet that brought closure to the stanza of exhortation.

If I am correct in tracing this stanzaic design in the 'Prologue,' it remains to summarize how these formal divisions organize the content of the poem thematically. We have already seen how the 'Prologue' divides easily into two equal sections each composed of a pair of stanzas. In the first half (1–20) Callimachus reports the attacks of his rivals and then quotes his own reply, using mainly quantitative measurements, such as length or weight, to contrast the themes and style of his poetry with that of his rivals.[21] He also disparages his rivals as a race (γένος) or tribe (φῦλον), whose poetics and themes are then unfavourably linked in the second stanza with barbarians like the Persians or Pygmies. In the second half of the 'Prologue', in contrast, he uses qualitative (i.e. not easily measured) distinctions of refinement, such as 'common' vs. 'untrodden' or 'clear sound' vs. 'din',[22] and (in the second half only) analogies to animals—the cicada and ass—rather than foreigners. It is clear, moreover, that Mimnermus plays a special role in the 'Prologue' as a model for Callimachus. He is, as far as we can tell, the only poet named explicitly in text, appearing prominently in the first verse of the second stanza as a counterweight to the harping Telchines, and he seems to be the model for the entire fourth stanza, which takes up the theme of old age.

Given this emphasis on Mimnermus it is fair to ask whether we find any traces of specifically Mimnerman technique in the

---

[21] For the emphasis on the quantitative, see Massimilla (1996) 199–216, who labels lines 1–20 as 'la poetica dell'esilità' (p. 199).

[22] Massimilla (1996, 217) summarizes the theme of lines 21–40 as 'la poetica della raffinatezza.'

'Prologue'. As we saw in Chapter 2, the shortness of the surviving fragments (the longest is eight couplets), does not allow us to know if Mimnermus ever used such an elaborate system of responding and parallel verses to link stanzas in a series as Callimachus does in his 'Prologue'. We did identify, however, at least two well-composed stanzas among his surviving fragments. His technique was particularly dazzling in the first section of Mimnermus 2, where he girded the stanza with an elaborate and sweeping scheme of triple ring-composition, with the key words ending lines 1–3 (ὥρη, ἠελίου, ἥβης) systematically answered in strictly reversed order by the same words, which appear in the second half of the stanza at the ends of lines 7–9 (ἥβης, ἠέλιος, ὥρης). We can now add to our appreciation of the artistry of these verses the fact that Mimnermus elaborates and sustains the repetition of the word ἠέλιος by embedding it in pentameters that share the same kind of parallel enjambment, word placement and sound pattern that we saw repeatedly in Callimachus' 'Prologue':

> ἔαρος, ὅτ᾽ αἶψ᾽ αὐγῆς αὔξεται ἠελίου (2)
> καρπός, ὅσον τ᾽ ἐπὶ γῆν κίδναται ἠέλιος (8)

Likewise, the repetition of the word ὥρη at the end of lines 1 and 9 is preceded in both cases by similarly shaped five-syllable words that begin with the same letter: πολυάνθεμος ὥρη (1) and παραμείψεται ὥρης (9). This relatively subtle kind of rhythmical repetition and syntactical parallelism prompts the suggestion that if we had a much longer, continuous section of Mimnermus' verses, we might observe that he (like the Callimachean imitation in the 'Prologue') used these same techniques as well to emphasize much wider verbal, syntactical and thematic parallels between responding verses placed in two or more different stanzas,

I should, finally, stress how both Mimnermus and Callimachus carefully design an individual stanza, by looking one last time at the best preserved and most Mimnerman stanza of the 'Prologue':

> τῷ πιθόμη]ν· ἐνὶ τοῖς γὰρ ἀείδομεν οἳ λιγὺν ἦχον
> τέττιγος, θ]όρυβον δ᾽ οὐκ ἐφίλησαν ὄνων.   30
> θηρὶ μὲν οὐατόεντι πανείκελον ὀγκήσαιτο
> ἄλλος, ἐγ]ὼ δ᾽ εἴην οὐλ[α]χύς, ὁ πτερόεις,

ἃ πάντως, ἵνα γῆρας ἵνα δρόσον ἣν μὲν ἀείδω
πρώκιον ἐκ δίης ἠέρος εἶδαρ ἔδων,
35   αὖθι τὸ δ᾽ ἐκδύοιμι, τό μοι βάρος ὅσσον ἔπεστι
τριγλώχιν ὀλοῷ νῆσος ἐπ᾽ Ἐγκελάδῳ.
...... Μοῦσαι γὰρ ὅσους ἴδον ὄθματι παῖδας
μὴ λοξῷ, πολιοὺς οὐκ ἀπέθεντο φίλους.

I obeyed him, for we sing among those who love the clear sound of the
cicada, not the din of asses. Let another bray like a long-eared beast; I would
be the small, the winged one, ah truly, that I may sing feeding upon the
moisture, the morning dew from the divine air, and that in turn I may shed
old age, which is a weight upon me, like his tricorn island upon destructive
Enceladus. [...] for whom the Muses look upon with favor as boys, these
they do not abandon as friends when they are old.

This is, as we have seen, a meditative stanza of a type popular in early
elegy, introduced by γάρ and intermixing present, optative, and
gnomic aorist verbs to describe and at the same time perform the
kind of poetry Callimachus prefers. And just as the meditative
stanzas of Tyrtaeus contrasted the brave man and the craven, these
verses compare and evaluate elegiac poetry in starkly opposed terms
such as the 'clear sound' of a cicada and the 'din' of an ass. If this
stanza were found alone (without the restoration at the start of line
28) on a tattered papyrus or in the manuscripts of a late Roman
florilegium, we might be tempted, as we are in the case of Mimnermus 1 and 2.1–10, to imagine that it was a complete poem that nicely
contrasts a heavy and light style of poetry and the heaviness of old
age and the lightness of youth. Even the underlined phrases at the
end of the first and last pentameters, although they are stripped from
the wider pattern of multiple responsions within the 'Prologue', work
extremely well within the single stanza to frame these contrasts
within the realm of φιλία. Callimachus sings for those who love the
better kinds of poetry, just as the Muses continue to love the elderly
poet who keeps singing such poetry.

The final couplet (37–38) moreover, regardless of its lost beginning, clearly brings the stanza to a climax, with a summary sweep
('For the Muses do not abandon...') that reverses the initial helplessness of the aged narrator. The feeling of closure here is further
intensified, as we saw earlier at the end of Callinus 1 and Xenophanes 2,
by the internal pentameter rhymes in the last two couplets: ὀλοῷ ...

Ἐγκελάδῳ (36) and πολιοὺς ... φίλους (38). Although there is little evidence among the few extant fragments that Mimnermus used such rhymes in his poetry, there seems to have been a tradition in the Hellenistic period that he did so. Hermesianax suggests, in fact, that Mimnermus invented them:[23]

> Μίμνερμος δὲ τὸν ἡδύν, ὃς εὕρετο πολλὸν ἀνατλὰς
> ἦχον καὶ μαλακοῦ πνεῦμα τὸ πενταμέτρου.

And Mimnermus, who after much suffering discovered the sweet echoing-sound and breath of the soft pentameter.

Despite the fact that Hermesianax often uses such medial rhymes in his work, it is difficult to resist the temptation in this case that he wishes us to hear the 'echoing-sound and breath' of Mimnermus' 'soft pentameter' precisely in the rhyme of μαλακοῦ and πενταμέτρου. Hermesianax, in short, appears to describe a notable and perhaps novel feature of Mimnerman verse (a rhyming echo in the pentameter) and at the same time cleverly demonstrates this echo with the word 'pentameter' itself. I suggest that Callimachus alludes to this same tradition, when he brings his own Mimnerman stanza to a close with the pair of pentameter rhymes in lines 36 and 38.[24] Thus here in the final stanza of his programmatic 'Prologue', where he at the start of the second stanza set forth the verses of Mimnermus as an important model for the best elegiac poetry, Callimachus seems to engage in the same kind of learned play as Hermesianax: he affirms his allegiance to Mimnermus by taking up the theme of old age, while at the same time playfully imitating the 'soft echo' of the old master in the final two couplets.[25]

---

[23] Powell (1925) Hermesianax, Fragment 7.35–36.

[24] In the 'Prologue', moreover, Callimachus, like Hermesianax, focuses on the sweetness of Mimnermus' shorter poems (11–12: Μίμνερμος ὅτι γλυκύς, αἱ κατὰ λεπτὸν [ῥήσεις] ἡ μεγάλη δ' οὐκ ἐδίδαξε γυνή), and then he deploys ἦχον, the same word that Hermesianax uses, in a similarly emphatic position at the end of the first hexameter of this last stanza (29–30: ἐνὶ τοῖς γὰρ ἀείδομεν οἳ λιγὺν ἦχον | τέττιγος, θ] ὅρυβον δ' οὐκ ἐφίλησαν ὄνων, where (as we have seen) it responds closely to the lines just quoted (11–12). Here, of course, the 'the clear ἦχον of the cicada,' is best understood in its more common meaning of 'sound' (as translated above), but nonetheless a sound that reverberates like that of a cicada.

[25] In the first couplet of this same elegiac stanza Callimachus contrasts the 'echo of the cicada' with the 'din of asses'. If the poet is, as I suggest, calling attention to his use

Finally, although it is quite beyond the scope of this study to offer a full and satisfying reading of a text as rich and as damaged as the 'Prologue', suffice it to say that it is entirely appropriate for Callimachus in this poem to adopt the critical elegiac tone of an elder upbraiding a group of contemporary or—perhaps more likely given the emphasis on his advanced age—younger poets, for this is precisely the role of a traditional elegiac poet, whether he gives advice to young men on war, politics, or affairs of the heart. One is reminded, for example, of the seal-poem at the start of the Theognidean 'Cyrnus Book' (19–38), where the poet recalls the time he learned proper behavior from his elders 'while still a youth' (28: παῖς ἔτ᾽ ἐών), and then goes on to teach these same things to Cyrnus in the second stanza (29–38).[26] Callimachus presents himself in similar fashion, I suggest, when he recalls what Apollo advised him, when as a young man he first began to compose poetry. Indeed, just as the Theognidean poet speaks the wise and presumably verbatim words of his elders in the stanza of traditional exhortation that follows the seal-poem, so, too, Callimachus quotes Apollo's advice directly and with a generic vocative 'o singer' (24: ἀοιδέ) that theoretically allows them to be repeated with each successive generation. In both cases, then, we are to imagine that the next generation of young men—the Telchines and the 'Cyrni'—are in some palpable way instructed directly by the teacher of the poet, whose advice is embedded directly in his song.

Callimachus has studied the archaic elegists carefully and his 'Prologue'—a tour de force of stanzaic technique—pays homage to them. His poem is, however, a product of the library, not the symposium, and his apparent revival of the style of long-dead poets like Mimnermus seems driven by a desire to rehabilitate the elegiac poetry of his day by imitating the best that archaic and classical poets have to offer. And he launches this revival in manner that is entirely appropriate to the genre of elegy: he imagines himself

of the pentameter rhyme in the final two pentameters of the 'Prologue', then it is perhaps significant that in his description of the 'anti-model' of the Telchines, he (playfully?) deploys a near-rhyme (in the first pentameter of the stanza) to describe the 'din of asses' (θ]όρυβον δ᾽ οὐκ ἐφίλησαν ὄνων), in a place where we might have expected a real one (cf. Callinus 1.13).

[26] Discussed earlier at the end of Section 3.1.

as an elder upbraiding and teaching a recalcitrant younger generation about what constitutes better or worse poetry. This is, I think, far different from Euripides' project, who at the end of the fifth century might also be said to archaize when he places in the mouth of Andromache a presumably older form of threnodic elegy. Euripides, however, was probably part of the last generation of poets who could have heard traditional elegies sung at symposia in Athens, and who may have even witnessed in his travels the kind of lament that Andromache sings. By bringing that lament to the Attic stage, however, he was not attempting to revive a lost art as Callimachus seems to do, but rather he was using and adapting to the stage yet another (barely) living song culture to enliven the tragic monodies for which he was justly famous. It is rather the case of one talented composer borrowing from the disappearing folk cultures of his day, somewhat in the manner that Chopin or Bartok imitated in their own music the forms of the eastern European folkdances. Callimachus, however, seems to be more conscious of great distance between the archaic poets and himself: they composed their stanzaic songs orally to the tune of an *aulos*, while in his encounter with Apollo Callimachus carefully places a wax tablet on his knees as he begins to inscribe his very first poem.

8

Conclusions

The five-couplet stanza appears to have been popular among early elegiac poets as a frame for a short poem or contribution to a sympotic performance, and also as a helpful unit for assembling longer compositions. Given the fragmentary evidence for early elegy, it is fruitless, of course, to invoke statistics in any probative way, but they do give us some sense, albeit *grosso modo*, of the importance of this feature. Of the extant fragments longer than four couplets it is remarkable how many are themselves either preserved as rhetorically complete and coherent five-couplet units or as longer stretches of two or more such stanzas. All of the longer fragments of Tyrtaeus (and probably Callinus 1, as well) seem to have been composed, at least originally, in five-couplet stanzas,[1] and among the fragments of Archilochean elegy only one sufficiently legible poem longer than four couplets survives and it is indeed a well-crafted stanza (Fragment 13).[2] The extant corpus of Mimner-

---

[1] As we saw in Section 3.1, Callinus 1 preserves one clearly coherent stanza at its end (lines 12–21), which is probably preceded by three and a half couplets from the end of another. Tyrtaeus 4 is itself a complete stanza (see Section 2.2) and his longer fragments (10, 11, and 12) contain eleven stanzas in total. Or to put it another way: of the 131 lines preserved in Tyrtaeus' longer poems 120 have survived in recognizable stanzaic form. I exclude from my count the Tyrtaeus papyri (Fragments 2 and 18–23), because they are too lacunose to allow any kind of close analysis, but Bowie (2001, 46–47) points out that Fragment 2—formed by the overlap of *POxy.* 2824 and a short quotation from Strabo 8.4.10—seems to begin with a section of exhortation (2–11, see 10: πειθώμεθα), followed by one of description or narrative (13–16). Since this second section begins with γάρ (13) and uses present and perfect indicative verbs, I suspect that this fragment might also have been part of a Tyrtaean poem composed in alternating stanzas, like Fragments 10 and 11.

[2] The recent publication of *POxy.* 4708 provides us with a tantalizing glimpse of a longer elegiac poem by Archilochus that mentions Telephus, Argives, and Trojans,

mus includes four longer fragments and of these, two are or contain well-designed stanzas (1 and 2), and a third includes a five-couplet digression from a longer poem (12).[3] Mimnermus 14, on the other hand, is an eleven-verse narrative fragment and shows no obvious signs of stanzaic boundaries. Of the four longer fragments of Solon, one is a complete stanza (24),[4] two use the elegiac stanza consistently as an important structural device (4 and 27),[5] and the last (13) has a stretch of three stanzaic catalogues at its centre.[6]

The *Theognidea* is, as we would expect, much more inconsistent. Of the forty-three lines that make up the beginning of the 'Cyrnus Book' (19–62) forty seem to be organized into elegiac stanzas.[7] The remaining four-fifths of the 'Cyrnus Book' (62–237), however, show a much smaller percentage of stanzas.[8] Solon 13 has a similarly odd mixture of three well-designed and continuous stanzas (the catalogues in lines 33–62) that are preceded and followed by a total of forty-eight verses that show almost no signs of the five-couplet stanza.[9] This is not, of course, unexpected, since, despite the ingenuity

---

and describes a river choked with corpses and a battle scene. It is either a mythological narrative or (more likely) part of an extended mythological exemplum. See Obbink (2006) for text and discussion. Although Fragment 1 of the papyrus is fifteen verses long, it is very damaged, missing the beginning and end of nearly every line and without any scholia to help with reconstruction. If it is composed in stanzas, I cannot tell.

[3] For the stanzaic architecture of Mimnermus 12, see Appendix I.

[4] Solon 24 and *Theognidea* 719–28 seem to record different performances of the same five-couplet elegiac poem that all editors treat as a complete poem.

[5] As we saw in Section 2.3, Solon 27 seems to have originally been two stanzas in length, but it has lost a single couplet that originally described the eighth hebdomad. Solon 4 has a coherent stanza at its start and finish, and has traces of two others in the lacunose middle of the poem; see Appendix II.

[6] Solon 13.33–62, for which see Section 2.3.

[7] The five-couplet stanzas include: 19–28, 29–38, 39–48, and 53–62; see above Sections 3.1 and 4.2 for discussion.

[8] 119–28, 133–42, and 183–92, which add up to thirty verses out of a total of 175. For the stanzaic design of 133–42, see Appendix III. Of the more than 1,100 verses that come after the 'Cyrnus Book' (255 ff.), only 110 are obviously composed in five-couplet stanzas: 341–50 (the prayer to Zeus discussed in Section 2.2); 429–38; 467–96 (the three symposium poems in Section 4.1); 657–66; 699–718 (the Sisyphus poem in Section 4.2); 773–82 (the prayer to Apollo in Section 2.3); 993–1002; 1135–44; 1341–50 (the Ganymede poem in Section 2.3)

[9] Weil (1862, 2–6) argued that all of Solon 13, except the final six-couplets, was composed in stanzas of four couplets each, but he was incorrect in this judgement, as

of some modern commentators, the unity and consistent authorship of both the *Theognidea* (even the 'Cyrnus Book') and of Solon 13 has been suspected on account of their internal disorder and discontinuities of thought, which seem to reflect more of the flotsam and jetsam of centuries of excerption, collection, and reproduction, than the unmitigated original design of a single author.[10] After the archaic period our evidence for new stanzaic compositions is slim. Indeed, aside from the six-couplet stanzas of Xenophanes and the Euripidean lament in the *Andromache*, original compositions in elegiac stanzas seem to disappear from the extant poetic repertoire.[11] Nearly all of the extant longer fragments of Xenophanes' contemporary Simonides are too lacunose for this kind of analysis, although Fragment 11 does show faint traces of a pair of coordinated stanzas

my analysis of the centre of the poem (33–62) demonstrates (see Section 2.3). It is true, however, that if we remove these three catalogue-stanzas, we are left with a series of five possible four-couplet stanzas, followed by a single three-couplet one. Nonetheless, because ancient authors clearly agree that the opening prayer to the Muses was by Solon, I suggest below that the first thirty-two lines of Solon 13 are probably genuine, but badly truncated or abbreviated by Stobaeus or his scribes.

[10] Excepting his assumption of a biographically discrete 'Theognis', few scholars would nowadays disagree with Gerber's description (1999, 7) of the *Theognidea* as 'an anthology containing genuine works of Theognis, selections from other elegists (e.g. Tyrtaeus, Mimnermus, Solon) and anonymous poems, together with numerous verses repeated throughout the corpus, usually with some slight variation'. With regard to Solon 13, Linforth (1919, 112) summed up 19th-cent. scholarship as follows: 'Some have found in it nothing but an aggregation of disjointed scraps; others have regarded it as a splendid work of genius.' According to Gerber (1970) not much had changed in a half century: 'Some have argued that only part or parts of it are genuine, the rest being excerpts from different gnomic writers rather carelessly joined together. Other have put forth a variety of theories in an attempt to explain the sequence of ideas.' Both Linforth and Gerber were, in fact, fairly staunch unitarians, as has generally been the trend in Anglo-American and German scholarship—see Mülke (2002) 232–35—but they understood that a wide range of opinions prevailed. I assumed the unity of Solon 13 as a given, until my research on the stanzaic architecture of elegy suggested otherwise; in reviewing the scholarship, it seems to me that in the end the 'Italian school' had it right from the very beginning; see e.g. Romagnoli (1898, 55–57), Perotta (1924), and Maddalena (1943, 12), who argue that Solon 13 is a 'cento' of different elegies, beginning with some that were Solon's and ending with some that were not: see my detailed discussion below in this chapter. See Lardinois (2006) on the whole question of the authenticity of Solonic verses.

[11] Of course, a discovery of a papyrus containing a sizable section of a longer lost elegiac poem like Antimachus' famous *Lyde* (late 5th cent.) could instantly change this perception.

(see the start of Chapter 6). Some short poems by Evenus (8a and c) and Ion of Chios (27) likewise suggest that the tradition may have lingered in the context of the symposium as well. It is clear, then, that although the five-couplet stanza was an important feature of early elegiac poetics, its importance dwindled during the fifth century, probably, as I have suggested throughout this study, around the same time that elegy is separated from its musical accompaniment.

It remains, then, to sum up the salient features of the elegiac stanza. Like most early Greek poets, the elegists made frequent use of ring-composition in individual stanzas and at the beginning and end of larger structures as well, such as the coordinated pairs of stanzas used by Solon and Xenophanes, the three-stanza run in Tyrtaeus 10, or, grandest of all, in the four-stanza frame of Tyrtaeus 12.[12] In this study I have, moreover, tried to isolate a number of other typical features that are crucial for identifying the elegiac stanza. With regard to the internal structure of the individual stanza, for example, we saw how Archilochus 13, Mimnermus 1, and other fragments exhibit a tell-tale twist in the very middle that unsettles the stanza and lends it a peculiar A–B shape. Also popular, especially in the *Theognidea*, is the single-stanza poem with a four-plus-one format: four lines of meditation capped by a single exhortation. The early elegists, moreover, often use stanzas to frame rhetorical set-pieces, which in turn display their own idiosyncratic features. Catalogues and priamels, for instance, often devote one regular end-stopped couplet to each item on the list, while prayers are often framed by the name of a god at the beginning and end of the stanza. Stanza-long digressions, like the one on Sisyphus' κατάβασις (*Theognidea* 703–12), are somewhat more complicated.[13]

Another notable feature of stanzaic composition is the frequent combination of stanzas into linked pairs. Sometimes these pairs connect a stanza of exhortation with one of meditation that explains or defends (γάρ) the exhortation (for example, the first two stanzas of Tyrtaeus 10), or in reversed order, where the meditation provides the rationale or trigger for the advice, which follows (Tyrtaeus 11.1–20 or

[12] See e.g. Fowler (1987) 64–82 *passim*.
[13] See the beginning of Ch. 5 and Appendix I for discussion.

Theognidea 19–38). Tyrtaeus 12 and the fragments of Solon, on the other hand, produce a different pattern, since they are almost entirely meditative or descriptive and the paired stanzas within them tend to be aligned, balanced and contrasted by formal responsion. The pattern is perhaps best illustrated by the poetry of Solon, where we find a number of continuous ten-couplet meditations composed as independent stanzas that are nonetheless closely linked by parallel structure and responsion, for example, the catalogue of the ages of man (Solon 27), which subtly compares the physical development of a boy's body in the first half of life (1–10) with the evolution of a mature man's cognitive and rhetorical skills in the second half (11–18). Likewise in the catalogue of vocations in Solon 13, which is designed as two elegiac stanzas (43–52 and 53–62) closely linked by the sixfold reiteration of various forms of the pronoun ἄλλος, each placed at the start of a hexameter. But here, too, Solon carefully distinguishes the individual stanzas by differences in content and structure, in the first stanza adapting the form of a priamel, which subtly praises the poet's vocation, while in the second focusing on the special gifts and limitations of the god-given roles of seer and healer.

Some evidence suggests, moreover, that when stanzas are composed in coordinated pairs, the internal boundary between them is felt to be weaker than the external boundary between pairs. We saw, for example, that the poet who re-performed the extant version of Tyrtaeus 12 overran the boundary between the first pair of stanzas (1–10 and 11–20), but not the boundary that separated this pair from the one that followed. Since, as we have seen, the sympotic tradition of performing elegy in the round probably admitted both single- and double-stanza contributions, I suspect that some post-archaic re-performers began to think in terms of two-stanza units and were less concerned about preserving the internal boundary between them. This tendency is, I think, nicely illustrated by the Theognidean poem with the long digression on Sisyphus: the poet who improvised this coherent ten-couplet poem completely ignores the division between stanzas, but nonetheless seems to respect the idea that the ten-couplet stanza is an appropriate length for an elegiac poem.

At the beginning of this study, I asked a few questions that my students had posed to me: What was the length of a typical elegiac poem? Which of the surviving fragments are complete poems? How did elegiac poets mark the beginning and end of their compositions? What formal devices did these poets use to lend internal structure to their poems? As we can now see more clearly, the answers to these questions are, in fact, all connected in one way or another with the use of the elegiac stanza. There are, for instance, a number of examples from the archaic period of brilliant and striking compositions of a single stanza—Mimnermus and Archilochus come to mind—which are either complete poems or sections of a longer poem or of a cycle of contributions recited in turn around the symposium. The symposiarch-poems and the city-poems suggest, moreover, that poets and singers at symposia could compose and improvise single-stanza poems that address common themes and even take a generic form, while at the same time correcting or disagreeing in various subtle and not so subtle ways with compositions on similar themes. There is, in short, little reason to doubt the existence of the complete five-couplet elegiac poem or sympotic contribution, although in the case of any individual five-couplet fragment, like Archilochus 13 or Mimnermus 1, we will never know for certain whether they are short poems of this type or stanzas belonging to a longer composition. The survival, moreover, of rhetorically well-rounded two-stanza fragments concerned with the symposium, such as Xenophanes 1 or the Theognidean 'Seal-Poem', suggest that at some symposia the length of each contribution could be doubled in size.

It is, however, more difficult to say for certain if any of our extant fragments stood at the beginning or end of a longer poem. In the past, the appearance of so-called continuative particles at the start of an elegiac fragment—for example: δέ, ἀλλά, and γάρ—suggested to some that it must have been extracted from the midst of a longer poem, but in recent times scholars have come to an understanding that such particles could very well appear at the beginning of a discrete elegiac poem, especially if it was thought to be part of a longer group performance at a symposium. Knowledge of stanzaic design helps us to enlarge and fine-tune these observations. We have seen, for example, that γάρ frequently appears at the start of a meditative stanza and ἀλλά (and occasionally τοι) at the start of an exhortation or a prayer. Other stanzas begin without such particles.

The sympotic contribution of Ion of Chios and the similar composition preserved on the Elephantine papyrus, for instance, both begin
with a bare imperative (χαιρέτω and χαίρετε) and the Theognidean
poet, especially in the 'Cyrnus Book', seems to start new poems with
an initial vocative (e.g. Κύρνε at lines 19, 39, and 53). It is, however,
impossible to document this as a regular tendency. Tyrtaeus 10, for
example, begins with a meditation introduced by γάρ, Tyrtaeus 11
with a series of imperatives introduced by ἀλλά, and Tyrtaeus 12 (an
entirely meditative poem) with a long conditional sentence that is
introduced without any particle at all! The only two cases of vocatives
in the Tyrtaean fragments, moreover, fall in the middle of their
stanzas, not at the start (10.15: ὦ νέοι and 11.35: ὦ γυμνῆτες). As
modern readers we may instinctively feel that the vigorous opening
lines of Tyrtaeus 11 ('Come, take courage, for your stock is from
unconquered Heracles!') would make an excellent beginning to a
longer martial elegy, but we cannot be sure.

Occasionally later authors tell us or imply that a fragment comes
from the very beginning of a poem, information that can sometimes
be confirmed by patterns of quotation. Clement of Alexandria
(6.11.1), for example, tells us that Solon's invocation of the Muses
(Fragment 13.1–6) stood at the beginning of the poem from which
they came, and since Crates (Fragment 1) begins an elegiac parody
with this same prayer, there seems to be solid ground for asserting
that these verses mark the start of Solon 13. But such evidence is hard
to come by, and even more so for the ends of poems. I can suggest—
as I have from time to time in this study—that elegiac poets often use
devices, such as ring-composition, as well as linguistic markers for
explanation (γάρ) and summary (οὕτως) to mark the close of an
individual stanza, but we have no reliable way of knowing when the
end of a stanza coincides with the end of a poem. We have noted a
few special cases where internal pentameter-rhymes are deployed in
two successive couplets at the end of a stanza and may serve (to
borrow a term from Herrnstein-Smith) as a 'terminal modification'
that signals to the audience that the poem is about to end.[14] English

---

[14] Herrnstein-Smith (1968, 44–46 and 51–52) discusses various forms of 'terminal
modification' at the ends of English songs and sonnets.

and Italian poets, for example, often use rhymed couplets as a regular marker of closure,[15] and Shakespeare even uses such rhymed couplets in his plays to signal the end of a scene.[16] Greek elegiac poets used other kinds of terminal modifications. Callinus, for example, enhanced the effect of the pentameter rhymes in the last two couplets of his Fragment 1 by also placing spondaic *hemiepe* at the beginning of each of the last four verses. The final stanza of Tyrtaeus 12 ends with spondaic rhythms and Solon likewise uses spondaic first feet in the final five verses of the 'Eunomia' fragment (4.35–39).[17] Xenophanes 1 ends in similar fashion, as does the final stanza of the Callimachean 'Prologue', the stanza that seems most influenced by Mimnermus. The combination, then, of these specifically elegiac forms of terminal modification, along with a satisfying sense of rhetorical closure in all of these fragments, at least, suggests that they may have stood at the very end of a longer composition.

My teacher and friend Jack Winkler, the second dedicatee of this study, once identified two basic kinds of scholarly books. There are those, for example, that aim at being the last word on a well-worn subject, in which the ultimate goal is explicitly or implicitly to close down an area of scholarly discourse forever by providing the best and irrefutable argument. But then there are those that aim to open a new or inactive area of inquiry by asking new questions and encouraging renewed debate with the expectation that some or even all of the arguments presented must in the end be refined or even abandoned. It should be clear at this point, if not earlier, that this study belongs to the latter category and that in attempting to revive, enlarge, and

---

[15] See Herrnstein-Smith (1968) 51–52, for the rhyming couplet that brings to a halt the forward motion of the English sonnet. Rutherford (1997, 56–57) draws a neat parallel between Herrnstein-Smith's 'epigrammatic ending' of the rhymed couplet of a sonnet and a type of Pindaric ending (e.g. the end of *Nemean* 8), which involves a terse μέν–δέ comparison that is coordinated with the metre.

[16] My colleague David Bevington kindly offers some examples of scenes that end with a rhymed couplet: *Love's Labors Lost* 5.1; *Comedy of Errors* 3.1; *A Midsummer Night's Dream* 3.1, and *Hamlet* 4.3 and 4.4. There are three rhymed couplets at the end of *Romeo and Juliet* 2.2.

[17] See van Raalte (1988) 148 n. 8 for the effect of the spondaic *hemiepe* at the end of Callinus 1 and Tyrtaeus 12. I discuss the last stanza in Solon 4 in Appendix II.

strengthen Weil's theory of the elegiac 'strophe', I endeavour to shift scholarly attention away from the content of archaic elegiac poetry and towards a fuller and more sustained inquiry into its basic poetic architecture and how over the centuries this architecture changed and adapted to new circumstances of performance, improvisation, and revival.

Elegiac Digressions (Mimnermus 12)

We saw in Chapter 5 how the Theognidean poet uses a five-couplet stanza to frame a digression in the midst of an ongoing poem: the description of Sisyphus' journey to Hades (699–718) that was inserted into the middle of a priamel. I suggest that Mimnermus 12 was deployed in similar fashion and I print the eleven-line fragment below to reflect this suggestion:

> Ἠέλιος μὲν γὰρ ἔλαχεν πόνον ἤματα πάντα,
> οὐδέ ποτ' ἄμπαυσις γίνεται οὐδεμία
> ἵπποισίν τε καὶ αὐτῷ, ἐπὴν ῥοδοδάκτυλος Ἠὼς
> Ὠκεανὸν προλιποῦσ' οὐρανὸν εἰσαναβῇ.
> τὸν μὲν γὰρ διὰ κῦμα φέρει πολυήρατος εὐνή,   5
> κοιίλη, Ἡφαίστου χερσὶν ἐληλαμένη,
> χρυσοῦ τιμήεντος, ὑπόπτερος, ἄκρον ἐφ' ὕδωρ
> εὕδονθ' ἁρπαλέως χώρου ἀφ' Ἑσπερίδων
> γαῖαν ἐς Αἰθιόπων, ἵνα δὴ θοὸν ἄρμα καὶ ἵπποι
> ἑστᾶσ', ὄφρ' Ἠὼς ἠριγένεια μόλῃ·   10
> ἔνθ' ἐπέβη ἑτέρων ὀχέων Ὑπερίονος υἱός.

For the Sun's lot is toil every day and there is never any respite for him and his horses, from the moment rose-fingered Dawn leaves Oceanus and goes up into the sky. A lovely bed, hollow, forged by the hands of Hephaestus, of precious gold and winged, carries him, as he sleeps soundly, over the waves on the water's surface from the place of the Hesperides to the land of the Ethiopians, where his swift chariot and horses stand until early-born Dawn comes.

There the son of Hyperion mounts his other vehicle.

The first ten verses are a nicely constructed stanza framed by a skilful bit of ring-composition that focuses on the movements of Dawn (Eos) and the presence of Helios' horses:

> οὐδέ ποτ' ἄμπαυσις γίνεται οὐδεμία
> ἵπποισίν τε καὶ αὐτῷ, ἐπὴν ῥοδοδάκτυλος Ἠὼς
> Ὠκεανὸν προλιποῦσ' οὐρανὸν εἰσαναβῇ. (2–4)
>
> γαῖαν ἐς Αἰθιόπων, ἵνα δὴ θοὸν ἄρμα καὶ ἵπποι
> ἑστᾶσ', ὄφρ' Ἠὼς ἠριγένεια μόλῃ· (9–10)

Helios cannot, it seems, stop working once Dawn ascends to the sky nor can he begin working the next morning until she arrives. Her importance is oddly underscored by the fact that the verbs describing her movements (εἰσαναβῇ and μόλῃ), although placed in syntactically subordinate temporal clauses in the two sentences, appear in the two most emphatic positions in the stanza: the only two points where sentence- and couplet-end coincide. And she alone of all the other gods mentioned in this fragment (Helios, Oceanus, Hephaestus, the Hesperides) is described twice in what appears to be a split rendition of her most traditional Homeric epithet.[1]

Mimnermus begins the fragment with an explanation, presumably of something that was just mentioned in the previous lines: 'For (γὰρ) the Sun has got toil as his share all his days…' and for the next nine verses, he describes the repeated routine of Helios in a series of present- and perfect-tense verbs. The first five couplets, in short, seem to share some of the features of the meditative stanzas described earlier in Section 3.1. The eleventh and final line of this fragment, however, with its aorist verb and the demonstrative adverb ἔνθα—'In *that* place (i.e. Ethiopia) the son of Hyperion mounts his other vehicle'—seems oddly concrete in comparison, and I suggest that it marks the beginning of a new stanza, one that perhaps returns to some ongoing narrative about nighttime, about Helios or about Ethiopia, the place whence he departs to the sky.[2] But regardless of the main narrative, this fragment is organized precisely like the digression on Sisyphus, which likewise interrupts an ongoing catalogue of heroes to insert a full stanza of narrative about his exploits in the underworld. Indeed, in both cases we observe a different kind of responsion than we saw earlier—one that might prove unique to stanza-long digressions, if only we had more comparanda.

Elsewhere in extant archaic elegy, when poets repeat a significant proper name, they most often do so in ring-composition within the confines of a stanza to provide internal ring-composition to the stanza itself, as for example in the Theognidean prayers to Zeus and Apollo, or the Delphic oracle described and quoted in Tyrtaeus 4 (all discussed in Section 3.3). As a result, if the stanza is removed from the longer poem in which it sits, the ring-composition remains intact. In the two cases of stanzaic digression

---

[1] Allen (1993, 141) notes how Mimnermus takes a well-established Homeric formula—ἦμος δ' ἠριγένεια φάνη ῥοδοδάκτυλος Ἠώς—and splits it in half, placing the last half at the end of line 3 (i.e. in its usual formulaic spot) and the first part near the end of line 10.

[2] Some scholars connect this fragment with Mimnermus 11 and 11a, which refer to the sun and the Golden Fleece in Aeetes' palace. They suggest that all three fragments are from a lost poem on Jason's journey, but the connections are slim. See Allen (1993) 99 and Barron and Easterling (1989) 93.

discussed here, however, the proper names appear to respond to each other from adjoining stanzas. Helios, for example, appears in the first line of the digression (1) and in the first line of the continuing narrative as 'the son of Hyperion' (11). This sequence is reversed, however, in the case of the digression on Sisyphus, for he is named in the last line before it (*Theognidea* 702) and then five couplets later in the last line of the digression itself (712).

Thus, it seems that in stanzaic composition the word or name that triggers a digression is treated not as the initial part of a ring-composition, but rather as the first of two responding couplets that set up parallel structures in successive stanzas. In both of the digressions under discussion, then, the poet finds another focus for the ring-composition that holds the stanza together. In the case of the Theognidean poem, the poet could not use Sisyphus' name to bracket the stanza-long digression itself, and instead we saw how he creates vigorous internal ring-composition around another detail (703 and 711–12): how the hero used his famous cleverness to escape from Hades. Mimnermus 12 works in similar fashion, except that the repetition of the god's name appears in the first, rather than the last couplet of the adjoining stanzas. In this case Mimnermus makes Eos and Helios' horses the focal points for the internal ring-composition of the stanza. I suspect, moreover, that Mimnermus may have crafted this digression with a playful and metapoetic wink at the technique of ring-composition itself, for Helios' daily journey takes him on a circuit that begins and ends at the very same place (Ethiopia) at which this stanza-long digression begins and ends.

Solon 4 ('Eunomia')

Solon 4, the so-called 'Eunomia' fragment, begins with a five-couplet section that frets, like the two Theognidean city-poems, about the future of 'our city' (1: ἡμετέρη δὲ πόλις) and expresses fears that both the citizens (6: ἀστοί) and the leaders (7: ἡγεμόνες) are acting in a manner that will doom the city.[1] I suggested at the end of Section 4.2 that this initial stanza probably takes the form of a generic 'city-poem': a pessimistic statement about the possible destruction of the city, followed by a close analysis of the sociological problems that are causing it. The two Theognidean versions seem to have been single contributions to a sympotic performance or perhaps as the first half of a coordinated pair of stanzas. The stanza at the start of Solon 4, on the other hand, introduces a much longer analysis and narrative of social decline, followed by a single stanza that proclaims the benefits of 'Good rule' (Eunomia).

The eighteen lines between the initial and final stanzas are in fact ruined, like the beginning of Callinus 1, by lacunae, but given Solon's use of stanzaic architecture elsewhere, we can speculate cautiously about the wider structure of Fragment 4. If we skip over for the moment the complete break in syntax before and after line 11, we can just barely make out the wreck of a coordinated pair of stanzas in the lines that follow (4.12–29):[2]

$$< \quad . \quad . \quad . \quad . \quad . \quad . \quad . \quad . \quad . \quad >$$

οὔθ' ἱερῶν κτεάνων οὔτε τι δημοσίων
φειδόμενοι κλέπτουσιν ἀφαρπαγῇ ἄλλοθεν ἄλλος,
οὐδὲ φυλάσσονται σεμνὰ Δίκης θέμεθλα,
15   ἣ σιγῶσα σύνοιδε τὰ γιγνόμενα πρό τ' ἐόντα,
τῷ δὲ χρόνῳ πάντως ἦλθ' ἀποτεισομένη.

---

[1] Quoted by Demosthenes 19.254–56. Fränkel (1975, 220) quotes and discusses lines 1–10 as a discrete rhetorical unit.

[2] The diamond brackets are mine and indicate a lacuna of a single verse in each stanza. Most editors are agnostic as to the length of the lacunae, and indeed the one before line 12 could be longer than the one line I have indicated above. I have not printed or translated line 11, a pentameter that stands isolated in our texts by lacunae before and after it.

τοῦτ᾽ ἤδη πάσῃ πόλει ἔρχεται ἕλκος ἄφυκτον,
ἐς δὲ κακὴν ταχέως ἤλυθε δουλοσύνην,
ἣ στάσιν ἔμφυλον πόλεμόν θ᾽ εὕδοντ᾽ ἐπεγείρει,
ὃς πολλῶν ἐρατὴν ὤλεσεν ἡλικίην·   20

ἐκ γὰρ δυσμενέων ταχέως πολυήρατον ἄστυ
τρύχεται ἐν συνόδοις τοῖς ἀδικέουσι φίλαις.
ταῦτα μὲν ἐν δήμῳ στρέφεται κακά· τῶν δὲ πενιχρῶν
ἱκνέονται πολλοὶ γαῖαν ἐς ἀλλοδαπὴν
πραθέντες δεσμοῖσί τ᾽ ἀεικελίοισι δεθέντες   25
       <   .   .   .   .   >
οὕτω δημόσιον κακὸν ἔρχεται οἴκαδ᾽ ἑκάστῳ,
αὔλειοι δ᾽ ἔτ᾽ ἔχειν οὐκ ἐθέλουσι θύραι,
ὑψηλὸν δ᾽ ὑπὲρ ἕρκος ὑπέρθορεν, εὗρε δὲ πάντως,
εἰ καί τις φεύγων ἐν μυχῷ ᾖ θαλάμου.

... sparing neither sacred nor private property, they steal with rapaciousness,
one from one source, one from another, and they have no regard for the august
foundations of Justice, who bears silent witness to the present and the past and
who in time assuredly comes to exact retribution. This is now coming upon the
whole city as an inescapable wound and the city has quickly approached
wretched slavery, which arouses civil strife and slumbering war, the loss for
many of their lovely youth.

For at the hands of its enemies the much-loved city is being swiftly worn down
amid conspiracies dear to the unjust. These are the evils that are rife among the
people, and many of the poor are going to a foreign land, sold and bound in
shameful fetters (25) ... And so the public evil comes home to each man and the
courtyard gates no longer have the will to hold it back, but it leaps over the high
barrier and assuredly finds him out, even if he takes refuge in an innermost
corner of his room

These lines are devoted to the pessimistic description of the poorly ruled city
and they are entirely meditative, switching back and forth between present
and gnomic aorist verbs.

The second stanza is better preserved. At line 21 Solon seems to begin a
section of explanation with γάρ, which, as we have seen, often marks the
start of a new stanza of meditation. And if we posit the loss of only one
pentameter after line 25, lines 21–29 comprise a rhetorically balanced stanza,
in which the adverb οὕτω at the beginning of the final sentence provides a
summary statement about the outcome of the 'conspiracies' mentioned at
the beginning of the stanza (22). Solon, moreover, frames the stanza by
echoing the second hexameter (23: ταῦτα μὲν ἐν δήμῳ στρέφεται κακά) with
a similar phrase in the fourth (26: οὕτω δημόσιον κακὸν ἔρχεται), common

points for ring-composition within the elegiac stanza.[3] There are similar reasons to suspect that the preceding lines (12–20) also constitute a full stanza, whose first hexameter has disappeared into the lacuna between lines 11 and 12. Firstly, Solon places medial rhymes in what I take to be the first and last pentameters of the stanza (12: κτεάνων ... δημοσίων and 20: ἐρατὴν ... ἡλικίην), an occasional feature of stanzaic construction that we have seen before.[4] This stanza is, moreover, formally unified by the repetition of the feminine relative pronouns at the beginning of lines 15 and 19, which describe the actions of the two abstract personifications at work in Athenian society: justice and slavery. Solon sets these descriptions in parallel motion by making them each the subjects of echoing and similarly structured pentameters: τῷ δὲ χρόνῳ πάντως ἦλθ᾽ ἀποτεισομένη (16) and ἐς δὲ κακὴν ταχέως ἤλυθε δουλοσύνην (18).[5] These verses are effective because they contrast deeply the roles of justice and slavery, and capture in a few succinct lines the continuous and nightmarish slide from slavery (18) to civil crisis and armed conflict (19) to the complete annihilation of the youth of Athens (20).

Taken individually these proposed internal markers of stanzaic structure in lines 13–29 are admittedly weaker than most discussed in this volume, but our view of the overall architecture of the fragment has undoubtedly been hampered by the loss of a single verse from each stanza, especially at the start of the first stanza, since the initial hexameter is so often involved in both ring-composition and responsion. But here, as elsewhere, the wider relationship between these two stanzas suggests that Solon composed them as a coordinated pair, which compares the public and private dangers that loom ominously before the people of Athens. In the fourth hexameter of the second stanza, for example, Solon, like Tyrtaeus in the second half of his Fragment 12, sets up a triple responsion:[6]

[3] Here the obvious echo in content and vocabulary is enhanced by a subtler than usual parallel in the prosody of the verses, which both have a penthemimeral caesura and a strong sense pause at the bucolic diaeresis, in between which we find the main verb and its subject: στρέφεται κακα (23) and κακὸν ἔρχεται (26).

[4] The rhyme in the final pentameter also echoes the ending of the final word in the preceding pentameter (δουλοσύνην).

[5] Note especially the similarities of sound and sense between πάντως ἦλθ᾽ (16) and ταχέως ἤλυθε (18), both of which straddle the mid-line diaeresis of their pentameters, and the placement of words with the feminine ending -η at the end of the last three couplets: ἀποτεισομένη (16); δουλοσύνην (18); and ἡλικίην (20), the last of which (as we noted earlier) is echoed in the rhyme in the final pentameter (20: ἐρατὴν and ἡλικίην).

[6] Siegman (1975, 276–77), Fowler (1987, 79), and Mülke (2002, 143) all note these verbal echoes. See the end of Ch. 5 for discussion of the triple responsion in Tyrtaeus 12, between the second and fourth stanza of one stanza (lines 37 and 41–42) and the fourth stanza of the preceding stanza (27).

τοῦτ᾽ ἤδη πάσῃ πόλει ἔρχεται ἕλκος ἄφυκτον (17 = 4th couplet)

('This is now coming upon the whole city as an inescapable wound')

ταῦτα μὲν ἐν δήμῳ στρέφεται κακά (23 = 2nd couplet)

('These are the evils that are rife among the people')

οὕτω δημόσιον κακὸν ἔρχεται οἴκαδ᾽ ἑκάστῳ (26 = 4th couplet)

('In this way the public evil comes home to each man')

We saw earlier how the fourth hexameter in the second of the two stanzas (26) echoed the language of the second hexameter (23) and thereby created ring-composition within the stanza, but now we can see that line 26 also recalls the syntax and wording of the corresponding fourth hexameter (17) in the preceding stanza. These two responding hexameters begin with a summary term (τοῦτ᾽ and οὕτω) that stands at the start of the final sentence of the stanza, a sentence which then runs on for two full couplets. The verb ἔρχεται, moreover, falls in the same metrical position and in both cases has a rather vague, neuter singular subject (ἕλκος and κακὸν). These verses draw attention, of course, to the thematic parallels between the two stanzas (both imagine the advent of some kind of relentless evil), but at the same time they highlight, as responding elegiac verses often do, the different public and private destinations of the impending disaster: the 'whole city' in the first stanza (πάσῃ πόλει ἔρχεται) and the home of each individual citizen in the second (ἔρχεται οἴκαδ᾽ ἑκάστῳ).[7] Solon also takes great care to distinguish these two stanzas stylistically from each other: in the first he uses four abstract political terms—justice, slavery, civil discord, and war—to describe the impending doom, whereas in the second he avoids such abstract terms entirely, and instead he imagines the threat first in the vivid image of the poor sold in chains to a foreign land (23–25) and then in very concrete, architectural terms, as he describes disaster overleaping the walls and penetrating the inner chambers of private houses.

The final ten lines of Solon 4 also appear to be an autonomous and well-knit stanza (30–39):[8]

> ταῦτα διδάξαι θυμὸς Ἀθηναίους με κελεύει,   30
> ὡς κακὰ πλεῖστα πόλει Δυσνομίη παρέχει.
> Εὐνομίη δ᾽ εὔκοσμα καὶ ἄρτια πάντ᾽ ἀποφαίνει,
> καὶ θαμὰ τοῖς ἀδίκοις ἀμφιτίθησι πέδας·

---

[7] Siegman (1975) 277.

[8] Campbell (1983, 94) and Irwin (2005, 183–93) discuss these ten lines as a discrete unit, and Adkins (1985, 128) suggests in passing that these lines 'if preserved with no context would have had the air of a complete poem'.

τραχέα λειαίνει, παύει κόρον, ὕβριν ἀμαυροῖ,
35   αὐαίνει δ' ἄτης ἄνθεα φυόμενα,
    εὐθύνει δὲ δίκας σκολιάς, ὑπερήφανά τ' ἔργα
    πραΰνει· παύει δ' ἔργα διχοστασίης,
    παύει δ' ἀργαλέης ἔριδος χόλον, ἔστι δ' ὑπ' αὐτῆς
    πάντα κατ' ἀνθρώπους ἄρτια καὶ πινυτά.

This is what my heart bids me teach the Athenians: that Lawlessness brings the city countless ills. But Lawfulness reveals all that is orderly and fitting, and often places fetters round the unjust. She makes the rough smooth, puts a stop to excess, weakens insolence, dries up the blooming flowers of ruin, straightens out crooked judgments, tames deeds of pride, and puts an end to acts of sedition and to the anger of grievous strife. Under her all things among men are fitting and rational.

Solon begins with a backward-looking pronoun in asyndeton (ταῦτα) that summarizes the preceding material—the long description of the evils that Dysnomia ('Lawlessness') is producing in the city,[9] in much the same way that Tyrtaeus, for example, uses οὕτως (11) at the beginning of the second stanza of Fragment 10 to summarize the previous discussion of the craven and homeless warrior, whom he has just finished describing.

In the remaining four couplets of this final stanza Solon contrasts the looming troubles of Dysnomia (ταῦτα) with the potential benefits of Eunomia, using ring-composition to bracket his description of the latter with two similarly global assertions: εὔκοσμα καὶ ἄρτια πάντ' in the second line (32) and πάντα...ἄρτια καὶ πινυτά in the last (39).[10] The intervening verses (33–38) describe the beneficial actions of Eunomia, using eight present-tense verbs, nearly all of which are spondaic and have a soothing effect thanks to the proliferation of diphthongs and long vowels: λειαίνει, παύει (three times), ἀμαυροῖ, αὐαίνει, εὐθύνει and πραΰνει.[11] And, like the sonorous pentameters

---

[9] In the fragment, as it is preserved, the pronoun ταῦτα presumably refers to all of the material from line 5 onward, but again the intervening lacunae leave this to the realm of hypothesis. For the asyndeton at the start of the stanza with a backward-looking demonstrative ταῦτα, see Denniston (1954) xliv. The syntax of the first couplet is not entirely clear. West (1992) and Gerber (1999) place a comma at the end of it (line 31) and presumably understand that all of the remaining verses are part of the indirect discourse signaled by the opening lines ταῦτα διδάξαι θυμὸς Ἀθηναίους με κελεύει | ὡς.... I have, however, followed Adkins (1985) and Mülke (2002) in replacing the comma with a stronger pause stop in both the Greek and English versions, and beginning a new sentence at the start of line 32. With either form of punctuation, however, these five couplets form a sensible stanza. For further discussion, see e.g. Jaeger (1966) 96, van Groningen (1958) 51–56, Gerber (1970) 133–34, and Adkins (1985) 121–22.

[10] Gerber (1970) 134.

[11] Jaeger (1966) 96–97 and Campbell (1983) 94.

in the final stanza of Callinus 1, the placement of all of these verbs at the beginning of four of the last five verses suggests that this stanza may have been the conclusion to the poem itself.[12] Thematic considerations, in fact, support this suggestion, since this stanza also recalls and in deliberate fashion negates or reverses many of the specific ills described in the foregoing verses.[13]

We might, then, outline—albeit very tentatively given the lacunose nature of the fragment—the stanzaic organization of Solon 4 as follows:

[lines 1–10] The Solonian city-poem
<Lacuna of at least one stanza that includes the isolated line 11>
[lines 12–20] Threat to the whole city [missing first hexameter]
[lines 21–29] Threat to individual homes [missing third pentameter]
[lines 30–39] Summation and optimistic discussion of Eunomia

As we have seen in other long fragments, these stanzas are distinguished from each other both thematically and stylistically. The first, as we have seen, seems to be a generic set-piece, a 'city-poem' of which we have two other Theognidean examples, and the two middle stanzas contrast thematically the different civic and private destinations of disaster. The final stanza is devoted almost entirely to a description of Eunomia and is stylistically marked by a profusion of spondee-shaped verbs that impress upon the audience the serenity of a well-ruled city. There are hints, moreover, of an alternating pattern among the last three stanzas: the second and the fourth primarily use female abstract concepts to describe the political scene, whereas the third section avoids abstractions entirely and opts instead for very concrete images of individuals and their homes.

It is a pity that time and circumstances have so mistreated this fragment. Preserved in the manuscripts of Demosthenes, one would have thought that its chances for complete survival would be great. Enough survives, however, to show that Solon was a master of stanzaic composition. For, although we have ample evidence in Solon 13.33–62 and Solon 27 of his competence in this area, such catalogues seem wooden in comparison, undoubtedly

---

[12] Adkins (1985) 123.
[13] See Halberstadt (1955), Siegman (1975), 277, Adkins (1985), 122–23, and Irwin (2005), 184, who collectively provide the following examples, among others. Verses 32–34, for instance, in their description of how Eunomia reveals all that is orderly (32: εὔκοσμα), puts a stop to excess (34: παύει κόρον) and weakens insolence (34: ὕβριν ἀμαυροῖ), echo and invert the description of the unruly ἡγεμόνες in lines 8–10, who on account of their great hybris (8: ὕβριος ἐκ μεγάλης) are destined to suffer, because they do not know how to restrain excess (9: κατέχειν κόρον) or bring order to the festivities of civic life (10: εὐφροσύνας κοσμεῖν).

because of their generic content. In Solon 4, however, we can see how Solon, like Tyrtaeus in his masterful Fragment 12, can begin a poem with a generic set-piece—Solon uses a 'city-poem', Tyrtaeus a priamel—and from it generate a long meditative poem, organized as pairs of coordinated stanzas, that uses alternation and responsion to tease out a deeper and more complicated understanding of the political inner workings of archaic Athens.

APPENDIX III

Theognidea 133–42

A five-couplet stanza at the middle of the *Theognidean* 'Cyrnus Book' displays an interesting hybrid form of the elegiac stanza that combines the catalogue format with ring-composition (133–42):

οὐδείς, Κύρν', ἄτης καὶ κέρδεος αἴτιος αὐτός,
   ἀλλὰ θεοὶ τούτων δώτορες ἀμφοτέρων·
οὐδέ τις ἀνθρώπων ἐργάζεται ἐν φρεσὶν εἰδὼς   135
   ἐς τέλος εἴτ' ἀγαθὸν γίνεται εἴτε κακόν.
πολλάκι γὰρ δοκέων θήσειν κακὸν ἐσθλὸν ἔθηκεν,
   καί τε δοκῶν θήσειν ἐσθλὸν ἔθηκε κακόν.
οὐδέ τῳ ἀνθρώπων παραγίνεται ὅσσα θέλησιν·
   ἴσχει γὰρ χαλεπῆς πείρατ' ἀμηχανίης   140
ἄνθρωποι δὲ μάταια νομίζομεν, εἰδότες οὐδέν·
   θεοὶ δὲ κατὰ σφέτερον πάντα τελοῦσι νόον.

No one, Cyrnus, is responsible on his own for ruin or profit, but it is the gods who give both. Nor does anyone know in his heart whether his toil will turn out well or badly in the end. For often a man who thought he would fail succeeds and a man who thought he would succeed fails. No one has at hand everything he wants, since the constraints of grievous helplessness hold him back. We mortals have vain thoughts, not knowledge; it is the gods who bring everything to pass according to their own intent.

Most scholars believe that this is a complete poem because the poet places the vocative Κύρν' near the beginning of the first line (133) and then another—this time his patronymic Πολυπαΐδη—in the line (143) that immediately follows these verses and is thematically unconnected to them.[1]

Formal signs of unity and completeness abound. Firstly, the poet has composed a rhetorically complete thought, by listing three types of common human failing, with a thematic focus on the limitations of human thinking or prediction. He introduces each instance with various forms of the pronoun 'no-one' at the beginning of three of the first four hexameters (οὐδείς [133]; οὐδέ τις ἀνθρώπων [135]; οὐδέ τῳ ἀνθρώπων [139]), and then

---

[1] See e.g. Garzya (1958) 160–61, Van Groningen (1966) ad loc., Gerber (1970) ad loc., and West (1992) ad loc.

provides an explanation for each in the following pentameter: ἀλλά (134); γάρ (137); and γάρ (140), a pattern that we have seen elsewhere in the design of elegiac catalogues. And like a catalogue these couplets have a uniformly structured and repetitive style: nearly all of them are end-stopped and all but the final hexameter break at the penthemimeral caesura creating an unbroken cadence of *hemiepe* at the beginning of the first eight lines.[2] The persistent rhymes in the pentameters—τούτων … ἀμφοτέρων (134); ἀγαθόν … κακόν (136); χαλεπῆς … ἀμηχανίης (140) and σφέτερον … νόον (142)—have a similar effect.[3] In fact this stanza shows a tendency, visible elsewhere in the *Theognidea*, of the bundling together a series of couplet-long wisdom-sayings on the same subject, and then summing up the content of all these verses with a general statement that in this case contrasts the ignorance of 'we mortals' with the effective knowledge and action of the gods (141: ἄνθρωποι δὲ μάταια νομίζομεν, εἰδότες οὐδέν).[4]

The poet emphasizes this feeling of closure by returning to the theme (raised in the first couplet) of the different roles of god and men and by placing the gods at or near the beginning of the first and last pentameters (θεοί at 134 and 142). The words εἰδότες and τελοῦσι in the final couplet similarly echo, at least superficially, εἰδώς and ἐς τέλος in the second. These verses also display some ring-composition in the second and fourth couplets, another common place for repetition in the architecture of an elegiac stanza: οὐδέ τις ἀνθρώπων ἐργάζεται (3) and οὐδέ τῳ ἀνθρώπων παραγίνεται (7). I should stress, however, that although this poem displays a significant amount of verbal ring-composition, its content does not take the form of an A–B–A stanza. Instead the three internal couplets comprise a list of related ideas that are connected in a paratactic manner and therefore resemble most of all the three central couplets that regularly list the individual contents of an elegiac catalogue. No one, of course, would claim that this is a good poem or a particularly interesting one, but it does illustrate nicely how ring-composition can bring closure and unity to stanzas whose thematic content is more loosely organized.

[2] Carrière (1948) 264–66 and van Raalte (1988) 154.

[3] Noted but not discussed by Gerber (1970) 282.

[4] The inclusive first-person plural focus of 'we mortals' here, is also a feature of catalogues like the Megarian epitaph and the first catalogue in Solon 13, both discussed in Section 2.3.

Glossary

The Glossary is primarily devoted to metrical terms, whose definitions are limited to phenomena of dactylic and elegiac verse. In preparing these definitions I have consulted West (1982) 191–202 and Rosenmeyer, Ostwald, and Halporn (1963) 121–28.

Antistrophe: see 'Strophe'

Bucolic diaeresis: a break in the dactylic hexameter between the fourth and fifth *metra*.

Caesura: a break within a *metron* where word ending is required or recommended.

Dactyl: a *metron* of the shape –∪∪. In the first four metra of a dactylic hexameter, the final two shorts often contract into a single long.

Diaeresis: a break between two *metra* where word ending is required or recommended.

Elegiac couplet: a metrical unit comprised of a dactylic hexameter followed by a pentameter.

Enjambment: the run-over of a sentence or syntactical unit from the end of one verse into the start of another.

Hemiepes (pl. *hemiepe*): a metrical unit of the shape –∪∪–∪∪–. In the first *hemiepes* of an elegiac pentameter the two shorts may contract into a single long, but not in the second *hemiepes*.

Hexameter: shorthand reference to the dactylic hexameter, a unit of verse comprised of six dactylic *metra*, the last of which is disyllabic. Epic verse is composed in stichic hexameters, whereas the elegiac couplet consists of a hexameter followed by a pentameter.

Metron (pl. *metra*): the smallest metrical unit in a verse, consisting of a sequence of long and short syllables. The elegiac couplet contains two different *metra*: the dactyl (–∪∪) and the hemiepes (–∪∪–∪∪–). It is sometimes referred to as a 'foot'.

Penthemimeral caesura: a caesura falling after the initial long syllable of the third foot of the dactylic hexameter. In an elegiac couplet, this produces a triple repetition of *hemiepe*, one at the start of the hexameter and two in the pentameter.

Pentameter: 'an absurd name for a verse which does not contain five of anything' (West, 1982) 44 n. 41). The second verse of the elegiac couplet, it is comprised of two *hemiepe* and has a midline diaresis.

Priamel: a type of rejected catalogue; see p. 34 for full definition.

Responsion: in choral poetry, the parallelism of metrical schemes between strophe and strophe or strophe, and antistrophe. In this volume I use it to refer to other kinds of parallelism (syntactical and verbal) between different elegiac strophes.

Ring-Composition: usually, parallelism (syntactical and verbal) between the start and finish of a poem or stanza of an A–B–A form.

Stanza: see pp. 5–6 for definition.

Stichic verse: a verse-form in which the same verse is repeated throughout a poem, for example, the dactylic hexameter in an epic poem.

Strophe: In choral poetry it represents a musical unity or melodic structure that is longer than a verse, and is usually followed by an antistrophe of equal length and shape. In describing non-choral poetry (e.g. Sappho) the strophe is sometimes used interchangeably with stanza.

Bibliography

Acosta-Hughes B. and S. Stephens (2002), "Rereading Callimachus' *Aetia* Fragment 1", *CP* 97: 238–55.

Adkins, A. W. H. (1972), *Moral Values and Political Behavior in Ancient Greece* (New York).

—— (1977), "Callinus 1 and Tyrtaeus 10 as Poetry", *HSCP* 81: 59–97.

—— (1985), *Poetic Craft in the Early Greek Elegists* (Chicago).

Alexiou, M. (2002), *The Ritual Lament in Greek Tradition*, rev. D. Yatromanolakis and P. Roilos (Boston).

Allan, W. (2000), *The Andromache and Euripidean Tragedy* (Oxford).

Allen, A. (1949), "Solon's Prayer to the Muses", *TAPA* 83: 50–65.

—— (1993), *The Fragments of Mimnermus: Text and Commentary*, Palingenesia 44 (Stuttgart).

Aloni, A. (1981), *Le muse di Archiloco* (Copenhagen).

—— (2001), "The Proem of Simonides' Plataea Elegy and the Circumstances of its Performance", in Boedeker and Sider (2001) 86–105.

Andrewes, A. (1938), "Eunomia", *CQ* 32: 89–102.

Anhalt, E. K. (1993), *Solon the Singer: Politics and Poetics* (Lanham).

Asper, M. (2004), *Kallimachos Werke* (Darmstadt).

Babut, D. (1971), "Semonide et Mimnerme", *Revue des études grecques* 84: 17–43.

Barnes, H. R. (1995), "The Structure of the Elegiac Hexameter: A Comparison of the Structure of Elegiac and Stichic Hexameter Verse", in Fantuzzi and Pretagostini (1995) 135–162.

Barron, J. P. and P. E. Easterling (1989), "Early Greek Elegy: Callinus, Tyrtaeus, Mimnermus", in Easterling and Kenney (1989) 87–94.

Bartól, K. (1987), "Literarische Quellen der Antike und das Problem des Vortragens der frühgriechischen Elegie", *Eos* 75: 261–78.

—— (1993), *Greek Elegy and Iambus: Studies in Literary Sources* (Poznán).

Baum, P. F. (1929), *The Principles of English Versification* (Cambridge, Mass.).

Boedeker, D. and D. Sider (eds.) (2001), *The New Simonides* (Oxford).

Bossi, F. (1990), *Studi su Archiloco* (Bari).

Bousquet, J. (1992), "Le polyandrion d'Ambracie", *BCH* 116: 596–606.

Bowie, E. L. (1986), "Early Greek Elegy, Symposium and Public Festival", *JHS* 106: 13–35.

Bowie, E. L. (1990), *"Miles Ludens?* The Problem with Martial Exhortation in Early Greek Elegy", in Murray (1990) 221–29.

—— (1993), "Greek Table-Talk before Plato", *Rhetorica* 11: 355–71.

—— (1997), "The *Theognidea*: A Step Towards a Collection of Fragments?", in G. W. Most (ed.), *Collecting Fragments/Fragmente sammeln*, (Göttingen 1997) 53–66.

—— (2001), "Ancestors of Historiography in Early Greek Elegiac and Iambic Poetry", in N. Luraghi (ed.), *The Historian's Craft in the Age of Herodotus* (Oxford 2001) 45–66.

Bowra, C. M. (1938*b*), "Xenophanes Frag. 1", *CP* 33: 353–67.

—— (1938*a*), "An Epigram for the Fallen at Coronea", *CQ* 32: 80–88.

—— (1934), "Simonides in the *Theognidea*", *CR* 48: 2–4.

—— (1961), *Greek Lyric Poetry from Alcman to Simonides* (Oxford).

—— (1969), *Early Greek Elegists*, Martin Classical Lectures 7 (New York).

Buchner, K. (1939), "Solons Musengedicht", *Hermes* 87: 163–90.

Bulloch, A. (1985), *Callimachus: The Fifth Hymn* (Cambridge).

Burkert, W. (1985), *Greek Religion*, trans. J. Raffan (Cambridge, Mass.).

Butrica, J. L. (1997), "Editing Propertius", *CQ* 47: 176–208.

Cameron, A. (1995), *Callimachus and his Critics* (Princeton).

Campbell, D. (1964), "Flutes and Elegiac Couplets", *JHS* 84: 63–68.

—— (1967), *Greek Lyric Poetry: A Selection of Early Greek Lyric, Elegiac and Iambic Poetry* (Bristol).

—— (1983), *The Golden Lyre: The Themes of the Greek Lyric Poets* (London).

—— (1984), "Stobaeus and Early Greek Lyric Poetry", in Gerber (1984) 51–57.

—— (1991), *Greek Lyric*, vol. 3: *Stesichorus, Ibycus, Simonides and Others* (London).

Carrière, J. (1948), *Theognis de Mégare: Étude sur le recueil élégiaque attribué à ce poète* (Paris).

—— (1962), "A propos d'un grand livre et d'un petit papyrus", *REG* 75: 37–44.

—— (1975), *Théognis: Poèmes élégiaques* (Paris).

Cassio, A. C. (1994), "I distici del polyandrion di Ambracia e l' 'Io Anonimo' nell' epigramma Greco", *SMEA* 33: 101–6.

Cavallotti, F. (1898), *Canti e frammenti di Tirteo* (Milan).

Clemm, W. (1883), "Zu den griechischen Elegikern", Jahrbuch für Klassische Philologie 127: 1–18.

Collins, D. (2004), *Master of the Game: Competition and Performance in Greek Poetry* (Cambridge, Mass.).

Crane, G. (1986), "Tithonus and the Prologue to Callimachus' *Aetia*", *ZPE* 66: 269–78.

Dale, A. M. (1965), *Collected Papers* (Cambridge).

D'Alessio, G. B. (1995), "Sull'epigramma dal polyandrion di Ambracia", *ZPE* 10: 22–26.

Day, J. (1989), "Rituals in Stone: Early Greek Epigrams and Monuments", *JHS* 109: 16–28.

Denniston, J. D. (1954), *Greek Particles*, 2nd edn. (Oxford).

Dingeldein, O. (1892), *Der Reim bei den Griechen und Römern* (Leipzig).

Donnet, D. (1995), Review of Allen (1993) in *CA* (1995) 64: 264–65.

Dover, K. J. (1967), "The Poetry of Archilochus", in *Archiloque*, Entretiens sur l'Antiquité Classique, Fondation Hardt 10 (Geneva) 181–222.

Dunbabin, K. M. D. and M. W. Dickie (1983), "*Invidia rumpantur pectora*: The Iconography of *Pthonos/Invidia* in Greco-Roman Art", *JAC* (1983) 26: 7–37.

Easterling, P. E. and E. J. Kenney (eds.) (1989), *The Cambridge History of Classical Literature*, vol. 1 (Cambridge).

Edmunds, L. and R. W. Wallace (eds.) (1997), *Poet, Public, and Performance in Ancient Greece* (Baltimore).

Falkner, T. M. (1995), *The Poetics of Old Age in Greek Epic, Lyric and Tragedy* (Norman, Okla.).

Fantuzzi, M. and R. Hunter (2004), *Tradition and Innovation in Hellenistic Poetry* (Cambridge).

—— and R. Pretagostini (eds.) (1995), *Struttura e storia dell' esametro Greco*, vol. 1 (Rome).

Faraone, C. A. (1986), "Callimachus *Epigram* 29.5–6 (Gow–Page)", *ZPE* 63: 53–56.

—— (1995), "The 'Performative Future' in Three Hellenistic Incantations and Theocritus' Second *Idyll*", *CP* (1995) 90: 1–15.

—— (2002), "A Drink from the Daughters of Mnemosyne: Poetry, Eschatology and Memory at the End of Pindar's *Isthmian* 6", in J. F. Miller, C. Damon and K. S. Myers (eds.) (2002), *Vertis in usum: Studies in Honor of Edward Courtney*, Beiträge zur Altertumskunde 161 (Munich) 259–70.

—— (2005*a*), "Catalogues, Priamels and Stanzaic Structure in Early Greek Elegy.", *TAPA* 135: 249–65.

—— (2005*b*), "Exhortation and Meditation: Alternating Stanzas as a Structural Device in Early Greek Elegy", *CP* 100: 317–36.

—— (2006), "Stanzaic Structure and Responsion in the Elegiac Poetry of Tyrtaeus", *Mnemosyne* 59: 19–52.

—— (forthcoming–*a*), "Stanzaic Structure in the Etiological Poetry of Phanocles and Callimachus".

—— (forthcoming–*b*), "Pseudepigraphy and Archaism: The Use of the Elegiac Stanza in Late Classical and Hellenistic Epigrams".

Fera, M. C. (1990), *Pindarus: Threnorum fragmenta* (Rome).

Ferrari, F. (1988), "P. Berol. Inv. 13270: I canti di Elefantina", *Studi Classici e Orientali* 38: 181–227.

Figueira, T. J. (1985), "The *Theognidea* and Megarian Society", in Figueira and Nagy (1985) 112–158.

—— and G. Nagy (eds.) (1985), *Theognis of Megara: Poetry and the Polis* (Baltimore).

Foley, H. P. (1993), "The Politics of Tragic Lamentation", in Sommerstein et al. (1993) 101–45.

Ford, A. (1985), "The Seal of Theognis: The Politics of Authorship in Archaic Greece", in Figueira and Nagy (1985) 82–95.

Fowler, R. L. (1987), *The Nature of Early Greek Lyric: Three Preliminary Studies* (Toronto).

Fränkel, H. (1975), *Early Greek Poetry and Philosophy*, trans. M. Hadas and J. Willis (Oxford).

Friedländer, P. and H. B. Hoffleit (1948), *Epigrammata: Greek Inscriptions in Verse from the Beginnings to the Persian Wars* (Berkeley).

Friis Johansen, H. (1991) "A Poem by Theognis (Thgn. 19–38)", *Classica et Mediaevalia* 42: 5–37.

Fussell, P. (1965), *Poetic Meter and Poetic Form* (New York).

Garzya, A. (1958), *Teognide Elegie, Libri I–II* (Florence).

—— (1963), *Studi sulla lirica greca* (Messina).

Gentili, B. (1967) "Epigramma ed elegia", in *L'épigramme grecque*. Entretiens sur l'Antiquité Classique, Fondation Hardt 14 (Geneva 1967) 37–90.

—— (1988), *Poetry and Its Public in Ancient Greece* (Baltimore).

—— and C. Prato (eds.) (1979–85), *Poetarum elegiacorum testimonia et fragmenta* (Leipzig).

Gerber, D. E. (1970), *Euterpe: An Anthology of Early Greek Lyric, Elegiac, and Iambic Poetry* (Amsterdam).

—— (1975), "Mimnermus, Fragment 2.4–5", *GRBS* 16: 263–8.

—— (ed.) (1984), *Greek Poetry and Philosophy: Studies in Honor of L. Woodbury* (Chico, Calif.).

—— (1991), "Early Greek Elegy and Iambus", *Lustrum* 33: 1–409.

—— (1997), "Elegy", in D. E. Gerber (ed.), *A Companion to the Greek Lyric Poets*, Mnemosyne Supplementum 173 (Leiden) 91–132.

—— (1999), *Greek Elegiac Poetry from the Seventh to the Fifth Centuries B.C.*, Loeb Classical Library 258 (Cambridge, Mass.).

Giangrande, G. (1967), "Sympotic Literature and Epigram", in *L'épigramme grecque*, Entretiens sur l'Antiquité Classique, Fondation Hardt 14 (Geneva 1967) 94–140.

Giannini, P. (1973), "Espressioni formulari nell'elegia greca arcaica", *QUCC* 15: 7–78.

Gianotti, G. F. (1978), "Alla ricerca di un poeta: Callino di Efeso", in E. Livrea and G.A. Privitera, (eds.), *Studi in onore di Anthos Ardizzoni*, vol. 1 (Rome) 405–30.

Goold, G. P. (1990), *Propertius*, Loeb Classical Library 18 (Cambridge, Mass.).

Gow, A. S. F. and D. Page (1965). *The Greek Anthology: Hellenistic Epigrams.* (Cambridge).

Greenberg, N. (1985*a*), "A Statistical Comparison of the Hexametrical Verse of *Iliad* 1, Theognis and Solon", *QUCC* 20: 63–75.

—— (1985*b*), "Appendix: Language, Meter and Sense in Theognis,", in Figueira and Nagy (1985) 245–60.

Griffith, M. (1976), "Man and the Leaves: A Study of Mimnermos fr. 2", *CSCA* 8: 73–88.

Gronewald, M. (1975), "Theognis 255 und P.Oxy. 2380", *ZPE* 19: 178–9.

—— and R.W. Daniel (2004), "Ein neuer Sappho-papyrus", *ZPE* 147: 1–8.

Halberstadt, M. (1955) "On Solon's Eunomia (Fragment 3D)", *Classical Weekly* 48: 197–203.

Harrison, E. (1902), *Studies in Theognis* (Cambridge).

Harvey, A. E. (1955), "The Classification of Greek Lyric Poetry", *CQ* 49: 157–75.

Hasler, F. S. (1959), *Untersuchungen zu Theognis (Zur Gruppenbildung im I. Theognisbuch)* (Winterthur).

Hauvette-Besnault, A. (1905), *Archiloque, sa vie et ses poésies* (Paris).

—— (1896), *De l'authenticité des épigrammes de Simonide* (Paris).

Henderson, W. J. (1982), "The Nature and Function of Solon's Poetry (Fr. 3D, 4 West)", *Acta Classica* 25: 21–33.

—— (1983), "Theognis 702–12: The Sisyphus-exemplum", *QUCC* 15: 83–90.

Herington, J. (1985), *Poetry into Drama: Early Tragedy and the Greek Poetic Tradition* (Berkeley).

Herrnstein-Smith, B. (1968), *Poetic Closure: A Study in How Poems End* (Chicago).

Higham, T. F. (1936), "*Teliambi*: A Review of 'Mouse-tailed', alias 'Miuric', Hexametrical Verse", in Page (1936) 299–324.

Holst-Warhaft, G. (1992), *Dangerous Voices: Women's Laments and Greek Literature* (London).

Hopkinson, N. (1988), *A Hellenistic Anthology* (Cambridge).

Hopwood, K. (ed.) (1999), *Organised Crime in Antiquity* (London).

Hudson-Williams, T. (1910), *The Elegies of Theognis* (London).

Hudson-Williams, T. (1926), *Early Greek Elegy: The Elegiac Fragments of Callinus, Archilochus, Mimnermus, Tyrtaeus, Solon, Xenophanes, & Others* (Cardiff).

Hunter, R. (1992), "Writing the God: Form and Meaning in Callimachus, *Hymn to Athena*", *MD* 29: 9–34.

—— (2001), "The Poet Unleaved: Simonides and Callimachus", in Boedeker and Sider (2001) 242–60.

Irwin, E. (2005), *Solon and Early Greek Poetry: The Politics of Exhortation* (Cambridge).

Isager, S. (1998), "The Pride of Halikarnassos: Editio Princeps of an Inscription from Salmakis", *ZPE* 123: 1–23.

Jacobs, F. (1813–17), *Anthologia Graeca*, 2nd edn. (Leipzig).

Jacoby, F. (1918), "Studien zu den älteren griechischen Elegikern", *Hermes* 53: 1–44 and 262–307.

—— (1945), "Some Athenian Epigrams from the Persian Wars", *Hesperia* 14: 157–211.

Jaeger, W. (1966), "Tyrtaeus on True Arete", in *Five Essays*, trans. A.M. Fiske (Montreal 1966) 103–42.

Kleinknecht, H. (1939), "*ΛΟΥΤΡΑ ΤΗΣ ΠΑΛΛΑΔΟΣ*", *Hermes* 74: 301–50.

Knox, B. M. W. (1989), "Theognis", and "Solon", in Easterling and Kenney (1989) 95–111.

Kotansky, R. (1993), "*P.Berol.* 21220 = Theognis, *Elegiae* 1.917–33", *ZPE* 96: 1–10 with plate VIIIa.

Kovacs, D. (1995), *Euripides* vol. 2, Loeb Classical Library 484 (Cambridge Mass.).

Kowerski, L. M. (2005), *Simonides on the Persian Wars: A Study of the Elegiac Verses from the "New Simonides"* (London).

Krevans, N. (1993), "Fighting against Antimachus: The *Lyde* and the *Aetia* Reconsidered", in M. A. Harder, R. F. Regtuit and G. C. Wakker (eds.) *Callimachus*, Hellenistic Groningana 1 (Groningen) 149–60.

Kurke, L. (1989), "*ΚΑΠΗΛΕΙΑ* and Deceit: Theognis 59–60", *AJP* 110: 535–44.

—— (1991), *The Traffic in Praise* (Ithaca).

Lambin, G. (1979) "'Dans un rameau de myrte...' (Aristophanes *Lysistrata* v. 632)", *REG* 92: 542–51.

Lardinois, A. P. M. H. (1995), *Wisdom in Context: The Use of Gnomic Statements in Archaic Greek Poetry* (Princeton Dissertation).

—— (2006), "Have We Solon's Verses?", in J. H. Blok and A. P. M. H. Lardinois (eds.), *Solon of Athens: New Historical and Philological Approaches* (Leiden) 15–37.

Lattimore, R. (1947), "The First Elegy of Solon", *AJP* 68: 161–79.

Lefkowitz, M. (1981), *Lives of the Greek Poets* (Baltimore).

Lesher, J. H. (1992), *Xenophanes of Colophon: Fragments*. Phoenix Supplementary Volume 30 (Toronto).

Lewis, D. M. (1987), "Bowie on Elegy: A Footnote", *JHS* 107 188.

Linforth, I. M. (1919), *Solon the Athenian*, University of California Publications in Classical Philology 6 (New York).

Lloyd-Jones, H. (1994), "Notes on the New Simonides", *ZPE* 101: 1–3.

Loraux, N. (1986), *The Invention of Athens: The Funeral Oration in the Classical City* (Cambridge, Mass.).

Luppe, W. (1997), "Kallimachos Aitien-Prologue v. 7–12", *ZPE* 115: 50–54.

MacDowell, D. M. (2000), *Demosthenes: On the False Embassy* (Oxford).

Mace, S. (2001), "Utopian and Erotic Fusion in a New Elegy by Simonides", in Boedeker and Sider (2001) 185–207.

Maddalena, A. (1943), "Per l'interpretazione dell'elegia di Solone alle Muse", *RFIC* 21: 1–12.

Malandra, W. W. (2001), "Gathas", in E. Yarshater (ed.), *Encyclopedia Iranica* 10 (New York 2001) 321–330.

Marcovich, M. (1978), *Studies in Greek Poetry*, ICS Supplement 1 (Atlanta).

Masaracchia, A. (1958), *Solone* (Florence).

Massimilla, G. (1996), *Callimacho: Aitia libri primo e secundo*, Biblioteca di studi antichi 77 (Pisa).

Molyneux, J. H. (1992), *Simonides: A Historical Study* (Wauconda).

Mülke, C. (2002), *Solons politische Elegien und Iamben* (Munich).

Murray, O. (1983), *Early Greece* (Stanford).

—— (ed.) (1990), *Sympotica: A Symposium on the Symposion*, vol. 1 (Oxford).

Nagy, G. (1974), *Comparative Studies in Greek and Indic Meter* (Harvard).

—— (1985), "Theognis and Megara: A Poet's Vision of his City", in Figuera and Nagy (1985) 22–81.

—— (1990*a*), *Greek Mythology and Poetics* (Ithaca).

—— (1990*b*), *Pindar's Homer* (Baltimore).

—— (1996), *Poetry As Performance* (Cambridge).

Noussia, M. and M. Fantuzzi (2001), *Solone: Frammenti dell'opera poetica* (Milan).

Obbink, D. (2001), "The Genre of *Plataea*: Generic Unity in the New Simonides", in Boedeker and Sider (2001) 65–85.

—— (2006), "A New Archilochus Poem", *ZPE* 156: 1–9.

Oliver, M. (1994), *A Poetry Handbook* (New York).

Page, D. L. (1936), "The Elegiacs in Euripides' *Andromache*", in *Greek Poetry and Life: Essays Presented to Gilbert Murray* (Oxford) 206–30.

—— (1957), *Literary Papyri: Poetry* (Cambridge, Mass.).

Page, D. L. (1981), *Further Greek Epigrams* (Cambridge).

Paton, W. R. (1917), *The Greek Anthology* (New York) 5 vols.

Pellizer, E. (1990), "Outlines of a Morphology of Sympotic Entertainment", in Murray (1990) 177–84.

Perrotta, G. (1924), "L'elegia di Solone alle Muse", *Atene e Roma*, NS 5: 251–60.

Pfeiffer, R. (1949), *Callimachus* (Oxford).

—— (1968), *History of Classical Scholarship* (Oxford).

Pfohl, G. (1972), *Die griechische Elegie* (Darmstadt).

Piper, W. B. (1969), *The Heroic Couplet* (Cleveland).

Podlecki, A. J. (1974), "Archilochus and Apollo", *Phoenix* 28: 1–17.

Positano, L. M. (1947), *L'elegia di Solone alle Muse*, Collana di Studi Greci 12 (Napoli).

Powell, J. U. (1925), *Collectanea Alexandrina* (Oxford).

Prato, C. (1968), *Tirteo* (Rome).

Race, W. H. (1982), *The Classical Priamel from Homer to Boethius*, Mnemosyne Supplementum 74 (Leiden).

—— (2002), "Framing Hyperbata in Pindar's *Odes*", *CJ* 98: 21–34.

Raubitschek, A. E. (1967), "Das Denkmal-Epigramm", in *L'épigramme grecque*. Entretiens sur l'Antiquité Classique, Fondation Hardt 14 (Geneva 1967) 3–26.

Reinhardt, K. (1916), "Solons Elegie *ΕΙΣ ΕΑΥΤΟΝ*", *RhM* 9: 128–35.

Reitzenstein, R. (1893), *Epigramm und Skolion* (Giessen).

Roberts, D. H., F. M. Dunn, and D. Fowler (eds.) (1997), *Classical Closure: Reading the End in Greek and Latin Literature* (Princeton).

Romagnoli, E. (1898), "Studi critici sui frammenti di Solone: La elegia XIII", *SIFC* 6: 35–59.

Rosenmeyer, T. G. (1969), "Elegiacs and Elegos", *CSCA* 1: 217–31.

—— M. Ostwald, and J. W. Halporn (1963), *The Meters of Greek and Latin Poetry* (Indianapolis).

Rösler, W. (1980), *Dichter und Gruppe: Eine Untersuchung zu den Bedingungen und zur historischen Funktion früher griechischer Lyrik am Beispiel Alkaios* (Munich).

Rossi, F. (1953/54), "Studi su Tirteo", *AIV* 112: 369–437.

Rutherford, I. (1997), "Odes and Ends: Closure in Greek Lyric", in Roberts, Dunn, and Fowler (1997) 43–61.

—— (2001), "The New Simonides: Towards a Commentary", in Boedeker and Sider (2001) 33–54.

Schmiel, R. (1974), "Youth and Mimnermus 1 and 2", *RFIC* 102: 283–9.

Schmitz, T. (1999), "'I hate all common things': The Reader's Role in Callimachus' *Aetia* Prologue", *HSCP* 99: 151–78.

Scodel, R. (1992), "Inscription, Absence and Memory: Epic and Early Epigram", *SIFC* 10: 57–76.

Shay, H. J. (1976), "Tyrtaeus and the Art of Propaganda", *Arethusa* 9: 5–28.

Sider. D. (1997), *The Epigrams of Philodemus* (Oxford).

—— (2001a),"Fragments 1–22 W²: Text, Apparatus Criticus and Translation", in Boedeker and Sider (2001) 13–32.

—— (2001b), "'As is the Generation of Leaves' in Homer, Simonides, Horace and Stobaeus", in Boedeker and Sider (2001) 272–88.

Siegman, E. (1970), "Die solonische Lebenslinie", *Philosophische Perspektiven* 2: 335–46.

—— (1975), "Solons Staatselegie", *Perspektiven der Philosophie* 1: 267–81.

Sitzler, J. (1880), *Theognidis Reliquiae* (Heidelberg).

Slings, S. R. (1991), "Sappho Fr. 1.8 V: Golden House or Golden Chariot?", *Mnemosyne* 44: 404–10.

—— (2000), *Symposium: Speech and Ideology: Two Hermeneutical Issues in Early Greek Lyric, with Special Reference to Mimnermus* (Amsterdam).

Snell, B. (1965), *Dichtung und Gesellschaft: Studien zum Einfluss der Dichter auf soziale Denken and Verhalten in alten Griechenland* (Hamburg).

—— (1969), *Tyrtaios und die Sprache des Epos* (Göttingen).

Snodgrass, A. (1964), *Early Greek Armour and Weapons from the End of the Bronze Age to 600 BC* (Edinburgh).

Solmsen, F. (1949), *Hesiod and Aeschylus* (Ithaca) 107–23.

Sommerstein, A. H. and S. Halliwell et. al. (eds.) (1993), *Tragedy, Comedy and the Polis* (Bari).

Steffen, V. (1986), *Die Kyrnos-Gedichte des Theognis* (Warsaw).

Stehle, E. (1997), *Performance and Gender in Ancient Greece: Non-Dramatic Poetry in its Setting* (Princeton).

—— (2001), "A Bard of the Iron Age and his Auxiliary Muse", in Boedeker and Sider (2001) 106–119.

Schwartz, E. (1899), "Tyrtaeos", *Hermes* 34: 428–68.

Tarditi, G. (1982), "Parenesi e areté nel corpus Tirtaico", *RFIC* 110: 257–76.

Tedeschi, G. (1995), "Solone e lo spazio della comunicazione elegiaca", in Fantuzzi and Pretagostini (1995) 33–46.

Trypanis, C. A. (1958), *Callimachus: Fragments* (Cambridge, Mass.).

Tuomi, R. (1986), *Solons Gedicht an Mimnermos im Licht der Tradition* (Turku, Finland).

van der Valk, M. H. (1955), "Theognis", *Humanitas* 6: 68–140.

van Groningen, B. A. (1958), *La Composition littéraire archaique grecque* (Amsterdam).

—— (1966), *Théognis: Le premier livre, édité avec un commentaire* (Amsterdam).

van Raalte, M. (1988), "Greek Elegiac Verse Rhythm", *Glotta* 66: 145–78.

van Wees, H. (1999), *The Mafia of Early Greece: Violent Exploitation in the Seventh and Sixth Centuries BC*, in K. Hopwood (1999) 1–51.

Verdenius, W. J. (1953), "Mimnermus 1 and 6", *Mnemosyne* 6: 197.

—— (1969), "Tyrtaeus 6–7 D: A Commentary", *Mnemosyne* 22: 337–55.

—— (1972), "Callinus fr. 1: A Commentary", *Mnemosyne* 25: 1–8.

—— (1974), "Inceptive *Δέ* Again", *Mnemosyne* 27: 173–4.

Verrall, A. W. (1896), "Tyrtaeus: A Graeco-Roman Tradition", *CR* 10: 269–77

Vetta, M. (ed.) (1980), *Theognis: Elegiarum liber secundus* (Rome).

—— (ed.) (1983), *Poesia e simposio nella Grecia antica: Guida storica e critica* (Rome).

—— (1984), "Identificazione di un caso di catena simposiale nel *Corpus Teognideo*", in *Lirica greca da Archiloco a Elitis: Studi in onore di F. M. Pontani* (Padua 1984).

Wade-Gray, H. T. (1968), "The Spartan Rhetra in Plutarch, *Lycurgus* VI", *Essays in Greek History* (Oxford) 37–85.

Wallace, M. B. (1984) "The Metres of Early Greek Epigrams", in Gerber (1984) 303–18.

Weil, H. (1862), "Über Spuren strophischer Composition bei den alten griechischen Elegikern", *RhM* 17: 1–13.

Welcker, F. T. (1826), *Theognidis reliquiae* (Frankfurt).

West, M. L. (1974), *Studies in Greek Elegy and Iambus* (Berlin).

—— (1982), *Greek Metre* (Oxford).

—— (ed.) (1992), *Iambi et Elegi Graeci ante Alexandrum Cantati*, 2nd edn. (Oxford) 2 vols.

—— (1995), "The Date of the *Iliad*", *Museum Helveticum* 52: 203–19

Willink, C. W. (2001) "Euripides *Andromache* 103–125: Metre and Text", *Mnemosyne* 54: 724–30.

Wood, C. (1940), *A Poet's Handbook* (New York).

von Wilamowitz-Moellendorf, U. (1900), *Textgeschichte der griechichen Lyriker* (Berlin).

—— (1913), *Sappho und Simonides* (Berlin).

Yatromanolakis, D. (2001), "To Sing or to Mourn? A Reappraisal of Simonides 22W²", in Boedeker and Sider (2001) 208–225.

Young, D. (1964), "Borrowings and Self-Adaptions in Theognis, with Reference to the Constitution of the Extant Sylloge and the *Suda* References to the Poet's Work", *Miscellanea Critica* 1: 307–90.

—— (ed.) (1976), *Theognis* (Leipzig).

Ziegler, C. (1880), *Theognidis Elegiae* (Tübingen).

Index of Passages

Index of Subjects

Pygmies 140, 142, 150
Pytho 30

recusatio 38 n. 55
Renaissance poetry 5–6, 9, 42,
	126–7, 162–3
reperformance 3, 8, 82, 93–113
	passim
repetition, verbatim 95–6, 107,
	142
responsion 3–4, 9, 12, 59, 60–9,
	80–1, 92, 102, 124–5, 146
responsion, triple 50, 64, 107–8,
	136 n. 52, 148, 170
Rhadamanthys 97–9
rhapsode 114, 116
ring-composition 16, 21 n. 16,
	22–31, 41, 47–8, 50, 53–4, 58–9,
	75–6, 77, 79, 87, 90, 124–5, 141,
	144–5, 159, 162, 165, 166–7,
	175–6
ring-composition between second and
	fourth couplets §2.2, §3.1, 54, 67,
	68 n. 41, 88–9, 107, 169–71

Sappho 7, 9, 103 n. 23
Sacadas of Argos 132 n. 36
scholia 131, 145 n. 14
scribes 22, 24, 66–7, 89–90, 95, 100,
	108, 111–13
Shakespeare 42, 163 n. 16
Simonides 1, 13, 14, 23 n. 21, 31 n.
	42, 82 n. 19, 86–7, 91, 108,
	(108 n. 35), 111 n. 41, 114,
	(114 n. 2), 115, (115 n. 4), 132–3,
	138 n. 2, 158
Sisyphus 97–100, (100 n. 17),
	157 n. 8, 159, 165–7
skolia 71, 72, (72 n. 3), 74 n. 7,
	75–6, 81–2, 92
Socrates 115 (115 n. 3)

Solon 3, (3 n. 10), (3 n. 12), 10, 11,
	13 n. 33, 14, 31, 35–41, (36 n.
	51), 60, 65–9, 82–6, (82 n. 19),
	93–4, (93 n. 2), (94 n. 4), 100,
	126 n. 22, 134, 146–7, 157,
	(157 n. 9), 158 n. 10, 159, 160,
	162–3, 168–74
Son of Hyperion, *see* Helios
σοφίη as special elegiac craft 38,
	122–3, 142
Sparta 30, 51–2, 136 n. 50
Spenser, Edmund 6, 9
spondaic *hemiepê* 56 n. 20
spondaic rhythms at ends of
	poems 56 n. 20, 163, 172–3
stanza beginning with conditional
	protasis 77 n. 12, 104–5,
	109–10
stanza with internal twist 16–22,
	26–8, 42, 159
stanza, definition of 5–6, 8–9, 16,
	44, 60
stanza, six-couplet 116–27
stanzaic boundaries 43–70 *passim*,
	110–11
stanzaic boundaries overrun 89, 97,
	102–5, 111, 160
stichic verse 7
Stobaeus 1 n. 4, 14–15, 17 n. 1,
	17 n. 3, 19 n. 9, 20 n. 15, 22,
	24 n. 23, 25 n. 25, 89 n. 30,
	100 n. 19, 102, 105 n. 28, 112 n.
	43, 158 n. 9
strophe 3–4, 12–13
subjunctive, hortative 47, 50, 74
Suda 94 n. 4
summary statement, *see* οὗτος and
	οὕτως
Sun, *see* Helios
symposiarch 75, 87, 91,
	114–15, 161

Index of Greek Words and Terms